Key Topics in Positive Psychology

Key Topics in Positive Psychology provides an insightful guide to this burgeoning, rebellious discipline. Exploring the science of the good life through theoretical foundations, empirical evidence, practical application, research methods, impacts and future trends, this book is a compelling call to consider mental health in a new light, where the focus shifts from treating illness to nurturing wellbeing.

In a concise yet comprehensive format, the book takes readers on an illuminating journey, beginning with the launch and historical evolution of Positive Psychology, highlighting its mission, vision, remit, the pivotal figures and moments that have shaped the discipline and its applied side – Positive Psychology Interventions. It then takes a dive into several applied domains, such as Positive Psychology Coaching, Positive Psychotherapy and Positive Psychiatry, demonstrating the integration of the field within applied psychological practices. Next, key scholarly interdisciplinary fields are discussed, including Positive Education, Positive Work and Organisations, Positive Health and Positive Economic Psychology, exploring the core principles and theories of each domain and innovative applications. The book also elucidates the vital research methodologies of the discipline, providing a foundation for understanding its evidence-based strategies. Further, the book critically discusses the impact of research and applications in the field, highlighting their influence in academia and beyond, in clinical practice, policy-making and in transforming people's lives. The book concludes by uncovering the emerging trends that are set to shape the future of the discipline.

Key Topics in Positive Psychology is valuable reading for students, researchers, practitioners and anyone interested in implementing Positive Psychology principles in their personal or professional life. It also seeks to promote the application of Positive Psychology in various settings and foster a widespread understanding of mental health and wellbeing.

Rona Hart is Associate Professor of Applied Positive Psychology at the School of Psychology, University of Sussex, UK. She is a lecturer, researcher, practitioner and author specialising in Positive Psychology and Economic Psychology. Recently, she launched a pioneering interdisciplinary field – Positive Economic Psychology – which integrates these two domains. Her textbook, *Positive Psychology: The Basics* (2020), is widely adopted in higher education and has been translated into several languages. Rona is also a long-standing member of the International Positive Psychology Association and holds several leadership roles: Member of the Leadership Team of the Work and Organisation Division; Director of Communities of Practice; Director of the Professionalising Positive Psychology Policy Initiative; Leader of a Community of Practice; and Member of the IPPA Taskforce on Accreditation. Rona is also Co-Editor of the *International Journal of Wellbeing* and has served as guest editor for several special issues on *Positive Economic Psychology, Flourishing at Work and Prosocial Organisational Behaviour.*

Key Topics in Parenting and Family Psychology

Key Topics in Identity Development

Key Topics in Psychobiology

Key Topics in Positive Psychology

BPS Key Topics in Psychology

British Psychological Society

Routledge, in partnership with the British Psychological Society (BPS), is pleased to present *BPS Key Topics in Psychology*, a series of short introductory books that focus on a specific field within psychology. Each book is broken down into bitesize chunks to provide a helpful overview of core psychology topics, made clear by a five-part structure: foundations, theories, methodologies, impacts, and emerging areas. Written by active and experienced authors, these essential books encourage students to approach fundamental concepts with confidence and critical thinking.

Books may incorporate student-friendly pedagogies, including tools such as: feature boxes; key terms and definitions; and links to further reading online. Concise yet comprehensive, these books offer a simple and accessible overview of core psychology topics for students looking for a summary of key concepts in the topic, or those new to the area.

Key Topics in Memory
Richard J. Allen and Charity Brown

Key Topics in Parenting and Family Psychology
Alina Morawska & Amy E. Mitchell

Key Topics in Identity Development
Theo A. Klimstra

Key Topics in Psychobiology
Emma M. Karlsson and Sebastian Ocklenburg

Key Topics in Positive Psychology
Rona Hart

For more information about this series, please visit: www.routledge.com/BPS-Key-Topics-in-Psychology/book-series/BPSKTP

Key Topics in Positive Psychology

Rona Hart

Routledge
Taylor & Francis Group
LONDON AND NEW YORK

Designed cover image: Getty Images via Ivcandy

First published 2027
by Routledge
4 Park Square, Milton Park, Abingdon, Oxon OX14 4RN

and by Routledge
605 Third Avenue, New York, NY 10158

Routledge is an imprint of the Taylor & Francis Group, an informa business

British Library Cataloguing-in-Publication Data
A catalogue record for this book is available from the British Library

ISBN: 978-1-032-66310-4 (hbk)
ISBN: 978-1-032-66309-8 (pbk)
ISBN: 978-1-032-66311-1 (ebk)

DOI: 10.4324/9781032663111

Typeset in Galliard
by Apex CoVantage, LLC

Access the Support Material: www.routledge.com/9781032663098

Contents

About the Author

Dr Rona Hart is Associate Professor of Applied Positive Psychology at the School of Psychology, University of Sussex, UK. She is a lecturer, researcher, practitioner and author specialising in Positive Psychology and Economic Psychology. Recently, she launched a pioneering interdisciplinary field – Positive Economic Psychology, which integrates these two domains. Her textbook, *Positive Psychology: The Basics* (Routledge), is widely adopted in higher education and has been translated into several languages. Rona is also a long-standing member of the International Positive Psychology Association and holds several leadership roles: Member of the Leadership Team of the Work and Organisation Division, Director of Communities of Practice, Director of the Professionalising Positive Psychology Policy Initiative, Leader of a Community of Practice and a member of the IPPA Taskforce on Accreditation. Rona is also Co-Editor of the *International Journal of Wellbeing* and served as guest editor for several special issues on Positive Economic Psychology, Flourishing at Work and Prosocial Organisational Behaviour.

Section 1

Key Foundations

This Section in Summary

Chapter 1: Introducing Positive Psychology

- **Positive Psychology** emerged as a disruptive movement, challenging Psychology's traditional focus on disease and dysfunction.
- Its mission was to balance Applied Psychology's remedial emphasis, by attending to the bright side of human psychology.
- It adopts positive assumptions about human nature, targets non-clinical populations, seeks to promote positive outcomes and operates positive processes in its interventions.
- It has evolved through three successive waves, shifting from an individual-centred focus on positive aspects of life to more complex, context-sensitive, and systems-oriented understandings.
- The discipline has faced sustained criticism, which has prompted reflection and learning, helping to drive progress.

Chapter 2: Key Concepts

- Positive Psychology is a broad field that combines new contributions with long-established psychological constructs.
- Its core research is centred on micro-level phenomena, especially intra-personal concepts, alongside a lesser emphasis on interpersonal experiences.
- The field has developed through two parallel paths: Deepening classic topics and expanding into interdisciplinary sub-disciplines and applied domains.
- Seven classic concepts are reviewed: Strengths, optimism, flow, meaning in life, **resilience**, kindness and love. These show how flourishing is supported by inner resources, meaningful activity and positive relationships.

DOI: 10.4324/9781032663111-1

Section 1

Key [illegible]

Chapter 1

Introducing Positive Psychology

Psychology has long been most visible in its efforts to explain and alleviate illness, distress and dysfunction. Positive Psychology expanded this agenda by placing the conditions for a good life at the centre of scientific inquiry. Emerging from a deliberate provocation to study what is strong, not only what is wrong, it shifted attention towards the conditions under which human **well-being** can be enhanced and sustained rather than merely restored. However, Positive Psychology is neither a feel-good movement nor a rejection of suffering. It is an evidence informed expansion of Psychology's explanatory lens, so that **flourishing** becomes a legitimate object of **theory**, measurement, **empirical research** and **intervention**.

> **Theory:** An organised set of ideas that explains how or why something happens.

> **Positive Psychology:** A branch of Psychology that focuses on studying the conditions and processes that contribute to the flourishing of people, groups and institutions.

This chapter outlines the origins and development of the field, what it claims and contests, and the field's aims, mission, vision and principles. It also traces its development and addresses several common critiques of the discipline.

The Emergence of Positive Psychology

The launch of Positive Psychology as a scientific and applied field is commonly dated to Seligman's 1999 APA presidential address, which challenged the field of **Applied Psychology** to reconsider what it had become and what it had left behind. Seligman argued that, prior to World War II, Psychology had been oriented around three broad aims: Alleviating mental illness, making people's lives more fulfilling and identifying and

DOI: 10.4324/9781032663111-2

nurturing talent (Seligman, 1999). In the decades that followed, however, the discipline's **remedial** mission came to dominate research and practice, leaving the other two aims comparatively marginal. The result, he suggested, was a professional culture shaped by a **disease model**: Diagnosing deficits and repairing damage, with far less attention to the capacities, **virtues** and resources that enable people to function well and flourish.

Applied Psychology: The use of psychological theory and research in practical settings such as psychological therapy.

Remedial: Something intended to correct, improve or address an illness, weakness, difficulty or problem.

Disease model: An approach that understands psychological problems mainly in terms of symptoms, diagnosis and treatment.

Importantly, this critique did not deny the importance of treating suffering. Seligman acknowledged the field's substantial progress in healing mental illness and restoring dispirited lives. Rather, he argued that Psychology had become intellectually and practically imbalanced, leaving it poorly equipped to develop preventive approaches that draw on what is right with people to buffer against the development of ailment (Seligman, 1999). Positive Psychology was therefore proposed as a corrective: An evidence-oriented discipline committed to studying wellbeing and human strengths with the same conceptual and methodological rigour traditionally applied to dysfunction.

The early vision of the field was shaped by a series of scholarly meetings and collaborations, including formative discussions between Seligman and Csikszentmihalyi that crystallised the need to broaden Psychology's agenda to include questions on happiness, meaning and what makes life worth living. Organisational infrastructure followed swiftly: Committees, research centres and early summits helped consolidate a shared identity, generate flagship publications and secure funding for research and education, accelerating the field's visibility and reach (Csikszentmihalyi & Nakamura, 2011).

While Seligman's leadership provided a clear rallying point, the subsequent growth of Positive Psychology reflected a broader appetite among researchers and practitioners to build a more complete Psychology, one that can account for both suffering and strengths, repair and prevention, vulnerability and flourishing.

Conceptualising Positive Psychology

Since its launch, Positive Psychology has undergone repeated efforts to clarify and refine its guiding philosophy, mission and scope.

The term **Positive Psychology** is attributed to Maslow (1987), who characterised it as the study of psychological health and optimal human functioning, encompassing attributes such as morality and virtue.

Following the formal launch of the movement, Seligman and Csikszentmihalyi (2000) articulated a multi-level definition. At the subjective level, they emphasised valued experiences such as wellbeing and happiness. At the individual level, they highlighted positive traits such as talent and wisdom. At the group level, they underscored civic virtues and the social institutions that enable constructive citizenship (Seligman & Csikszentmihalyi, 2000).

In a more concise formulation, Gable and Haidt (2005) defined Positive Psychology as "the study of the conditions and processes that contribute to the flourishing or optimal functioning of people, groups, and institutions" (p.104).

Across these definitions, a shared core is evident: A focus on wellbeing, a commitment to scientific inquiry and an emphasis on understanding positive functioning alongside, rather than instead of, distress and disorder. At the same time, differences in emphasis remain, particularly concerning how broadly the field's remit should be drawn.

The Mission of Positive Psychology

Positive Psychology articulated an explicitly expansive ambition: To instigate a shift in Psychology from its preoccupation with repairing what is worst in life towards also understanding and cultivating what is best in human experience (Seligman & Csikszentmihalyi, 2000). To advance this shift, several interrelated objectives were proposed (Seligman et al., 2004):

- To elevate a new set of topics and questions within Psychology's scientific agenda, with particular emphasis on healthy functioning;
- To develop a shared language to support communication across the field;
- To design and empirically assess interventions intended to enhance wellbeing;
- To integrate positive and negative perspectives within applied work.

Collectively, these objectives outline a programme that is both empirically grounded and practically oriented. They also bring systematic attention to the enabling conditions of a good life while remaining attentive to suffering and dysfunction.

Core Principles Underpinning Positive Psychology

The principles of Positive Psychology articulate the field's guiding commitments. They align with its key goals and provide a framework for its scientific work and applications, while emphasising **conceptual clarity**, methodological rigour and ethical responsibility.

> **Conceptual clarity:** The extent to which key ideas are clearly defined and distinguished from one another.

- **Positive assumptions about human nature:** Applied work in Psychology often rests on particular, **value-laden** assumptions about human nature that are rarely made explicit. Seligman (2005) argued that mainstream Psychology had been strongly shaped by a Freudian view, in which human behaviour is understood as driven by conflict and aggressive or pleasure-seeking impulses. By contrast, Positive Psychology is aligned with humanistic traditions that frame human nature as oriented towards goodness and morality, and portray people as motivated to grow and realise their potential.

> **Value-laden:** Carrying assumptions about what is good, desirable or worthwhile.

- **Holistic ideology:** In line with its assumptions about human nature, Maddux (2005) argues that much of Clinical Psychology has been shaped by an **illness ideology** – a set of guiding principles that define the field's mission, target population and professional territory, including what counts as normal versus abnormal, clinical versus non-clinical concerns and how **psychopathology** and dysfunction are conceptualised, diagnosed and treated. By questioning the dominance of this illness-oriented framework and its close ties to the **medical model**, Positive Psychology advanced a more **holistic** agenda, one

> **Illness ideology:** A framework that treats psychological life mainly through the lens of illness, diagnosis and treatment of disorders.
>
> **Psychopathology:** Mental disorders, symptoms and abnormal psychological processes.
>
> **Medical model:** An approach that prioritises diagnosing problems or difficulties and offering treatment.
>
> **Holistic:** A perspective that considers studying a person as a whole.

that complements remedial work by emphasising the promotion of wellbeing.

- **Mental health is not the absence of illness:** A central implication of Positive Psychology's stance is that mental health cannot be reduced to the absence of disorder or dysfunction. Instead, it argues that psychological health should also be evaluated by the presence of wellbeing and flourishing (Seligman, 1999).
- **Positive aim and orientation:** This principle foregrounds the field's emphasis on strengths and wellbeing and signals the priorities that shape its research agenda, teaching and applied practice (Pawelski, 2016).
- **Positive outcomes:** Positive Psychology seeks "to provide an empirical vision for understanding and cultivating the good life" (Pawelski, 2016, p. 343). Accordingly, its applied work is explicitly oriented towards producing identifiable positive outcomes at individual and collective levels, including the enhancement of positive states and the development of positive traits and capacities.
- **Positive target population:** This principle highlights the primary population that Positive Psychology seeks to benefit, which is mainly non-clinical (Pawelski, 2016).
- **Positive processes:** These refer to the mechanisms through which Positive Psychology seeks to bring about change, often operationalised in its interventions. Such processes are intended to cultivate, mobilise or strengthen psychological and social capacities that help individuals or groups move towards desired outcomes (Pawelski, 2016), for example through character strengths use, **mindfulness** practices or conveying gratitude.
- **Positive topography:** This refers to the core topics typically regarded as falling within the domain of Positive Psychology, such as happiness, strengths, optimism and wisdom (Pawelski, 2016).
- **Positive language:** The illness-oriented lexicon is dominated by terms such as disorder, pathology, symptom, **diagnosis**, treatment, patient and clinician. In seeking a more balanced Psychology, Positive Psychology scholars and practitioners aim to develop an alternative vocabulary that enables the description and analysis of strengths, wellbeing and optimal functioning. Maddux (2005,

Diagnosis: The process of identifying a condition, disorder or problem by assessing its signs, symptoms or other relevant evidence.

Maladaptive: A behaviour, cognition or emotion that undermines a person's functioning.

Adaptive: A behaviour, cognition or emotion that supports a person's functioning.

p. 66) argued that, within this linguistic frame, **maladaptive** patterns of behaviour, cognition and emotion may be conceptualised as "problems in living" rather than as disorders or diseases.

- **Positive value position:** Positive Psychology researchers and practitioners recognise that concepts such as "the good life" and "positive traits" are inherently value-laden, insofar as they imply judgements about what is desirable or worthwhile. This sits uneasily with traditional expectations that scientific inquiry should be value-neutral and leaves such terms open to critical debate and scrutiny. In response, Positive Psychology has articulated an explicitly facilitative, non-prescriptive stance: It does not mandate how people ought to live; rather, it offers **evidence-based** resources and tools that can support individuals in pursuing their own valued goals (Linley et al., 2006).

Evidence-based/evidence-informed: Action guided by research evidence rather than opinion or unsupported claims.

Taken together, these principles position Positive Psychology as an integrative enterprise: One that complements Applied Psychology's concern with suffering by systematically examining strengths, resources and the conditions that sustain wellbeing. They clarify the field's assumptions, scope and preferred language, while underscoring commitments to scientific rigour and ethical responsibility in application. As such, they provide a useful framework for interpreting positive psychological research and for evaluating interventions in terms of effectiveness and appropriateness in real-world contexts.

The Conceptual Roots of Positive Psychology

The roots of Positive Psychology can be traced to four influential foundations:

- **Ancient Greek** philosophers **Aristotle** and **Epicurus** examined ideas around what makes a good life, paying attention to the concepts of hedonia and **eudaimonia** (see Chapter 3) and the importance of virtues for leading a good life (Tiberius & Mason, 2009).
- **Utilitarian philosophers Mill** and **Bentham** advanced the **principle of utility**, arguing that government actions and public policy should be evaluated in terms of whether they promote the greatest happiness for the greatest number of people. They also pioneered early efforts to conceptualise and measure happiness, while drawing attention to the limitations

of pleasure as a comprehensive account of wellbeing (Pawelski & Gupta, 2009).

- **Within Psychology,** early scholarly attention to positive themes is often linked to **James'** (1890/1950) discussions of healthy-mindedness and happiness. James treated happiness as a central concern of human life and encouraged scholars to investigate the conditions that enable it to be attained and sustained.

Principle of utility: The idea that actions or policies should be judged by their consequences for overall benefit.

- **Humanistic Psychology** is frequently described as a strategic forerunner of Positive Psychology (Waterman, 2013), given their shared assumptions about human nature and their emphasis on the healthy, growth-oriented aspects of psychological functioning. Associated with figures such as Maslow and Rogers, Humanistic Psychology advanced the idea that people are motivated by an inherent drive to develop and realise their potential, often expressed as the striving for **self-actualisation**.

Humanistic Psychology: A psychological tradition that emphasises growth, meaning, potential and the positive possibilities of human life.

During the field's early formation, Positive Psychology scholars were criticised for giving insufficient attention to the intellectual origins of the discipline (Taylor, 2001). More recently, however, these roots have been more explicitly acknowledged, alongside a growing appreciation of the broader traditions that helped to shape Positive Psychology and continue to inform its development (Snyder et al., 2011).

Is Positive Psychology a Discipline, a Collective Identity, an Ideology, or a Social Movement?

In the years following its emergence, Linley and Joseph (2004b) questioned whether Positive Psychology should be regarded as a new sub-discipline within Psychology and proposed that it may be better understood as a "**collective identity**" encompassing scholars from diverse disciplinary backgrounds who share an interest in "the brighter sides of human nature" (p. 4). From this perspective, the field may be viewed as an ethos, together with a body of concepts and tools, that can be adopted by researchers and practitioners across different areas of Psychology.

Collective identity: A shared sense of belonging among people who see themselves as part of the same community.

Later on, Lomas and Ivtzan (2016) argued that Positive Psychology has evolved into a distinct **applied discipline** within Psychology. On this view, it warrants formal recognition and **accreditation** to reflect the professional identity of those engaged in its research, teaching and applications.

Applied discipline: A field that develops practical methods and interventions for use in real-world settings.

Positive Psychology has also been characterised as a movement seeking to challenge the status quo and thus as carrying an **ideological position** regarding the focus of Psychology (Peterson & Park, 2003). Consistent with this interpretation, Biswas-Diener et al. (2011) portrayed the discipline as a vehicle for social change and described its practitioners as transformative activists.

Ideology: A set of ideas and values that shapes how a field understands its purpose and priorities.

Positive Psychology's Evolution

Positive Psychology's evolution is frequently framed as three successive "waves," charting a movement from an initially individual-centred focus on the positive facets of human experience towards more complex, **dialectical**, context-sensitive and systems-oriented accounts of human life (Lomas et al., 2020):

Dialectical: Understanding a phenomenon through the tension, interaction or opposition between contrasting ideas, forces or perspectives.

- **The first wave** is linked to early work in the field which sought to counterbalance Applied Psychology's long-standing emphasis on pathology by developing a robust empirical programme on the positive aspects of life (Seligman & Csikszentmihalyi, 2000). Frequently framed as a science of happiness, this phase foregrounded constructs such as happiness, life satisfaction, optimism, hope, character strengths and flow. Critics argued, however, that it over-privileged positivity, engaged insufficiently with distress and framed flourishing in excessively individualistic terms (Lomas et al., 2020).

- **The second wave** redirected the field towards the dialectical interdependence of positive and negative experience, with greater attention to **meaning-making**, existential themes, and cultural variation (Wong, 2011; Ivtzan et al., 2015). From this perspective, enduring wellbeing is not achieved by minimising the negative, but by engaging with adversity, ambiguity and the darker aspects of life, and by integrating difficult emotions into coherent narratives of meaning and growth. This wave also expanded the scope of the field beyond Western, happiness-centric formulations by incorporating existential–spiritual perspectives and insights from indigenous psychologies.

> **Meaning-making:** The process of interpreting experiences in ways that create understanding.

- **The third wave,** as described by Lomas et al. (2020), extended the earlier dialectical turn by widening the field's **interdisciplinary** engagement, deepening inquiry and tackling more complex questions. It places greater emphasis on context and systems, conceptualising wellbeing as emerging from dynamic interactions between individuals and their environments, including institutions, cultures, ecological conditions and policy settings, rather than as a purely intra-individual state. Consequently, it calls for applications in areas such as education, work and public policy that address social as well as personal determinants of wellbeing.

> **Interdisciplinary:** Drawing on ideas, methods or applications from more than one academic discipline.

The three waves mark a maturation journey of Positive Psychology from a corrective venture within Psychology into a more consolidative science of flourishing that can accommodate suffering, diversity and the complex conditions that enable or constrain wellbeing.

Challenges and Critique

Since its launch, Positive Psychology has attracted relentless criticism. Commentators have questioned the field's philosophical foundations,

Table 1.1 Overview of critiques of Positive Psychology and proposed responses

Key critiques	*Proposed ways to address the critique*
Insufficient theorising and conceptual clarity: Positive Psychology has been criticised for lacking a coherent metatheoretical foundation to anchor its philosophical assumptions and for offering limited guidance on how key concepts should be defined and approached.	**Broaden perspectives:** • Draw on diverse philosophical traditions • Integrate insights from other disciplines • Strengthen multidisciplinary collaboration **Build holistic meta-theories:** • Develop overarching frameworks • Make connections and linkages across concepts and models **Use bottom-up development and shared language:** • Prioritise inductive approaches • Work towards clearer, more consistent terminology **Co-produce theory:** • Clarify and coordinate academic versus applied priorities • Develop theory collaboratively with practitioners and stakeholders
Methodological weaknesses: Critics have contended that the field relies mainly on quantitative research methods. Measurement practices, cross-sectional designs, and experimental research were scrutinised for weak designs that undermine the validity, credibility and generalisability of findings.	**Diversify methods:** • Use alternative assessment tools • Balance quantitative measures with qualitative evidence • Capture collective/relational experiences **Advance open science and data sharing:** • Publish null and non-significant findings • Adopt open science practices (transparency, sharing) **Reduce bias:** • Minimise social desirability effects • Strengthen checks on response accuracy **Improve public-facing science communication:** • Support public understanding of science • Encourage responsible media reporting • Develop and apply ethical guidelines

(*Continued*)

Table 1.1 (Continued)

Key critiques	*Proposed ways to address the critique*
Questionable evidence base and replicability: Some critics portrayed Positive Psychology as pseudoscience, arguing that certain claims outpace the evidence, that intervention benefits are overstated, and that replication failures call the reliability of key findings into question	**Centralise evidence communication:** • Enable professional societies to publish accessible, comprehensive evidence summaries **Engage constructively with critics:** • Test and clearly communicate responses to pseudoscience claims • Co-develop solutions where possible
Limited novelty and self-isolation from mainstream Psychology: A common critique has been that the field offers few novel ideas, instead rebranding established concepts, and that it has reinforced an artificial divide between Positive Psychology and other Applied Psychology sub-disciplines	**Bridge disciplinary divides** • Clarify how the field differs from mainstream Psychology • Offer competing explanations where appropriate • Explore complementarities and tensions across perspectives
Neo-liberal orientation: A further line of critique characterised Positive Psychology as promoting Western, individualised values as universal, inadequately attending to culture and context, and placing disproportionate responsibility for wellbeing on individuals, thereby risking victim-blaming, marginalisation, and neglect of structural determinants of wellbeing.	**Strengthen cultural responsiveness:** • Test cross-cultural applicability of constructs and interventions • Develop bottom-up, context-sensitive theory • Prioritise local contexts in research and practice **Adopt a social responsibility stance:** • Acknowledge contextual impacts in research and practice • Attend to diverse and marginalised populations • Apply a clear "do no harm" principle **Balance positive and negative:** • Examine costs, limits and potential downsides • Avoid overly one-sided accounts of wellbeing **Verify intervention quality and ethics:** • Tailor interventions to individuals and contexts • Formalise training pathways and professional standards
Commercialisation and capitalist incentives: Critics suggested that commercial interests may shape the field's priorities and public messaging, potentially compromising objectivity and scientific standards	**Balance access with affordability:** • Provide free or low-cost basic provision where feasible • Support open-access research initiatives

Sources: Van Zyl et al. (2023) and Van Zyl (2025)

theoretical coherence, methodological standards, cultural assumptions and the delivery and impact of its applications (Van Zyl et al., 2023). These debates have been further intensified by wider credibility challenges within Psychology, including failures to replicate key findings (see Chapter 11) and the prevalence of questionable research practices. To synthesise contemporary critiques, Van Zyl et al. (2023) conducted a **systematic review** that identified 117 distinct criticisms, which they organised into six overarching themes. In a subsequent study, Van Zyl (2025) engaged Positive Psychology scholars and practitioners in action research to elicit ways of addressing the prevalent critiques. The findings from the two studies are reported in Table 1.1.

> **Theoretical coherence:** The extent to which a field's ideas fit together in a clear and consistent way.

Hart (2020) noted that while it can be expected that a field that challenges the status quo will attract criticism, some critiques have been misdirected or exaggerated. At the same time, constructive engagement with well-founded criticisms has fostered reflection and learning, contributing to substantial progress in the field's underlying philosophy, theories, methods and interventions.

Conclusion

Positive Psychology emerged as a deliberate rebalancing act within a discipline long dominated by **deficit models**, insisting that flourishing is a legitimate scientific concern alongside suffering. This chapter has traced the emergence of the discipline, clarified how the field has been defined, mapped its principles and situated its development within classic philosophical and psychological traditions. It has also highlighted the field's maturation across successive waves, moving from an early emphasis on intra-individual factors towards more dialectical, culturally attuned, systems-oriented and interdisciplinary accounts of wellbeing.

> **Deficit model:** An approach that focuses on weaknesses, problems or what is lacking, rather than on strengths and resources.

At the same time, the chapter has shown that Positive Psychology's visibility has brought scrutiny. Critiques concerning theoretical coherence, measurement and design limitations, evidential robustness, cultural assumptions, disciplinary positioning and commercial incentives have prompted debates about what the field is and what it should become. These debates have generated concrete proposals for improvement: Broadening perspectives, strengthening conceptual work, diversifying methods, engaging critics, enhancing cultural responsiveness and reinforcing ethical and social responsibility in research and practice.

Taken together, the field's future relevance depends on its capacity to retain the original ambition of a more complete Psychology while addressing these limitations with intellectual humility and methodological rigour. With these foundations established, the next chapter turns to the core concepts that have shaped Positive Psychology's scholarly identity and applied work.

References

Biswas-Diener, R., Linley, A.P., Govindji, R., & Woolfston, L. (2011). Positive psychology as a force for social change. In K.M. Sheldon, T.B. Kashdan, & M.F. Steger (Eds.), Designing positive psychology (pp. 410–420). Oxford University Press.

Csikszentmihalyi, M., & Nakamura, J. (2011). Positive psychology: Where did it come from, where is it going? In K.M. Sheldon, T.B. Kashdan, & M.F. Steger (Eds.), Designing positive psychology (pp. 3–8). Oxford University Press.

Gable, S.L., & Haidt, J. (2005). What (and why) is positive psychology? Review of General Psychology, (9), 103–110.

Hart, R. (2020). Positive psychology: The basics. Routledge.

Ivtzan, I., Lomas, T., Hefferon, K., & Worth, P. (2015). Second wave positive psychology. Routledge.

James, W. (1890/1950). The principles of psychology. Dover.

Linley, P.A., & Joseph, S. (2004). Applied positive psychology: A new perspective for professional practice. In P.A. Linley, & S. Joseph (Eds.), Positive psychology in practice (pp. 3–12). Wiley.

Linley, P.A., Joseph, S., Harrington, S., & Wood, A.M. (2006). Positive psychology: Past, present, and (possible) future. The Journal of Positive Psychology, 1(1), 3–16.

Lomas, T., & Ivtzan, I. (2016). Professionalising positive psychology: Developing guidelines for training and regulation. International Journal of Wellbeing, 6(3), 96–112.

Lomas, T., Waters, L., Williams, P., Oades, L.G., & Kern, M.L. (2020). Third wave positive psychology: Broadening towards complexity. The Journal of Positive Psychology, 16(5), 660–674.

Maddux, J.E. (2005). Stopping the "madness": Positive psychology and the deconstruction of the illness ideology and the DSM. In C.R. Snyder, & S.J. Lopez (Eds.), Handbook of positive psychology (pp. 13–25). Oxford University Press.

Maslow, A.H. (1987). Motivation and personality. Pearson Education.

Pawelski, J.O. (2016). Defining the 'positive' in positive psychology: Part II. A normative analysis. The Journal of Positive Psychology, 11(4), 357–365.

Pawelski, J.O., & Gupta, M. (2009). Utilitarianism. In S. Lopez (Ed.), The encyclopedia of positive psychology (pp. 998–1001). Blackwell.

Peterson, C., & Park, N. (2003). Positive psychology as the evenhanded positive psychologist views it. Psychological Inquiry, 14(2), 143–147.
Seligman, M.E.P. (1999). The president's address. American Psychologist, 54, 559–562.
Seligman, M.E.P. (2005). Positive psychology, positive prevention, and positive therapy. In C.R. Snyder, & S.J. Lopez (Eds.), Handbook of positive psychology (pp. 3–9). Oxford University Press.
Seligman, M.E.P., & Csikszentmihalyi, M. (2000). Positive psychology: An introduction. American Psychologist, (55), 5–14.
Seligman, M.E.P., Parks, A.C., & Steen, T. (2004). A balanced psychology and a full life. Philosophical Transactions of the Royal Society of London. Series B: Biological Sciences, 359(1449), 1379–1381.
Snyder, C.R., Lopez, S.J., & Pedrotti, J.T. (2011). Positive psychology. Sage.
Taylor, S. (2001). Positive psychology and humanistic psychology: A reply to Seligman. Journal of Humanistic Psychology, 41, 13–29.
Tiberius, V., & Mason, M. (2009). Eudaimonia. In S. Lopez (Ed.), Encyclopedia of positive psychology (pp. 351–355). Blackwell.
Van Zyl, L.E. (2025). Exploring the potential solutions to the criticisms of positive psychology: But can the bold, idealistic visions of positive psychologists survive real-world scrutiny? Frontiers in Psychology, 16, 1511128.
Van Zyl, L.E., Gaffaney, J., van der Vaart, L., Dik, B.J., & Donaldson, S.I. (2023). The critiques and criticisms of positive psychology: A systematic review. The Journal of Positive Psychology, 19(2), 206–235.
Waterman, A.S. (2013). The humanistic psychology–positive psychology divide: Contrasts in philosophical foundations. American Psychologist, 68(3), 124–133.
Wong, P.T.P. (2011). Positive psychology 2.0: Towards a balanced interactive model of the good life. Canadian Psychology, 52(2), 69–81.

Chapter 2

Key Concepts

Positive Psychology has matured rapidly into a recognised discipline with its own research questions, methods, applications and professional communities. As with any new field, its legitimacy and progress depend on clarifying what the discipline is concerned with. Demarcating boundaries provides a shared conceptual architecture that enables coherent programmes of research and applied work and meaningful integration with other disciplines.

This chapter introduces the concepts that define Positive Psychology and organise its scholarly landscape. The chapter also provides brief reviews of seven concepts most central to Positive Psychology's identity, highlighting their conceptual contours and distinctive contributions.

The Scope of Positive Psychology

> **Self-efficacy:** A person's belief in their ability to successfully manage tasks, challenges or goals.
>
> **Hardiness:** A personality trait associated with coping well under pressure and dealing effectively with stress.

In a comprehensive mapping exercise, Rusk and Waters (2013) charted the range of topics being studied under the banner of Positive Psychology. They identified 233 distinct topics (see Figure 2.1), which they organised into 21 overarching themes: Life satisfaction, happiness, positive emotions, mood, **self-efficacy**, motivation, **self-regulation**, creativity, optimism, resilience, **hardiness**, mental toughness, posttraumatic growth, behavioural change, relationships, altruism, leadership, citizenship behaviour, education, mindfulness and gratitude.

Notably, around 30% of these topics represent new themes that gained prominence after the field's formal emergence (e.g. positive emotions,

DOI: 10.4324/9781032663111-3

Figure 2.1 A wordle depicting the key themes that featured in Positive Psychology publications.

Source: Rusk and Waters (2013)

character strengths, gratitude, mental toughness and psychological capital (PsyCap)). However, the majority of topics (approximately 70%, including optimism, self-efficacy, self-determination, resilience, self-regulation, mindfulness and wisdom) had substantial research histories prior to the advent of Positive Psychology. This raises questions about disciplinary boundaries and ownership: To what extent do these long-established constructs belong within Positive Psychology's remit? As it stands, the discipline's remit is typically framed broadly, such that its boundaries encompass these well-established constructs that are regarded as allied with the discipline rather than originated by it (Hart, 2020). Moreover, several of these concepts had remained comparatively underdeveloped prior to the establishment of the field. One of Positive Psychology's central contributions was to consolidate this dispersed work, placing it higher on the research agenda, extending it theoretically and empirically, and integrating it into a more coherent body of knowledge (Linley & Joseph, 2004).

A closer examination of the topics which dominated the field in its first 15 years of existence suggests several patterns. First, most research focused on adults, while only a relatively small proportion examined children. Much of this child-focused work falls within the domain of **Positive Education** (see Chapter 7). Second, most topics were situated at the **micro-level** and, within this level, the dominant emphasis was on intrapersonal constructs. These can be grouped into three broad categories:

Positive traits, which encompass concepts such as strengths and virtues, emotional intelligence and optimism; positive states and processes, such as flow, coping and resilience; and positive outcomes and experiences, most notably wellbeing and happiness (see Chapters 3 and 4), with less attention given to other constructs such as self-actualisation and wisdom. This may explain why wellbeing and happiness have developed into more theoretically rich areas than other Positive Psychology concepts. Alongside this intra-personal emphasis, there is also a distinct body of research on **interpersonal positive experiences**, which includes topics such as **kindness**, social support and love. A relatively small number of concepts are examined at the **meso level** (groups, communities or organisations). These are mainly organisational in focus and largely fall within the domain of **Positive Work and Organisations** (see Chapter 8). Relevant concepts include teamwork, collaboration and leadership. Finally, **macro-level research** mainly consists of large-scale surveys centred on wellbeing and happiness as the primary positive outcomes, typically examining their key predictors (see Chapters 3 and 4).

> **Micro-level:** A level of analysis focused mainly on individuals and their personal psychological characteristics or experiences.
>
> **Meso level:** A middle level of analysis focusing on groups, communities, organisations or other social units.
>
> **Macro level:** The largest level of analysis, focusing on large-scale social patterns, populations or systems.

Since 2013, no updated global mapping analysis has been published. However, several other reviews (Kim et al., 2018; Wang et al., 2023) alongside an assessment of the topics covered in recently published textbooks (Boniwell & Tunariu, 2019; Carr, 2022; Compton & Hoffman, 2019; Hart, 2020; Pedrotti et al., 2024; Snyder et al., 2020) indicate that despite a distinctive increase in publications (Wang et al., 2023) this broad thematic classification of the field continues to be reflected in contemporary texts. This suggests that within Psychology, Positive Psychology mainly integrated with Applied, Individual and Personality Psychology and with Social Psychology.

At the same time, Positive Psychology has also developed along other trajectories, several of which have consolidated into interdisciplinary sub-disciplines. These include two well-established sub-disciplines: Positive Education (see Chapter 7) and Positive Work and Organisations (see Chapter 8). Another growing area is **Positive Health** (see Chapter 9), while a newer domain, **Positive Economic Psychology**, has only recently been introduced (see Chapter 10). Beyond these, a range of additional interdisciplinary sub-domains are developing, including Positive Body (Hefferon,

2013), Positive Ageing (Minichiello & Coulson, 2012), Positive Neuroscience (Greene & Seligman, 2016), Positive Environment and Architecture (Menezes et al., 2021), and Positive Tourism (Filep et al., 2016). In parallel, several integrated applied fields have developed, such as **Positive Psychology Coaching**, **Positive Psychotherapy**, Quality of Life Therapy, Positive **Cognitive Behavioural Therapy** and **Positive Psychiatry** (reviewed in Chapter 6).

These developments indicate that Positive Psychology has progressed along two parallel yet complementary paths. On the one hand, its core knowledge base within Psychology remains centred largely on micro-level phenomena, particularly intra-personal strengths, processes and wellbeing-related outcomes and, to a lesser extent, interpersonal processes and experiences. On the other hand, its expansion into interdisciplinary and applied domains reflects an increasing effort to move beyond its original psychological boundaries and engage with diverse contexts of human functioning. This pattern points to a tension between depth and breadth. The field has developed a relatively coherent centre of gravity, yet its scope remains uneven, combining limited depth in some areas with incomplete theoretical development in several of its core themes. At the same time, much of its maturation trajectory appears through the expansion of its boundaries into adjacent domains. Future progress is therefore likely to depend both on deepening and extending existing lines of inquiry and on more carefully developing stronger conceptual cores within interdisciplinary integrations.

Classic Topics

As the scope of Positive Psychology expanded, a small number of themes came to occupy a central place in its identity. Two core themes are highly theoretically developed and extensively researched – wellbeing and happiness (discussed in Chapters 3 and 4). Alongside these, seven classic topics stand out: Strengths, optimism, flow, meaning in life, resilience, kindness and love. These topics, which emerged during its first wave of development (see Chapter 1), reflect the discipline's defining concern with understanding the conditions and processes that enable individuals and communities to flourish. The sections below briefly summarise each of these foundational themes.

Character Strengths and Virtues

Character strengths and virtues are among the most influential and distinctive contributions of Positive Psychology. Aligned with its aim to redress the traditional imbalance in Psychology by attending to the qualities that enable individuals and communities to thrive, the Values in Action **(VIA) classification** of character strengths and virtues developed by Peterson and Seligman's (2004) represents a landmark development. Its aim was to "reclaim the study of character and virtue as legitimate topics of psychological inquiry" (Peterson & Seligman, 2004, p. 3) and to create "a manual of the sanities" comparable to the Diagnostic and Statistical Manual of Mental Disorders (DSM) in its breadth, depth, detail and practical utility for researchers and practitioners.

> **VIA classification:** The Values in Action framework that organises 24 character strengths under six broad virtues.

The VIA project was highly ambitious in both scope and intent. Drawing on major philosophical traditions and religious texts from across cultures and historical periods, Peterson and Seligman (2004) sought to identify traits that have been widely regarded as fundamental to good character. The result was a classification of 24 character strengths organised under six broad virtues (see Table 2.1).

Virtues are acquired excellences of character that contribute to a person's wholeness, while **character strengths** are the more specific, psychologically meaningful qualities through which virtues are expressed in everyday life. These strengths are seen as core positive traits that reflect a person's identity and values. They are intrinsically rewarding and contribute to beneficial outcomes for both the self and others (Niemiec, 2017). A further distinction is that of **signature strengths**. These are strengths that individuals

> **Virtues:** Broad, valued qualities of character, such as wisdom, courage, humanity, justice, temperance and transcendence.
>
> **Character strengths:** Positive personal qualities, such as kindness, curiosity or perseverance, that help people function well and express good character.
>
> **Signature strengths:** The strengths that are most characteristic of a person. They are frequently used, valued and experienced as authentic.

Table 2.1 The VIA classification of character strengths and virtues

Virtues	*Strength*	*Details*
Wisdom and knowledge (Cognitive strengths)	**Creativity**	Producing original or novel ideas and showing cognitive flexibility
	Curiosity	Taking an interest in the world and in ongoing experiences
	Judgement/Open mindedness	Thinking things through and examining them from all sides
	Love of learning	Mastering new skills, topics, or knowledge
	Perspective	Being wise and knowledgeable, able to reflect and take stock, and provide counsel to others
Courage (Emotional strengths)	**Bravery**	Not shrinking from threat, challenge, difficulty, or pain
	Industry/perseverance	Finishing what we start
	Authenticity/Honesty	Being open and honest, leading life authentically and with integrity
	Zest	Approaching life with excitement and energy
Humanity (Social strengths)	**Kindness**	Doing good deeds for others
	Love	Valuing close relationships with others
	Social intelligence	Adept in understanding our own as well as other people's motives and feelings
Justice (Community strengths)	**Fairness**	Treating people equally, with fairness and justice
	Leadership	Influencing and helping others, directing and motivating others towards collective achievements
	Teamwork	Working well as a member of a group or team
Temperance (Protective Strengths)	**Forgiveness**	Forgiving those who have done wrong
	Modesty	Letting our accomplishments speak for themselves
	Prudence	Being careful about life choices; not saying or doing things that might later be regretted.
	Self-regulation	Applying self-control and self-discipline
Transcendence (Spiritual strengths)	**Appreciation of beauty and excellence**	Noticing and appreciating beauty, excellence or skilled performance in all domains of life
	Gratitude	Being aware of and thankful for the good things that happen
	Hope	Expecting the best in the future and working to achieve it
	Humour	Enjoy laughing and teasing, bringing happiness to other people
	Spirituality	Having coherent beliefs about the higher purpose and meaning of life

Source: Peterson and Park (2009).

"own, celebrate and frequently exercise" (Peterson & Park, 2009, p. 29). Signature strengths are considered authentic and energising since they capture what is most characteristic of a person. By contrast, **lower strengths** are those that are less developed or less frequently expressed.

The VIA approach assumes that everyone possesses strengths and that all strengths have value. It also proposes that flourishing is supported by identifying and using one's assets more effectively (Niemiec, 2017).

Strengths-based perspective/approach: An approach that focuses on people's assets, capacities and resources rather than only on their problems or deficits.

The **strengths-based perspective** marked a significant shift in psychological thinking, since it emphasised what is right with people and how these qualities can be cultivated. This is particularly important given the well-established tendency for negative information to command greater attention than positive information (Baumeister et al., 2001). However, the strengths approach is not naïvely optimistic. It does not deny problems or weaknesses. Rather, it offers an alternative lens through which individuals can draw on personal resources to address challenges.

VIA Measures

The VIA measures are designed to help individuals assess their personal strengths profile. Several versions have been developed, with the shortest version including 24 items. Versions are available for adults and children (Niemiec, 2017).

Research on character strengths, much of which includes assessing the impact of the strength spotting intervention (see Chapter 5), has shown that strengths awareness and use are associated with a range of desirable outcomes. These include greater wellbeing, life satisfaction, meaning, optimism, resilience, confidence, vitality and positive relationships, as well as lower levels of depression. In workplaces, strengths use has been linked with engagement, productivity, job satisfaction, creativity and reduced stress. In educational settings, it has been associated with student wellbeing, engagement, achievement, and social competence (Niemiec, 2017). Together, these findings underline the importance of character strengths and virtues as pathways to individual fulfilment and to healthier institutions and communities.

Optimism

Optimism is one of the foundational constructs in Positive Psychology and has played a significant role in reshaping how Psychology understands mental health and human functioning. Until the late 1960s, influential traditions in Psychology regarded mental health as closely tied to realism, namely the accurate perception of oneself and the world. Within this framework, optimism was treated with suspicion, seen as a form of self-deception, distortion or illusion that might impair judgement and functioning. From the 1970s onwards, however, this view was increasingly challenged by research findings which indicated that optimism is common, as well as **adaptive** and beneficial (Taylor & Brown, 1988; Seligman, 2006). This shift proved conceptually important since it challenged the assumption that realism is the hallmark of psychological health.

> **Optimism** refers to positive expectations regarding the future. It has been described as a generalised expectation that good things will happen (Carver & Scheier, 2014) and, in some formulations, as the tendency to overestimate positive events and underestimate negative ones (Sharot et al., 2011).

One of the most influential accounts is Seligman's theory of learned optimism, which conceptualises optimism as an **explanatory style**. According to this view, people differ in how they habitually explain the causes of events in their lives and these patterns shape their expectations for the future (Seligman, 2006). Optimists tend to explain negative events using external, temporary and specific **attributions**, while interpreting positive events as resulting from internal, stable and global causes. Pessimists show the opposite pattern. These explanatory habits are consequential since they affect how people make decisions, pursue life goals and whether they respond to setbacks with persistence or helplessness. Seligman argued that pessimistic explanatory styles can contribute to learned helplessness and depression, whereas optimism can help protect against them (Seligman, 2006).

> **Explanatory style:** A person's habitual way of explaining why events happen.
>
> **Attribution:** Explanation of what caused an outcome and why it happened.

Measures of Optimism

Explanatory style is commonly assessed using the Optimistic–Pessimistic Explanatory Style Questionnaire (Peterson et al., 1982). The measure presents 48 hypothetical negative events and asks respondents to indicate the causes they would most likely attribute to each event.

The significance of optimism lies in its wide-ranging associations with positive functioning. Peterson (2000) referred to optimism as a "velcro concept" as it was found to be linked to a broad array of desirable outcomes. Research suggests that optimism is associated with greater happiness and wellbeing, higher self-esteem, self-efficacy, confidence, motivation, planning and persistence in goal pursuit (Carver et al., 2010; Forgeard & Seligman, 2012). Optimists also appear to cope more adaptively with adversity, show greater resilience and engage more readily in effective problem-solving and learning from failure (Forgeard & Seligman, 2012). Optimism has also been linked with better physical health, greater longevity and lower risk of heart disease (DuBois et al., 2015; Rozanski et al., 2019). In the social domain, it is associated with having larger social networks, more satisfying relationships and better conflict management (Carver et al., 2010).

At the same time, optimism is not an unqualified good. Peterson (2000) cautioned that it can become problematic when it leads to wishful thinking, neglect of risks or failure to act appropriately. Thus, the value of optimism lies not in blind positivity, but in fostering hopeful expectations while remaining responsive to reality. Understood in this balanced way, optimism remains one of the central concepts through which Positive Psychology has illuminated the cognitive and motivational foundations of flourishing.

Flow

Flow is one of the classic topics in Positive Psychology and has become central to understanding engagement and optimal functioning. The concept originated in early attempts to understand why people willingly engage in demanding forms of play and performance, including rock climbing, chess, dance, music, art and sport. Across these diverse activities, participants described a distinctive state of deep absorption in which they became fully immersed in what they were doing, often losing awareness of time, bodily needs, and surrounding events. Csikszentmihalyi (2014) termed this experience flow, drawing on participants' descriptions of being carried along effortlessly, like riding a current.

Flow can be defined as a state of intense experiential involvement in an activity in the present moment, in which attention is fully invested in the task at hand and performance operates at one's highest capacity (Csikszentmihalyi, 2014). It is therefore both action- and performance-oriented and typically arises in relation to a specific task. Although flow can occur in many domains, it is especially common in relatively complex and structured activities such as writing, music, painting, dancing, gaming and sport.

Flow: A state of deep absorption in an activity, in which attention is fully focused and the person becomes highly engaged in the task.

Research suggests that flow does not arise randomly, but depends on several conditions. First, the activity typically involves clear goals and rules, so that the person knows what is required at each stage. Second, flow is more likely when there is clear and immediate feedback, enabling continuous adjustment of action. Third, flow depends on a balance between challenge and skill. The task needs to be demanding enough to stretch the person, but not so difficult that it produces anxiety, nor so easy that it leads to boredom. Flow is most likely when both challenge and skill are relatively high, creating a state of dynamic equilibrium (Csikszentmihalyi, 2014).

Several defining characteristics accompany this state. These include intense concentration, a merging of action and awareness, a sense of control, reduced self-consciousness and an altered sense of time. Flow is also **autotelic**, meaning that the activity is rewarding in itself rather than pursued solely for an external outcome.

Autotelic: An activity that is rewarding in itself, rather than done mainly for some external outcome.

Measuring Flow

Early research on flow was primarily qualitative, relying on in-depth interviews with artists, scientists, writers, athletes and others. Later, the Flow Questionnaire was developed (Csikszentmihalyi & Csikszentmihalyi, 1988), which includes three open-ended questions and 12 closed items assessing key features of the flow experience.

Flow is associated with a range of beneficial outcomes. Studies have linked it to greater happiness, positive affect, motivation, engagement and enjoyment, as well as improved performance, productivity and progress in educational and occupational settings (Csikszentmihalyi, 2014). Importantly, because flow is intrinsically rewarding, it motivates repeated engagement. Over time, this can foster skill development, mastery and personal growth, since continued flow requires progressively greater challenges as competence increases.

However, flow also has a darker side. It can arise in maladaptive or morally problematic activities, including gambling, excessive gaming or high-risk pursuits. Its intensely rewarding quality may also make it addictive (Csikszentmihalyi, 2014). Thus, while flow is often beneficial, it is not inherently good in every context.

Overall, flow has made a major contribution to Positive Psychology by illuminating how deep engagement, disciplined attention and optimal challenge can enrich human functioning. It highlights that fulfilment often emerges not from passive pleasure, but from immersion in meaningful and demanding activity.

Meaning in Life

Meaning in life is a topic that predates Positive Psychology, having been discussed extensively in religion, literature, and philosophy. Frankl (1963) is widely regarded as a leader in the study of meaning. Reflecting on his survival in Nazi concentration camps during the Second World War, he argued that a sense of purpose and meaning helped him endure profound suffering. He later developed **Logotherapy**, a meaning-centred therapeutic approach based on the premise that the striving to find meaning is a primary human motivation (Frankl, 1986). Later scholars, including Steger (2012) and Wong (2012a), advanced this work theoretically

Logotherapy: A meaning-centred therapeutic approach developed by Frankl, based on the idea that finding meaning is a central human motivation.

and empirically, helping to establish meaning in life as a central construct in Positive Psychology.

> **Meaning in life** is defined as the extent to which individuals experience their lives as making sense, being guided by worthy goals and mattering in the world (King et al., 2016).

Heintzelman and King (2014) conceptualised meaning in life as comprising three interrelated components:

- **Comprehension** refers to the cognitive component of meaning and concerns the extent to which life feels coherent, intelligible and understandable. When comprehension is high, people feel that their experiences make sense; when it is low, life may appear fragmented or confusing.
- **Purpose** is the behavioural dimension and reflects the extent to which people are oriented towards worthwhile goals. A strong sense of purpose provides direction, whereas its absence is often experienced as aimlessness.
- **Mattering** is the emotional factor and refers to the sense that one's existence has significance and that one's actions make a difference. Low mattering, by contrast, is associated with feelings of insignificance.

Meaning in life shapes how people interpret their experiences, direct their actions and pursue their goals. Wong (2012a) argued that life without meaning is like "being on a ship without a rudder" (p. 6). At the same time, meaning is not static. It is often reconfigured during existential crises or major life transitions (Wong, 2012a). Yalom (1980) proposed that perceiving life as empty or pointless can precipitate a crisis of meaning and substantial psychological distress. Wong (2012b) suggested that common sources of meaning include achievement, relationships, spirituality, **self-transcendence**, self-acceptance and fairness.

Measures of Meaning in Life

Several validated scales have been developed to assess meaning in life. The Meaning in Life Questionnaire (Steger et al., 2006) is a ten-item measure comprising two subscales: The presence of meaning and the search for meaning.

The Personal Meaning Profile (MacDonald et al., 2012) contains 21 items assessing individuals' sources of meaning across seven domains: Achievement, relationships, religion, self-transcendence, self-acceptance, intimacy and fairness.

The Purpose in Life Test (Crumbaugh & Maholick, 1964) is a 20-item scale designed to assess the extent to which a person experiences meaning and purpose in life.

A substantial body of research shows that meaning in life is positively associated with wellbeing, happiness and adaptive functioning, including vitality, optimism, hope, resilience, self-esteem, self-acceptance, internal locus of control, responsibility, ambition, self-control and personal growth, while low meaning is linked to depression, anxiety, hopelessness, hostility, aggression, substance misuse and suicidality (Steger, 2017). It has also been associated with better physical health, quicker recovery from illness, better adjustment to chronic conditions and conducive health behaviours, and with lower mortality risk (Cross et al., 2018). Meaning in life is also positively associated with several relational outcomes, including a sense of belonging, closeness to others, social support, effective social functioning and social appeal. By contrast, social isolation and exclusion are associated with lower meaning in life (Steger, 2017).

Research on meaning in life has advanced considerably, deepening the understanding of the construct, its lived experience and its many benefits. Current work suggests that cultivating meaning involves reflection, self-awareness, self-evaluation, clarifying one's purpose and contributing to wider goals in ways that make a difference.

Resilience

Stressful experiences are a normal part of life, yet individuals vary considerably in how well they adapt when facing everyday difficulties, major life disruptions or prolonged hardship. Resilience research emerged from the observation that many people maintain relatively healthy functioning despite severe adversity. Across both developmental and adult research, one consistent finding stands out: Resilience is common rather than exceptional (Long & Bonanno, 2018; Masten, 2015).

Resilience: Positive adaptation in the face of adversity, stress or hardship.

Resilience is defined as "patterns of positive adaptation in the context of past and present adversity" (Riley & Masten, 2005, p. 13). Some scholars conceptualised resilience as a set of **protective factors** that buffer individuals against risk. Others viewed it as a dynamic process involving the interaction between the person, the adversity and the coping responses that unfold over time (Long & Bonanno, 2018). From this perspective, resilience is an evolving process shaped by personal and contextual factors.

Protective factors: Qualities or conditions that reduce risk and help people cope effectively with adversity.

Several patterns of resilience have been identified in the literature (Lepore & Revenson, 2006):

- **Resistance** refers to maintaining relatively stable functioning with minimal disruption;
- **Recovery** describes an initial period of distress followed by a return to previous levels of functioning;
- **Reconfiguration** involves adapting by creating a new equilibrium after major disruption;
- By contrast, low resilience may result in **succumbing**, where distress persists and functioning remains impaired.

A large body of research has identified factors that support resilience (Long & Bonanno, 2018; Masten, 2015; Reivich et al., 2011; Lahad, 2017; Windle & Bennett, 2012). These include:

- **Cognitive capacities** such as realistic thinking, problem-solving, goal setting and learning from mistakes appear important;
- **Emotional resources,** including self-regulation, emotional intelligence and the ability to generate positive emotions, also play a protective role;
- **Social support** is one of the most consistently reported predictors of resilience, including close relationships and wider community involvement;
- **Beliefs and outlooks** such as optimism, meaning in life and values strongly shape resilience;

- **Self-knowledge** is also essential for facing adversity, including positive self-esteem, knowing one's boundaries and accepting strengths and weaknesses;
- **Resourcefulness and creativity** can help people improvise and find solutions during times of hardship;
- **Physiology and good health habits** have been found to contribute significantly to resilience;
- **Resources** such as education, time and money have also been associated with more positive adaptation.

Measures of Resilience

The Connor–Davidson Resilience Scale (Connor & Davidson, 2003) is a 25-item measure that has been used widely.

Another instrument is the Resilience Scale for Adults (Friborg et al., 2003), a 37-item scale assessing protective factors associated with healthy adaptation.

The outcomes of resilience are wide-ranging. Most fundamentally, resilience enables people to endure, recover or adapt positively in the face of hardship. Beyond this, it has been linked with improved physical health, lower stress, depression and anxiety, and greater wellbeing, hope, self-efficacy, life satisfaction and quality of life. In work settings, resilience is associated with motivation, productivity, self-regulation and goal attainment (Zautra et al., 2010; Long & Bonanno, 2018). Research on resilience interventions has also demonstrated moderate effectiveness, indicating that resilience skills can be developed (see Chapter 5). Overall, resilience is best understood not as invulnerability, but as the ordinary yet powerful capacity to adapt well under pressure.

Kindness

Kindness is a central interpersonal theme in Positive Psychology and is commonly defined as actions intended to benefit others (Curry et al., 2018).

Kindness: Actions intended to benefit others, often through everyday behaviours that communicate care, respect or goodwill.

Contemporary scholarship conceptualises kindness as a multidimensional construct. It can be understood as a trait and a state, a virtue and a character strength, a moral emotion, a motivation, an attitude and a form of behaviour. It is also more than an individual attribute: Kindness may function as a norm, value, ethos or cultural feature within organisations, communities and societies. In this sense, kindness can be viewed as a meta-concept grounded in the idea of human interdependence.

> **Prosocial behaviour:** Behaviour intended to benefit others, such as helping, sharing, donating, supporting or volunteering.

Kindness belongs to the broader domain of **prosocial behaviour** (Eisenberg & Spinrad, 2014). Examples include helping, sharing, donating, supporting, comforting, and volunteering. However, kindness is often treated as a more specific subset of prosociality. Whereas prosocial behaviour may be directed towards individuals, groups, communities or wider social causes, acts of kindness are more commonly directed towards a person or small group, often through everyday, relatively low-cost actions such as listening, offering reassurance, or giving a compliment (Sanderson & McQuilkin, 2017). These ordinary acts may appear small, but they are socially significant because they communicate care, respect and goodwill.

Malti (2020) proposed that kindness involves three components:

- **Kind cognitions** involve perspective taking, openness and a respectful effort to understand others' standpoints;
- **Kind emotions** include empathy, sympathy, compassion, tenderness and gratitude, as well as self-conscious moral emotions such as guilt or shame when one regrets harming another;
- **Kind behaviours** refer to actions that express care and concern, ranging from simple gestures to more effortful forms of help and support.

Malti (2020) also referred to self-kindness, comprising kind thoughts, emotions and behaviours directed towards oneself, such as self-care, self-soothing and reduced self-criticism.

A major line of research examines why people behave kindly. Some theories emphasise evolutionary and biological foundations, suggesting that prosocial tendencies support survival and group cohesion (Bierhoff, 2002). Neuroscientific work indicates that humans are equipped for empathic responding: Observing another person's pain can activate neural systems associated with one's own pain, and vagal activity has also been linked to prosocial behaviour (Kogan et al., 2014; Singer & Lamm, 2009). Other perspectives focus on personality, identifying attributes such as empathy, social responsibility and helpfulness as part of a broader prosocial orientation (Penner et al., 2005). Situational accounts highlight the role of emotions, social norms, reciprocity and contextual judgements in shaping whether people act prosocially in a given moment (Batson, 2014).

Kindness Measures

The Kindness Scale developed by Youngs et al. (2021) assesses kindness as a trait. It comprises 40 items across four subscales.

Kindness matters since it benefits both the actor and the receipients. Research on kindness interventions shows that prosocial actions can enhance happiness, life satisfaction, positive affect, meaning, and self-worth, strengthen social connection, and allow the person to see the difference they have made (Aknin et al., 2019; Klein, 2017). Kindness has also been linked with better mental and physical health, including lower depression and stress, and reduced risk of morbidity and cardiovascular disease (Burr et al., 2016; Brown et al., 2003). In intimate relationships, work, and healthcare, kindness contributes to trust, cooperation, engagement, and relational quality (Gottman & Gottman, 2015; Bradbury & Karney, 2004; Bakker & Schaufeli, 2008; Berry et al., 2017). At the same time, kindness is not always uncomplicated: Well-intentioned acts may be misguided, and recipients may sometimes experience indebtedness or inadequacy. Even so, kindness remains a foundational expression of our social nature and an important pathway to both relational and personal flourishing.

Love

The desire for intimate and loving relationships is a major driving force in human life. Many people devote substantial time, effort and emotional energy to finding and sustaining close bonds, reflecting the central role of love in wellbeing. Within Psychology, love has been conceptualised in different ways, with some scholars emphasising its emotional qualities and others focusing on its relational structure.

Fredrickson (2013) conceptualised **love** as a supreme emotion, describing it as a "micro-moment of warmth and connection" shared with another living being (p. 10).

Fredrickson argued that love is a form of connection that is felt when positive emotions are shared, there is synchrony in people's behaviour and biochemistry and there is an underlying impulse to care for one another.

When these elements coincide, they create moments of positive resonance in which emotional energy is exchanged. Fredrickson also maintained that two conditions are necessary for love to emerge: Face-to-face interaction and a sense of safety within the relationship.

While Fredrickson (2013) conceptualised love as an emotional experience, Sternberg (1987; 2006) viewed love as a type of relationship, which comprises three components:

- **Intimacy**: Feelings of closeness expressed through shared knowledge and understanding, warmth, mutual trust and support. Intimacy is the emotional component of relationships.
- **Passion**: Physical and psychological arousal, excitement or desire, including sexual attraction. Passion is considered the motivational component of relationships.
- **Commitment**: A sense of durability, continuity or stability in a relationship, often grounded in a conscious decision to remain invested in it and to sustain it over time. Commitment is the cognitive component of relationships.

According to the model, each of these elements characterises the love shared between any two individuals. Since each component can vary in intensity from low to high, they can combine in numerous ways, giving rise to a wide range of possible forms of love. The principal prototypes are outlined below.

- **Nonlove:** When intimacy, passion and commitment are all absent, love is not present. Such relationships are typically experienced as casual acquaintances that are superficial and uncommitted.
- **Liking:** When intimacy is high, but passion and commitment are low, the relationship reflects liking. This is characteristic of friendship, where warmth and closeness are present, but without strong desire or long-term commitment.
- **Infatuation:** This type of love occurs when passion is intense, but intimacy and commitment are absent. It is often seen when people who hardly know one another experience strong attraction.
- **Empty love:** This form of love is characterised by commitment in the absence of intimacy and passion. It may occur in depleted relationships that continue due to a decision to remain together. In arranged marriages, it may also represent the starting point of the relationship.
- **Romantic love:** This highly desired type of love combines intimacy and passion but does not include commitment. Although commitment may later develop, Sternberg argued that it is not a defining feature of this type of relationship.
- **Companionate love**: Here, intimacy and commitment are strong, while passion is low. It is marked by deep affection, care and long-term

investment and is often found in enduring marriages in which passion has faded.

- **Fatuous love**: This type of love consists of passion and commitment without intimacy. It may arise when two people commit quickly on the basis of intense attraction, despite not knowing each other well.
- **Consummate love**: Marked by the presence of intimacy, passion and commitment, it is regarded as the fullest expression of love. Although often seen as the ideal, Sternberg suggested that it is difficult to maintain over time.

Measuring Love

The Passionate Love Scale (Hatfield & Sprecher, 1986) includes 15 items and is designed to measure romantic love.

Research suggests that love changes over time. Passion tends to diminish more quickly, whereas intimacy and commitment develop more gradually (Sternberg, 1987). As a result, relationships may shift from romantic love towards companionate love. Evidence also indicates that relationship satisfaction is more strongly predicted by intimacy and passion than by commitment (Cusack et al., 2014; Sternberg, 1987). Research also found that intimacy and commitment are stronger in women compared to men, in both heterosexual and same-gender relations (Duffy & Rusbult, 1986). As a result, commitment in gay men is slow to develop, compared to mix-gender couples and lesbians (Brown & Trevethan, 2010). Further studies suggested that same-gender couples report higher relationship satisfaction than heterosexual couples (Garcia & Umberson, 2019).

Overall, psychological research suggests that love is a dynamic and multifaceted phenomenon, shaped by emotional connection, relational processes and changing patterns of intimacy, passion and commitment over time.

Conclusion

Positive Psychology is a broad and evolving field whose boundaries encompass both novel contributions and long-established constructs that have been re-examined, extended and integrated in new ways. As this chapter has shown, its scope has been defined expansively and both publication output and public interest have grown steadily. Despite this breadth, the field's core research remains concentrated primarily at the micro-level. Two clusters are especially prominent: **Intrapersonal** constructs and **interpersonal positive experiences**. This suggests that, within Psychology, Positive Psychology has developed most strongly through integration with Applied, Individual and Personality Psychology, as well as with Social Psychology.

Intrapersonal: Psychological qualities or processes located within the individual, such as optimism, resilience or self-regulation.

Interpersonal experiences: Experiences that arise in relationships with others.

At the same time, the field has expanded beyond these psychological foundations through the emergence of a growing number of interdisciplinary sub-disciplines and applied domains. Positive Education and Positive Work and Organisations are now well-established, while newer areas such as Positive Health and Positive Economic Psychology point to an ongoing process of expansion. This suggests that the field's development has followed two parallel trajectories: A slower deepening and extension of its classic psychological concerns and a stronger expansion through interdisciplinary integration. As a result, Positive Psychology has acquired a relatively coherent centre of gravity within Psychology, but its broader development remains somewhat uneven, with greater progress in extending its boundaries than in fully consolidating the theoretical foundations of some of its central themes.

The classic concepts reviewed here illustrate the field's distinctive concern with human potential, adaptive functioning and positive experience. Taken together, they suggest that flourishing emerges through the interplay of inner resources, meaningful activity, supportive relationships and constructive engagement with life's challenges.

The chapters that follow build on this conceptual foundation by examining in greater detail two of the most theoretically developed concepts and central outcomes in Positive Psychology: wellbeing and happiness.

References

Aknin, L.B., Whillans, A.V., Norton, M.I., & Dunn, E.W. (2019). Happiness and prosocial behavior: An evaluation of the evidence. In J. De-Neve, H. Huang, S. Wang, & L.B. Aknin (Eds.), World happiness report (pp. 67–86). Sustainable Development Solutions Network.

Bakker, A.B., & Schaufeli, W.B. (2008). Positive organizational behavior: Engaged employees in flourishing organizations. Journal of Organizational Behavior, 29(2), 147–154.

Batson, C.D. (2014). The altruism question. Psychology Press.

Baumeister, R.F., Bratslavsky, E., Finkenauer, C., & Vohs, K.D. (2001). Bad is stronger than good. Review of General Psychology, (5), 323–370.

Berry, L.L., Danaher, T.S., Chapman, R.A., & Awdish, R.L. (2017). Role of kindness in cancer care. Journal of Oncology Practice, 13(11), 744–750.
Bierhoff, H.W. (2002). Prosocial behaviour. Psychology Press.
Boniwell, I., & Tunariu, A.D. (2019). Positive psychology. McGraw-Hill Education.
Bradbury, T.N., & Karney, B.R. (2004). Understanding and altering the longitudinal course of marriage. Journal of Marriage and Family, 66(4), 862–879.
Brown, J., & Trevethan, R. (2010). Shame, internalized homophobia, identity formation, attachment style, and the connection to relationship status in gay men. American Journal of Men's Health, 4(3), 267–276.
Brown, S.L., Nesse, R.M., Vinokur, A.D., & Smith, D.M. (2003). Providing social support may be more beneficial than receiving it: Results from a prospective study of mortality. Psychological Science, 14(4), 320–327.
Burr, J.A., Han, S.H., & Tavares, J.L. (2016). Volunteering and cardiovascular disease risk: Does helping others get "under the skin"? Gerontologist, 56(5), 937–947.
Carr, A. (2022). Positive psychology. Routledge.
Carver, C.S., & Scheier, M.F. (2014). Dispositional optimism. Trends in Cognitive Sciences, 18(6), 293–299.
Carver, C.S., Scheier, M.F., & Segerstrom, S.C. (2010). Optimism. Clinical Psychology Review, 30(7), 879–889.
Compton, W.C., & Hoffman, E. (2019). Positive psychology. Sage.
Connor, K.M., & Davidson, J.R.T. (2003). Development of a new resilience scale: The Connor–Davidson Resilience Scale (CDRISC). Depression and Anxiety, (18), 76–82.
Cross, M.P., Hofschneider, L., Grimm, M., & Pressman, S.D. (2018). Subjective well-being and physical health. In E. Diener, S. Oishi, & L. Tay (Eds.), Handbook of well-being. DEF Publishers.
Crumbaugh, J.C., & Maholick, L.T. (1964). An experimental study in existentialism: The psychometric approach to Frankl's concept of noogenic neurosis. Journal of Clinical Psychology, 20(2), 200–207.
Csikszentmihalyi, M. (2014). Flow and the foundations of positive psychology. Springer.
Csikszentmihalyi, M., & Csikszentmihalyi, I. (1988). Optimal experience. Cambridge University Press.
Curry, O.S., Rowland, L.A., Van Lissa, C.J., Zlotowitz, S., McAlaney, J., & Whitehouse, H. (2018). Happy to help? A systematic review and meta-analysis of the effects of performing acts of kindness on the well-being of the actor. Journal of Experimental Social Psychology, 76, 320–329.
Cusack, C.E., Hughes, J.L., & Cook, R.E. (2014). Components of love and relationship satisfaction: Lesbians and heterosexual women. Psi Chi Journal of Psychological Research, 17(4), 171.
DuBois, C.M., Lopez, O.V., Beale, E.E., Healy, B.C., Boehm, J.K., & Huffman, J.C. (2015). Relationships between positive psychological

constructs and health outcomes in patients with cardiovascular disease: A systematic review. International Journal of Cardiology, 195, 265–280.
Duffy, S.M., & Rusbult, C.E. (1986). Satisfaction and commitment in homosexual and heterosexual relationships. Journal of Homosexuality, 12(2), 1–23.
Eisenberg, N., & Spinrad, T.L. (2014). Multidimensionality of prosocial behavior: Rethinking the conceptualization and development of prosocial behavior. In L.M. Padilla-Walker, & G. Carlo (Eds.), Prosocial development (pp. 17–39). Oxford University Press.
Filep, S., Laing, J., & Csikszentmihalyi, M. (Eds.) (2016). Positive tourism. Routledge.
Forgeard, M.J.C., & Seligman, M.E.P. (2012). Seeing the glass half full: A review of the causes and consequences of optimism. Pratiques Psychologiques, 18(2), 107–120.
Frankl, V. (1963). Man's search for meaning. Pocket Books.
Frankl, V. (1986). The doctor and the soul. Vintage Books.
Fredrickson, B.L. (2013). Love 2.0. Penguin.
Friborg, O., Hjemdal, O., Rosenvinge, J.H., & Martinussen, M. (2003). A new rating scale for adult resilience: What are the central protective resources behind health adjustment? International Journal of Methods in Psychiatric Research, 12, 65–76.
Garcia, M.A., & Umberson, D. (2019). Marital strain and psychological distress in same-sex and different-sex couples. Journal of Marriage and Family, 81(5), 1253–1268.
Gottman, J.M., & Gottman, J.S. (2015). Gottman couple therapy. In A.S. Gurman, J.I. Lebow, & D.K. Snyder (Eds.), Clinical handbook of couple therapy (pp. 129–157). Guilford Press.
Greene, J.D., & Seligman, M.E.P. (Eds.). (2016). Positive neuroscience. Oxford University Press.
Hart, R. (2020). Positive psychology: The basics. Routledge.
Hatfield, E., & Sprecher, S. (1986). Measuring passionate love in intimate relationships. Journal of Adolescence, 9, 383–410.
Hefferon, K. (2013). Positive psychology and the body. Open University Press.
Heintzelman, S.J., & King, L.A. (2014). Life is pretty meaningful. American Psychologist, 69, 561–574.
Kim, H., Doiron, K., Warren, M., & Donaldson, S. (2018). The international landscape of positive psychology research: A systematic review. International Journal of Wellbeing, 8(1), 50–70.
King, L.A., Heintzelman, S.J., & Ward, S.J. (2016). Beyond the search for meaning: A contemporary science of the experience of meaning in life. Current Directions in Psychological Science, 25(4), 211–216.
Klein, N. (2017). Prosocial behavior increases perceptions of meaning in life. The Journal of Positive Psychology, 12(4), 354–361.
Kogan, A., Oveis, C., Carr, E.W., Gruber, J., Mauss, I.B., Shallcross, A., Impett, E.A., Van der Lowe, I., Hui, B., & Keltner, D. (2014). Vagal activity is quadratically related to prosocial traits, prosocial emotions, and observer perceptions of prosociality. Journal of Personality and Social Psychology, 107(6), 1051–1063.
Lahad, M. (2017). From victim to victor: The development of the BASIC PH model of coping and resiliency. Traumatology, 23(1), 27.

Lepore, S.J., & Revenson, T.A. (2006). Resilience and posttraumatic growth: Recovery, resistance, and reconfiguration. In L.G. Calhoun, & R.G. Tedeschi (Eds.), Handbook of posttraumatic growth (pp. 24–46). Lawrence Erlbaum.

Linley, P.A., & Joseph, S. (2004). Toward a theoretical foundation for positive psychology in practice. In P.A. Linley, & S. Joseph (Eds.), Positive psychology in practice (pp. 713–731). Wiley.

Long, K., & Bonanno, G.A. (2018). An integrative temporal framework for psychological resilience. In J.G. Noll, & I. Shalev (Eds.), The biology of early life stress (pp. 121–146). Springer.

MacDonald, M.J., Wong, P.T., & Gingras, D.T. (2012). Meaning in life measures and development of a brief version of the personal meaning profile. In P.T. Wong (Ed.), The human quest for meaning (pp. 357–382). Routledge.

Malti, T. (2020). Kindness: A perspective from developmental psychology. European Journal of Developmental Psychology, 18(5), 1–29.

Masten, A.S. (2015). Ordinary magic: Resilience in development. Guilford.

Menezes, K., de Oliveira-Smith, P., & Woodworth, A.V. (Eds.). (2021). Programming for health and well-being in architecture. Routledge.

Minichiello, V., & Coulson, I. (Eds.). (2012). Contemporary issues in gerontology. Routledge.

Niemiec, R.M. (2017). Character strengths interventions. Hogrefe.

Pedrotti, J.T., Lopez, S.J., McDermott, R.C., & Snyder, C.R. (2024). Positive psychology. Sage Publications.

Penner, L.A., Dovidio, J.F., Piliavin, J.A., & Schroeder, D.A. (2005). Prosocial behavior: Multilevel perspectives. Annual Review of Psychology, 56, 365–392.

Peterson, C. (2000). The future of optimism. American Psychologist, 55, 44–55.

Peterson, C., & Park, N. (2009). Classifying and measuring strengths of character. In S.J. Lopex, & C.R. Snyder (Eds.), Oxford handbook of positive psychology (pp. 25–34). Oxford University Press.

Peterson, C., & Seligman, M.E.P. (2004). Character strengths and virtues. APA.

Peterson, C., Semmel, A., von Baeyer, C., Abramson, L.Y., Metalsky, G.I., & Seligman, M.E.P. (1982). The attributional style questionnaire. Cognitive Therapy and Research, 6, 287–299.

Reivich, K.J., Seligman, M.E., & McBride, S. (2011). Master resilience training in the US Army. American Psychologist, 66(1), 25.

Riley, J.R., & Masten, A.S. (2005). Resilience in context. In R. Peters, R. B. Leadbeater, & R. McMahon (Eds.), Resilience in children, families, and communities (pp. 13–25). Springer.

Rozanski, A., Bavishi, C., Kubzansky, L.D., & Cohen, R. (2019). Association of optimism with cardiovascular events and all-cause mortality: A systematic review and meta-analysis. JAMA Network Open, 2(9), e1912200–e1912200.

Rusk, R.D., & Waters, L.E. (2013). Tracing the size, reach, impact, and breadth of positive psychology. The Journal of Positive Psychology, 8(3), 207–221. https://doi.org/10.1080/17439760.2013.777766.

Sanderson, R., & McQuilkin, J. (2017). Many kinds of kindness: The relationship between values and prosocial behaviour. In S. Roccas, & L. Sagiv (Eds.), Values and behavior (pp. 75–96). Springer.
Seligman, M.E. (2006). Learned optimism. Vintage.
Sharot, T., Korn, C.W., & Dolan, R.J. (2011). How unrealistic optimism is maintained in the face of reality. Nature Neuroscience, 1475–1479.
Singer, T., & Lamm, C. (2009). The social neuroscience of empathy. Annals of the New York Academy of Sciences, 1156, 81–96.
Snyder, C.R., Lopez, S.J., Edwards, L.M., & Marques, S.C. (Eds.). (2020). The Oxford handbook of positive psychology. Oxford University Press.
Steger, M.F. (2012). Making meaning in life. Psychological Inquiry, 23(4), 381–385.
Steger, M.F. (2017). Meaning in life and wellbeing. In M. Slade, L. Oades, & A. Jarden (Eds.), Wellbeing, recovery and mental health (pp. 75–85). Cambridge University Press.
Steger, M.F., Frazier, P., Oishi, S., & Kaler, M. (2006). The meaning in life questionnaire: Assessing the presence of and search for meaning in life. Journal of Counseling Psychology, 53(1), 80–93.
Sternberg, R.J. (1987). The triangle of love: Intimacy, passion, commitment. Basic Books.
Sternberg, R.J. (2006). A duplex theory of love. In R.J. Sternberg, & K. Weis (Eds.), The new psychology of love (pp. 184–199). Yale University Press.
Taylor, S.E., & Brown, J.D. (1988). Illusions and well-being: A social psychological perspective on mental health. Psychological Bulletin, 103(2), 193–210.
Wang, F., Guo, J., & Yang, G. (2023). Study on positive psychology from 1999 to 2021: A bibliometric analysis. Frontiers in Psychology, 14, 1101157.
Windle, G., & Bennett, K.M. (2012). Caring relationships: How to promote resilience in challenging times. In M. Ungar (Ed.), The social ecology of resilience (pp. 219–231). Springer.
Wong, P.T. (2012a). Toward a dual-systems model of what makes life worth living. In P.T. Wong (Ed.), The human quest for meaning (pp. 3–23). Routledge.
Wong, P.T. (2012b). From logotherapy to meaning-centered counseling and therapy. In P.T. Wong (Ed.), The human quest for meaning (pp. 619–647). Routledge.
Yalom, I. (1980). Existential psychotherapy. Basic Books.
Youngs, D.E., Yaneva, M.A., & Canter, D.V. (2021). Development of a measure of kindness. Current Psychology, 1–13.
Zautra, A.J., Hall, J.S., & Murray, K.E. (2010). Resilience: A new definition of health for people and communities. In J.W. Reich, A.J. Zautra, & J.S. Hall (Eds.), Handbook of adult resilience (pp. 3–34). Guilford.

Section 2

Key Theories

This Section in Summary

Chapter 3: Wellbeing

- Wellbeing refers to a life that is lived well and reflects an individual's **subjective evaluation** of the extent to which they have achieved an optimal quality of life.
- Two meta-theoretical frameworks have been used to map the core components of wellbeing: The widely applied distinction between hedonia and eudaimonia, and the more recent meta-model of having, loving, doing, and being.
- Overall wellbeing captures the wellbeing of individuals across varied life domains.
- Psychological wellbeing is a domain of overall wellbeing, regarded as a core concept in Positive Psychology, with multiple models identifying its components and offering compatible measures.
- Research on psychological wellbeing's antecedents and outcomes, indicates that social ties are especially important, while personality, health, work, and financial status also appear to be significant correlates.

Chapter 4: Happiness

- Happiness is defined as a continuum reflecting an individual's overall life evaluation and emotional experience.
- Set-Point Theory suggests that people have a typical baseline level of happiness, partly shaped by genetics.
- The Sustainable Happiness Model proposes that happiness is determined by genetics, life circumstances and intentional activities.
- **Hedonic Adaptation** describes the tendency for life events to affect happiness only temporarily.
- The Broaden-and-Build Theory proposes that positive emotions widen thought – action repertoires, build lasting resources, and help undo the effects of negative emotions.

DOI: 10.4324/9781032663111-4

- Several frameworks aim to optimise the pursuit of happiness: The Eudaimonic Activity Model, the Positive Activity Model, the Hedonic Adaptation Prevention Model, and Prioritising Positivity.
- Common pitfalls in pursuing happiness include striving for happiness, **social comparison**, and **affective forecasting** errors.
- Happiness is associated with better health, stronger relationships, and more positive work and economic outcomes, while also being influenced by demographics, personality and contextual factors.

Chapter 3

Wellbeing

Wellbeing is the beating heart of Positive Psychology, so integral to its identity that some have described the field as "the science and practice of improving wellbeing" (Lomas et al., 2014, p. ix). Across the literature, wellbeing functions not only as a flagship outcome but also as the organising thread that ties together the field's questions, methods and interventions (Seligman, 2012). Precisely because it plays this foundational role, wellbeing has also been one of Positive Psychology's most contested ideas, debated conceptually, semantically and methodologically. Yet recent developments indicate a notable shift in this long-standing discussion, with signs of convergence in how wellbeing is conceptualised (Lomas et al., 2024).

Much of Positive Psychology's empirical energy has focused on *psychological* wellbeing, while *overall* wellbeing, understood as a broader, multidomain phenomenon, has received less sustained attention. Reflecting this imbalance, the chapter begins with a definition of wellbeing, setting out its core domains, components and levels. It then examines overall wellbeing, briefly reviewing influential models that map its constituent domains. The discussion subsequently narrows to psychological wellbeing, surveying leading conceptual frameworks and measures, and synthesising evidence on its principal correlates.

Conceptualising Wellbeing

For nearly three decades, a key challenge in the wellbeing literature has been the persistent lack of clarity around its definition. Lomas et al. (2024) observed that, despite sustained scholarly effort, the question of how wellbeing should be defined has remained largely unresolved.

Wellbeing: A broad, multidimensional evaluation of how well a person is doing across life as a whole.

Subjective evaluation: A person's own evaluation of an aspect of their life.

DOI: 10.4324/9781032663111-5

Against the backdrop of this long-running debate, the definitions offered below indicate a potential breakthrough.

> **Wellbeing** is often framed as a "life well lived" (Hart, 2020, p. 47), and conceptualised as a fundamental human aim, reflecting the desire to meet our needs, pursue valued life goals and lead a life that is balanced and fulfilling.
>
> Lomas et al. (2024, p. 8) conceptualised overall human wellbeing as a continuum reflecting "the relative attainment of a personal subjective state of quality." This implies that wellbeing represents a person's subjective evaluation of how far they have attained an optimal level of quality of life and functioning, with quality denoting a level of goodness in this context.

Facets of Wellbeing

Scholars often refer to several facets that together structure and draw the boundaries around the construct of wellbeing (Hart & Hart, 2026):

- **Context-free wellbeing concept:** This concept refers to the overall wellbeing construct – an overarching, high-level, subjective evaluation of the extent to which a person has achieved a state of quality across different life domains. The concept integrates several key life domains to provide an overall evaluation.
- **Wellbeing domains:** These are specific life areas in which wellbeing can be experienced and evaluated, such as physical, occupational, social or financial wellbeing.
- **Components of wellbeing:** There are several core elements that make up wellbeing within or across domains. These refer to terms such as satisfaction, happiness, hedonic or eudaimonic wellbeing.
- **Meta-theoretical frameworks:** These are high-level frameworks that organise and define the broad facets of wellbeing, clarifying what should count as wellbeing and how its major components relate.
- **Models of wellbeing:** Structured accounts that elaborate meta-theories by specifying particular domains and/or components are considered models of wellbeing. They may be primarily theoretical or empirically grounded, and they offer a coherent map of the construct that informs both measurement decisions and the design of interventions.
- **Population segmentations:** Wellbeing is often conceptualised and measured in different ways across groups, for example, child wellbeing, employee wellbeing and immigrant wellbeing. Such segmentation matters since the salience, expression and determinants of wellbeing vary across populations.

- **Levels of wellbeing:** Terms such as flourishing, **languishing**, suffering or **illbeing** describe distinct gradations of wellbeing. They can be applied both to overall wellbeing and to wellbeing within specific domains.
- **Predictors of wellbeing:** The factors that are thought to shape wellbeing are often referred to as predictors of wellbeing. They are often grouped into demographic characteristics and internal and external influences.
- **Wellbeing outcomes:** Research on the downstream effects of wellbeing positions wellbeing as a potential driver that influences other life outcomes.
- **Correlates of wellbeing:** Factors that co-vary with wellbeing are often referred to as correlates of wellbeing. They are useful for describing patterns while remaining agnostic about whether one influences the other or whether a third factor accounts for both.
- **Wellbeing interventions:** These are evidence-based programmes or strategies intended to enhance wellbeing by cultivating positive states, bolstering functioning or mitigating influences that erode wellbeing. They can be delivered at individual, group, organisational and national levels. Typically, they are assessed in terms of whether they produce measurable improvements in wellbeing over time, with attention to who benefits, in which circumstances and via what mechanisms.
- **Measures of wellbeing:** There are numerous instruments used to operationalise and quantify wellbeing for research, evaluation or practice purposes. They can take the form of self-report questionnaires, experience-based methods, behavioural indicators, clinician ratings or administrative data. Importantly, measures do not all target the same domain of the construct: Some are designed to capture overall wellbeing, while others assess domain-specific wellbeing. Most measures draw on particular models of wellbeing, meaning that the scales are structured around those models' proposed components (see examples below).
- **Indicators of wellbeing**: Observable signs or metrics used to represent wellbeing overall or in a given context are commonly referred to as wellbeing indicators. Two types are often applied in the literature:
    - **Direct indicators** include people's own reports of their wellbeing.
    - **Indirect indicators** include behavioural, social or other signals that tend to track wellbeing.
        - **Proxies** are indirect indicators used as stand-ins for wellbeing when direct measurement is not feasible. Proxies can be useful pragmatically, but they are conceptually risky: They may capture only one aspect of wellbeing, reflect correlates or predictors, or be influenced by third factors that weaken their validity as wellbeing indicators.

Taken together, these facets offer a useful scaffold for organising the wellbeing literature. However, they also expose a persistent conceptual conundrum in the field: These concepts are frequently conflated, with researchers highlighting a lack of differentiation between context-free constructs, such as *overall wellbeing*, and domain-specific constructs, such as *psychological wellbeing* or *work wellbeing* (Pincus, 2023; Wijngaards et al., 2022). This **conceptual slippage** matters since it can undermine the development of measures, generate inconsistent findings across studies and obscure mechanisms of change.

Conceptual slippage: A lack of clarity caused by using terms in overlapping or inconsistent ways across disciplines.

Meta-Theories of Wellbeing: Mapping Its Core Components

Meta-theories of wellbeing provide an overarching conceptual platform for organising how the field defines, partitions and relates the core constituents of a "good life." A meta-theory functions at a higher level of abstraction, clarifying the organising principles that determine what counts as wellbeing and how its major domains should be distinguished. In this sense, meta-theories shape the conceptual "map" of wellbeing, whereas theoretical and empirical models translate this map into more fine-grained components and specify their structure, interrelations and, at times, causal dynamics.

Since the emergence of Positive Psychology, one meta-theoretical framework – the hedonia–eudaimonia distinction (Huta, 2016) has been extensively debated and has become widely adopted and highly influential. The other framework outlined next (Martela, 2025), is comparatively recent and challenges this dominant lens. It is worth noting that both are rooted in Western perspectives and may not translate well to other cultural contexts. Beyond the two meta-theories outlined next, other meta-theoretical accounts of wellbeing appear in the wider literature (see Hall's (2016) discussion of wellbeing in medicine); however, these are not typically linked to Positive Psychology.

Hedonia and Eudaimonia

Positive Psychology scholars often encapsulate wellbeing as a concept that comprises two central elements: **Feeling good** and **functioning well** (Keyes & Annas, 2009; Deci & Ryan, 2008). These dimensions draw on two long-standing philosophical traditions (Huta & Waterman, 2014):

- **Hedonia** refers to the experience of pleasure, contentment or gratification (Huta, 2016). It is typically understood as the experiential dimension of wellbeing and is treated as synonymous with happiness.

- **Eudaimonia** captures the behavioural dimension of wellbeing, involving functioning across life domains, alongside the enactment of virtues, engagement in morally worthwhile activities and the realisation of one's potential (Huta, 2016).

Hedonia: A component of wellbeing centred on happiness.

Eudaimonia: A component of wellbeing centred on functioning well.

The hedonia–eudaimonia distinction is often traced to Aristotle, who coined the term eudaimonia to describe a life worth living, a way of life that enables the attainment of a heightened state of quality and value (Huta, 2016). Aristotle positioned eudaimonic wellbeing as central to the good life and distinct from hedonia (Henderson & Knight, 2012), while also recognising that hedonic experience can arise from eudaimonic living and functioning (Huta, 2016). This view underpinned a foundational divide in the wellbeing literature, with scholars treating hedonia and eudaimonia as distinct concepts, a dichotomy that has remained influential in Psychology.

With the rise of Positive Psychology, empirical work on both constructs has grown, with evidence indicating a strong association between hedonia and eudaimonia (Goodman et al., 2017). The relationship is often characterised as bidirectional: How well people function shapes how happy they feel, and happiness can, in turn, support functioning and performance (Sheldon & Lyubomirsky, 2021). This has contributed to an emerging view that overall wellbeing comprises both hedonic and eudaimonic elements, each integral to a fulfilling life (Seligman, 2018).

Today, these perspectives coexist: One frames wellbeing as an integration of hedonic and eudaimonic facets, whereas the other treats eudaimonia as the essence of wellbeing (Hart, 2020). Another complication is that many studies blur hedonic and eudaimonic components in their operationalisations, with some authors arguing that, because the hedonic and eudaimonic aspects correlate strongly, treating eudaimonia as a separate component may be redundant (Goodman et al., 2017).

Despite these challenges, the hedonia–eudaimonia distinction has become firmly established across disciplines and is widely treated as a leading meta-theoretical lens for conceptualising wellbeing. However, models that break these components into more specific elements vary in the extent to which they integrate both dimensions.

Having, Loving, Doing and Being

Martela's (2025) meta-theory of wellbeing is a needs-based account rooted in the philosophical premise that a theory of wellbeing should specify the universal requirements that enable humans to survive, function and flourish.

Building on Allardt's (1976) framework, which organises wellbeing into domains of need satisfaction, Martela (2025) extended Allardt's (1993) classic triad of having, loving, and being into four modes of existence:

- **Having**: The material–biological preconditions for living well, which include secure access to resources and conditions that sustain life and protect basic functioning.
- **Loving**: The relational and social foundations of wellbeing – belonging, being cared for (and caring for others) and feeling valued within supportive communities.
- **Doing**: The agentic dimension of wellbeing – being able to act with volition and effectiveness, pursuing goals through autonomy and competence in everyday life.
- **Being**: The experiential–evaluative dimension of wellbeing – how life feels and is appraised, including affective states and life evaluation. This facet is shaped by the extent to which core needs in having, loving and doing are being fulfilled.

In this model, wellbeing is conceptualised as a structured outcome of need fulfilment across these domains. Although it aims to move beyond the hedonia–eudaimonia framework, critics might contend that it largely rearticulates similar elements: The hedonic facet maps onto the being component, while the eudaimonic facet is disaggregated into the need-based conditions for functioning represented by having, loving and doing.

Levels of Wellbeing

Across the wellbeing literature, researchers have developed an extensive – though at times inconsistent – lexicon for referring to different levels of wellbeing. Labels such as flourishing, languishing and illbeing are commonly used to capture distinct positions along a wellbeing continuum (Keyes, 2002). These descriptors are applied both to global wellbeing and to wellbeing within particular life domains. Despite their widespread use, few scholars have offered explicit definitions of these terms:

- **Flourishing** refers to a desirable state of overall wellbeing, reflecting the relative attainment of a condition in which the major facets of a person's life

Flourishing: High level of wellbeing.

Languishing: A medium level of wellbeing, whereby a person is not flourishing but not ill either.

Illbeing: A low state of wellbeing.

are positive and their environment supports sustained wellbeing (Lomas & VanderWeele, 2023).

- **Thriving** is framed as a desirable state of overall wellbeing that is achieved despite exposure to difficult, adverse or otherwise unsupportive contexts (Lomas et al., 2024).
- **Languishing** denotes a low level of wellbeing situated around the midpoint of the wellbeing continuum (Keyes, 2002). It can be characterised as an ambivalent state marked by a relative absence of positive, high-quality experiences, without the clear presence of distinctly negative or low-quality states.
- **Struggling** describes a lower wellbeing state in which individuals experience a mixed profile: Some personal states are experienced as high quality, while others are simultaneously experienced as lacking quality (Lomas et al., 2024).
- **Illbeing** (also termed floundering or ailing) can be understood as a condition characterised by the absence of personal states of quality alongside the presence of personal states that lack quality (Lomas et al., 2024).

These constructs provide a useful shorthand for describing broad gradations in wellbeing, but they also underscore the need for conceptual and methodological precision, since they are often used interchangeably with wellbeing (Hart & Hart, 2026).

Overall Wellbeing

Overall wellbeing is an umbrella construct that captures how well a person is faring as a whole, integrating multiple life domains. Because it spans domains and draws on varied theoretical traditions and measurements, overall wellbeing is treated as an interdisciplinary concept. As such, it often sits somewhat alongside, rather than fully within, the conceptual boundaries of Positive Psychology, with less consistent adherence to its terminology and theoretical frameworks. Additionally, it is often operationalised in large-scale population research and official statistics, where the priority is comparability, brevity and policy relevance.

> **Overall wellbeing** can be defined as "the quality of one's personal subjective state across the physical, mental, social, and spiritual dimensions of existence" (Lomas et al., 2024, p.11).

Models of Overall Wellbeing

Models of overall wellbeing typically disaggregate the broad construct into a set of constituent domains, each representing a distinct facet of life.

These models are commonly paired with measures that assess the hedonic and/or eudaimonic aspects specific to each domain, which can be aggregated across domains into an overall index.

Pincus (2023) reviewed the domains represented across overall wellbeing surveys and found substantial inconsistency: The number of domains ranged from 4 to 17. Most frameworks include physical, social and mental dimensions, while some also incorporate spiritual, intellectual, occupational, financial and environmental domains.

While approaches vary in their theoretical assumptions and the number or broadness of domains, the shared aim is to provide a coherent structure for conceptualising wellbeing and a pragmatic basis for measurement and comparison. The section below outlines two illustrative examples from the models currently in use.

The Gallup Wellbeing Model

The Gallup Wellbeing Model is one of the most widely applied frameworks in large-scale survey research, with Gallup's long-standing programmes enabling the examination of wellbeing patterns between countries and across time. The model distinguishes five **wellbeing domains** that can be analysed separately or combined into an overall composite score and includes subjective assessments of one's wellbeing in each domain. These assessments refer to the eudaimonic and hedonic aspects of wellbeing (Rath & Harter, 2010):

> **Wellbeing domains:** Specific areas of life in which wellbeing can be experienced and assessed, such as physical, social, occupational or financial wellbeing.

- **Career/purpose:** This domain concerns everyday activities, particularly work and productive pursuits;
- **Physical:** This component centres on health and vitality;
- **Social:** This domain reflects the presence of supportive, meaningful connections and experiences of love and belonging;
- **Community:** This aspect refers to a person's interest in, participation in and engagement with community life and civic matters at local and/or national levels;
- **Financial:** This domain focuses on managing one's finances effectively to reduce hardship and promote financial stability and security.

The Gallup Wellbeing Scale

To provide an overall wellbeing score, Gallup introduced a set of wellbeing benchmarks (Rath & Harter, 2010). The measure yields a

0–100 score for each of the five domains and uses predefined cut-off points to distinguish optimal from sub-optimal levels of wellbeing:

- **Thriving:** Individuals in this category report strong functioning across domains and tend to experience positive day-to-day states, such as feeling well-rested, enjoying activities and experiencing comfort. Thriving is defined by scores of 70 or above.
- **Struggling:** This group reflects moderate functioning in one or more domains and more frequent experiences of stress and difficulties. Struggling corresponds to scores between 40 and 69.
- **Suffering:** Individuals in this category rate their functioning and daily experiences as low across most or all domains, with scores below 40. Gallup's findings associate this profile with difficulties meeting basic needs, poorer physical health and elevated psychological distress.

The survey format and items have undergone periodic revisions, which should be borne in mind when interpreting trends across waves. Intriguingly, the model and measure do not refer to psychological wellbeing. Nevertheless, the index offers a pragmatic, policy-relevant way of conceptualising overall wellbeing that is multidimensional, subjective and combines hedonic and eudaimonic elements.

The State of Global Wellbeing

The Gallup (2014) State of Global Wellbeing report presented sobering findings on the state of wellbeing globally. Across each element of wellbeing, only around one in four people were thriving, the majority were struggling and a substantial minority were in the suffering category.

A decade later, data from the Gallup (2024) Global Life Evaluation Index suggested that global wellbeing has changed only marginally: On average, 28% of people were classified as thriving, struggling remained the largest group at 60% and 12% were suffering.

These averages inevitably mask substantial regional and national variation: Western countries generally report higher levels of thriving and lower levels of suffering across wellbeing domains, reflecting differences in economic security, health systems and institutional supports.

Nevertheless, these sobering statistics suggest that current approaches to improving human wellbeing have not translated into meaningful worldwide gains.

The Perceived Wellness Model

Adams et al.'s (1997) model draws on Systems Theory (Seeman, 1989), which treats each component as both part of a larger whole and a whole in itself. Because system elements are interdependent, disruptions to homeostasis at any level prompt adjustment across the entire system. Wellbeing can thus be seen as integrative functioning across multiple dimensions and levels.

The model encompasses six life domains:

- **Physical wellbeing:** Incorporates physical functioning and one's appraisal of their health and illness;
- **Intellectual wellbeing**: Feeling internally energised through an optimal level of intellectually stimulating activity;
- **Psychological wellbeing:** Optimism – a general expectation of positive outcomes across life events and circumstances;
- **Emotional wellbeing:** A secure sense of identity and positive self-regard;
- **Social wellbeing**: Perceiving support as available from others when needed and seeing oneself as a valued source of support;
- **Spiritual wellbeing:** A positive sense of meaning and purpose in life.

The Perceived Wellness Scale

The scale developed to measure the model (Adams et al., 1997) comprises 36 items across six subscales. It assesses individuals' subjective evaluations of wellbeing in each domain, with an emphasis on eudaimonic aspects.

The Perceived Wellness Model is one of the few overall wellbeing models to include psychological wellbeing as a core domain. This systems-informed framing implies that perceived change or strain in one domain may reverberate through others as individuals seek to restore equilibrium, making the measure well suited for capturing the eudaimonic aspects of functioning as they are experienced by the person.

The models reviewed here are a small subset of the numerous models of overall wellbeing. Across these models, several common commitments are clear. Each treats wellbeing as multidimensional, disaggregating overall wellbeing into constituent domains (work, health, social relations and finance) and enabling both domain-level diagnosis and aggregate scoring. The models either blend hedonic elements with eudaimonic elements or capture only the eudaimonic facets of wellbeing. The models also differ in the domains they foreground and in how they treat the psychological aspects of wellbeing. The relative absence of psychological wellbeing as a clearly specified domain in most overall wellbeing models may explain why Positive Psychology scholars felt compelled to focus on, develop, refine and foreground psychological wellbeing constructs and measures.

A common critique of these models, however, most of which derive from large-scale surveys, is that they often remain limited in the granularity needed to unpack mechanisms, provide an analysis of correlates or identify the conditions under which they operate.

Psychological Wellbeing

Psychological (or mental) wellbeing is a central concept in Positive Psychology, attracting substantial theoretical and empirical attention as scholars have sought to map its key components and examine its antecedents and correlates, alongside a large and growing evidence base on interventions designed to cultivate it.

> Within broader accounts of wellbeing, **psychological wellbeing** is treated as a distinct domain, capturing the quality of one's personal subjective state in the mental dimension of existence (Lomas et al., 2024).

However, this definition raises an important conceptual and semantic question: How does *mental wellbeing* differ from *mental health*? To address this point, Lomas et al. (2024) distinguished between the broader concepts of health and wellbeing. They contended that, when the two are not used interchangeably, wellbeing typically foregrounds a subjective perspective – how individuals experience and appraise their own state – whereas health often refers to an **objective evaluation**: The extent to which a desirable state has been achieved as judged by external criteria. From this standpoint, they proposed that a useful way to differentiate health from wellbeing is via the subjective–objective divide, defining health as "the relative attainment of a personal *objective* state of quality" (p. 8). Applied to the mental domain, this framing suggests that mental health refers to the relative attainment of one's *objectively* assessed psychological functioning, in contrast to the subjectively experienced quality captured by mental wellbeing.

> **Objective evaluation:** An evaluation of a person's aspect of life through external objective measures.

While this objective–subjective distinction is useful, the authors did not clarify how it should be operationalised. The binary distinction also becomes difficult to sustain for constructs that incorporate both objective and subjective elements. Moreover, the distinction sits uneasily with prominent large-scale measures of overall wellbeing, several of which incorporate objective indicators within their operationalisations of wellbeing (e.g. The Canadian Index of Wellbeing, 2016).

Models of Mental Wellbeing

Models of psychological wellbeing vary considerably in what they treat as the key constituents of the construct. Some are explicitly eudaimonic, whereas others incorporate both hedonic and eudaimonic elements. Some models include antecedents, while others focus on pathways – action-oriented means through which wellbeing can be cultivated. Consistent with their psychological framing, these models concentrate primarily on internal factors such as cognitions, emotions and motivations, typically leaving physical wellbeing and broader structural or environmental conditions outside their scope. Notably, however, social dimensions feature prominently across most accounts, suggesting that, even within psychologically centred models, wellbeing is rarely conceptualised as purely intrapsychic and is understood as inherently relational.

Hierarchy of Human Needs

Maslow's (1987) Hierarchy of Needs can be read as a mental wellbeing model insofar as it links human flourishing to the fulfilment of fundamental needs. The central claim is that wellbeing declines when needs are unmet and improves as needs are satisfied, culminating in optimal functioning. Although often presented as a rigid ladder, Maslow's own framing allows for movement and individual variation in how needs are prioritised.

The original model included five levels. Physiological needs form the base, reflecting the bodily requirements for survival. Safety needs involve protection, predictability and stability. Love and belonging needs capture social connection and affiliation. Esteem needs refer to feeling competent and valued, including both self-respect and recognition from others. At the apex, self-actualisation concerns realising one's potential and the pursuit of meaningful goals that express one's capabilities and values.

> **Self-actualisation:** Realising and developing one's fullest potential.
>
> **Self-transcendence:** Contributing beyond the self through service, spirituality or commitment to something larger than oneself.

Maslow's later writings also discuss self-transcendence – service, spirituality and commitment to a goal larger than the self as an extension beyond self-actualisation (Koltko-Rivera, 2006).

Maslow's model is best understood as a model of mental wellbeing rather than a comprehensive model of overall wellbeing, since its core concern is the organisation of human motivation and psychological functioning. Although it includes physiological and safety needs, these appear primarily as preconditions that enable psychological stability, functioning and development, not as wellbeing outcomes in their own right.

As a wellbeing account, the hierarchy is eudaimonic in emphasis, since wellbeing is framed in terms of functioning rather than in terms of happiness, contentment or **affect balance**. Notably, Maslow's model is distinctive in articulating an end-state of psychological flourishing: Self-actualisation and self-transcendence.

Affect balance: An overall emotional score of a person calculated by comparing positive affect and negative affect.

Self-Determination Theory

Self-Determination Theory (SDT) is a prominent needs-based, eudaimonic framework that explains psychological wellbeing in terms of the satisfaction of basic psychological needs (Ryan & Deci, 2017). SDT theorises that these needs are universal and foundational to growth, motivation and vitality. The model has been applied extensively not only in Psychology but also across fields such as healthcare and organisational studies, where it informs research and intervention design.

The three fundamental psychological needs are:

- **Autonomy:** Experiencing a sense of volition and psychological freedom, such that one's actions feel self-endorsed rather than pressured or coerced;
- **Competence:** Feeling effective and capable in one's activities, including opportunities to develop skills and achieve desired outcomes;
- **Relatedness:** Experiencing mutual care, connection and belonging with others, characterised by feeling valued and able to value others in return.

SDT Measures

Several measures gauge the extent to which basic psychological needs are satisfied. One widely used option is a nine-item scale (Sheldon et al., 2001).

When comparing scores across the three needs, the authors observed that a more balanced pattern of need satisfaction tends to be more supportive of wellness than marked variability between needs.

Overall, SDT offers a robust account of psychological wellbeing by examining the extent to which autonomy, competence and relatedness are supported in everyday life. This needs-based approach is useful for research and practice since it directs attention to modifiable social and contextual conditions that can strengthen wellbeing outcomes (Ryan & Deci, 2017).

The Psychological Wellbeing Model

Ryff's (1989) model of Psychological Wellbeing (PWB) is one of the most widely used eudaimonic frameworks for understanding optimal psychological functioning. The model conceptualises psychological wellbeing as multidimensional, comprising the core drivers of wellbeing. Each component is anchored in classic traditions within Psychology and has been operationalised in ways that enable extensive empirical testing across diverse populations and contexts.

PWB includes six key dimensions (Ryff, 1989):

- **Purpose in life:** The experience of meaning, direction and goal orientation that provides coherence and significance to one's life;
- **Autonomy:** The capacity to self-govern by acting in line with one's values and convictions, even when these diverge from social pressures;
- **Environmental mastery:** The ability to effectively manage life demands by navigating, selecting or shaping environments that support one's needs and goals;
- **Self-acceptance:** A positive, realistic attitude towards oneself, including acknowledgement and integration of both strengths and limitations;
- **Personal growth:** A sense of ongoing development characterised by openness to new experiences, learning and realising one's potential;
- **Positive relationships:** The tendency to form warm, trusting and mutually supportive relationships marked by empathy, intimacy and care.

Ryff's framework has generated a large evidence base demonstrating robust links between these eudaimonic dimensions and a wide range of psychological, behavioural and health-related outcomes (Ryff, 2018) (see below).

PWB Measures

The original scale (Ryff, 1989) comprised 120 items, with subsequent revisions evaluating shorter versions (Ryff & Singer, 1996), the shortest of which contains 18 items. The scale has been translated into more than 30 languages and applied across cultures and settings.

The model provides a comprehensive account of eudaimonic wellbeing, enabling scholars and practitioners to examine distinct profiles of psychological functioning and supporting more nuanced theorising about antecedents, mechanisms and outcomes of wellbeing, as well as more targeted intervention efforts (Ryff, 2018).

The PERMA Model

Seligman's (2012) PERMA model emerged from, and extends, his earlier Authentic Happiness framework, which conceptualised wellbeing in terms of three broad domains that lead to a good life: The pleasant life, the engaged life and the meaningful life. PERMA broadened this foundation into five subjectively assessed components, combining hedonic and eudaimonic elements. Importantly, PERMA is framed as a set of pathways to wellbeing: Rather than treating wellbeing as a fixed outcome, it proposes actions that individuals can intentionally practise to strengthen their mental wellbeing.

The model includes five key pathways to wellbeing:

- **Positive emotions:** This refers to the hedonic element of PERMA. The model encourages people to engage more frequently and intentionally in pleasurable activities to elicit positive emotions, since the capacity to experience emotions is widely recognised as fundamental to wellbeing.

  However, pleasure-focused actions have limits: It is neither realistic nor healthy to expect a constant emotional "high," as people typically experience ups and downs. Additionally, the effects of enjoyable activities are often short-lived, which can lead to the perpetual pursuit of pleasurable activities. Furthermore, more is not always better, since pleasure tends to diminish with repetition and some pleasure-seeking can carry long-term costs. Finally, people vary in how much (and what type of) pleasure they need, hence this pathway is best calibrated to individual differences.
- **Engagement:** The second route to wellbeing is engagement, most notably in its heightened form – flow. The model highlights the value of seeking opportunities to become immersed in tasks that are intrinsically interesting, that draw on a person's strengths, skills or talents and that offer the experience of challenge and mastery. When the challenge–skill balance is well matched, individuals experience flow, which manifests in deep absorption, concentration and sustained focus, often accompanied by peak performance. Flow can arise in almost any activity and highlights the notion that a life requiring no effort or challenge may not be very fulfilling. This pathway can support wellbeing by cultivating interest, competence, self-efficacy and mastery. A key caveat, however, is that flow can occur in harmful or addictive pursuits, hence the nature and consequences of the chosen activity matter.
- **Relationships:** This element is neatly conveyed by Peterson's (2006) widely cited claim that "other people matter." It aligns with the relational

emphasis evident in earlier wellbeing models and its consistent inclusion reflects the broad scholarly view that supportive relationships (or the lack thereof) exert a profound influence on mental wellbeing. Accordingly, the model encourages individuals to invest in relationships intentionally and as an end in itself, recognising their value for wellbeing and attending to how relationships can be created, nurtured and sustained.

- **Meaning:** This pathway reflects what individuals genuinely value and care about, fostering a sense of mattering and worth. The model proposes that meaning is cultivated through activities that align with valued goals or contribute to a purpose beyond the self, for example, belonging to a community or volunteering. Paradoxically, such activities are not always pleasurable. Instead, they tend to elicit experiences such as purpose and direction, value and significance, spirituality or belonging. Unlike pleasure- or flow-based pursuits, meaning is not addictive, as the sense of meaningfulness can endure even when the person is not engaged in the activity.
- **Accomplishment:** The final pathway to wellbeing involves pursuing and attaining objectives that require the investment of skills, effort and time. The model emphasises setting goals and working towards those that reflect one's genuine interests and values. This pathway overlaps with engagement, but the emphasis is different: Accomplishment centres on the goal and its attainment, and the gratification that accompanies reaching a milestone, rather than the process of immersion or mastery involved in getting there. This pathway recognises that a life in which very little is achieved will not be very fulfilling.

The PERMA Scale

The PERMA-Profiler (Butler & Kern, 2016) comprises 23 items: 15 assess the 5 PERMA facets, while a further eight items capture positive and negative emotions, loneliness and physical health.

The measure was evaluated across several large-scale surveys involving more than 30,000 participants, with mean scores on the five PERMA domains typically falling between 6.7 and 7.2.

PERMA is distinctive in offering an integrative account of wellbeing that brings together hedonic experiences with eudaimonic functioning within a single framework. The model frames its components as actionable pathways that can be intentionally cultivated through everyday choices. PERMA's clarity and practical orientation have supported its uptake across multiple disciplines and applied settings (education, management, health and coaching). However, this broad diffusion also has a drawback: Although PERMA was developed as a psychological model of wellbeing, it is often used as a proxy for overall wellbeing and, at times, conflated with other wellbeing domains (such as work wellbeing).

The Mental Health Continuum

Keyes' (2002) Mental Health Continuum (MHC) model is grounded in the premise that, much like mental illness, which is identified through patterns of symptoms, mental wellbeing can be understood as a constellation of *positive* symptoms. Building on this logic, Keyes (2005) specified several core indicators of mental wellbeing:

- **Emotional wellbeing:**
    - **Ongoing positive affect:** Feeling cheerful or in good spirits – happy, zestful, calm or peaceful.
    - **Life satisfaction:** Overall satisfaction with life, or satisfaction within specific life domains.
- **Positive functioning:**
    - **Self-acceptance:** Holding a positive view of oneself and one's life.
    - **Social acceptance:** Maintaining a positive orientation towards others.
    - **Personal growth:** Recognising one's potential, valuing development and being open to new experiences.
    - **Social actualisation:** Believing that people, groups, organisations and communities can develop in positive directions.
    - **Purpose in life:** Having goals and a sense of direction, meaning and purpose.
    - **Social contribution:** Feeling that one's life is valuable and that one can contribute to, or make a difference for, others.
    - **Environmental mastery:** Effectively managing, shaping, or navigating one's environment.
    - **Social coherence:** Taking an interest in society and being able to make sense of social and cultural life.
    - **Autonomy:** Being self-directed and guided by internal standards.
    - **Positive relationships:** Sustaining close, nurturing, trusting, and satisfying relationships.
    - **Social integration:** Experiencing belonging within a group or community.

The model is explicitly subjective, internally anchored and encompasses both hedonic and eudaimonic dimensions of wellbeing.

The Mental Health Continuum Scale

The MHC questionnaire (Keyes & Haidt, 2010) comprises 14 items: Three assess the hedonic aspects of the model and 11 pertain to the eudaimonic.

Beyond identifying the symptoms (or indicators) of mental wellbeing, Keyes (2005) also addressed the question of how mental illness relates to mental health. This question underpinned the development of the Dual Continua Model (Keyes, 2013), outlined next.

The Dual Continua Model

In Psychology, a common perception is that mental health and illness lie at opposite ends of a single spectrum, such that mental health is defined primarily as the absence of illness (Huppert, 2014). However, Keyes (2005) challenged this view, proposing instead that mental health and illness represent two distinct, orthogonal axes. From this perspective, mental health entails more than not being ill, as it requires the presence of positive emotional states and constructive forms of functioning.

Keyes' (2005, 2013) Dual Continua Model (DCM), later refined by Lomas and VanderWeele (2023), positions individuals across two dimensions – mental health and mental illness – hence yielding four quadrants:

- **Thriving** describes individuals who experience positive emotions and function well psychologically, alongside a low level of mental illness;
- **Struggling** refers to people who function reasonably well despite experiencing mental illness;
- **Languishing** captures a state of quiet despair in which individuals show low psychological functioning but do not meet criteria for mental illness. That is, they are neither mentally ill nor mentally healthy;
- **Faltering** denotes a combination of mental illness and poor psychological functioning.

A central implication of the DCM is that the presence of mental illness does not necessarily equate to poor mental wellbeing. This proposition is supported by empirical evidence indicating that, among those diagnosed with a mental illness, a meaningful proportion function well (Keyes, 2005; Franken et al., 2018; Iasiello et al., 2019; Kinderman et al., 2015).

The Dual Continua Measures

In studies applying the model, researchers administer measures of wellbeing and mental illness in parallel. For instance, Keyes (2002) assessed mental illness using the Composite International Diagnostic Interview and the Functioning–Impairment Inventory. Emotional wellbeing was measured using an affect-based scale, while eudaimonic wellbeing was assessed with Ryff's Psychological Wellbeing questionnaire.

Unlike the models cited earlier that aim to identify the components or pathways to psychological wellbeing, the Dual Continua Model is principally concerned with the *relationship* between health and illness. By conceptualising mental health and illness as independent dimensions, it provides a framework for locating individuals across a shared space in which both can vary.

The models reviewed in this section indicate substantial overlap across mental wellbeing models, and there is currently no clear scholarly consensus regarding the relative importance of their respective components. Notably, relational factors recur across multiple frameworks. Two common features cut across these models: They are inherently subjective and mostly internally oriented. Beyond relationships, there is little explicit attention to contextual conditions that may shape mental health.

Huta and Waterman (2014) argued that a central challenge in wellbeing models is that they rest on different underlying philosophical rationales. Some are organised around needs, others emphasise key components or pathways to wellbeing and others focus on wellbeing gradations or levels. Certain approaches focus specifically on eudaimonic wellbeing and delineate its constituent dimensions, whereas others integrate both hedonic and eudaimonic elements. These differences complicate comparisons.

Another challenge in this domain of research that has attracted critique is that most wellbeing models and scales were developed in English and have been validated within WEIRD contexts (Western, Educated, Industrialised, Rich and Democratic; Henrich et al., 2010). As a result, these models and measures may not translate well to other cultural settings (Lomas et al., 2024).

As for the measures discussed in this chapter, these are drawn from a wide array of instruments designed to assess psychological wellbeing. However, the sheer number of available questionnaires complicates the comparison and synthesis of findings across studies. Notwithstanding their limitations, these instruments signal a notable shift in how wellbeing is conceptualised and assessed. Until recently, many measures implicitly equated wellbeing with the absence of illbeing, reflecting a pathogenetic orientation. By contrast, the more recent measures reviewed earlier are salutogenetic in emphasis, prioritising the presence of positive functioning and resources rather than the absence of deficits.

Despite differences across models and measures, there is considerable convergence in the empirical research assessing the correlates of psychological wellbeing, which are reviewed next.

Factors Associated With Mental Wellbeing

Much of the research on mental wellbeing, regardless of how it is conceptualised or measured, has sought to identify what predicts it, while its downstream effects have received less attention. Several reviews have collated and synthesised this evidence base, and key points are summarised next.

Demographic Factors

To what extent is mental wellbeing predicted by demographic characteristics? Findings are surprisingly inconsistent. Keyes (2007) found minimal gender disparities between the dual continua categories, echoed in a PERMA study (Butler & Kern, 2016). Huppert (2009) also reported no gender differences in mental wellbeing. However, on the illbeing dimension, women exhibited higher levels of depression and anxiety compared to men.

The age–mental wellbeing association is often described as U-shaped: Younger and older adults tend to report slightly higher mental wellbeing than middle-aged adults (Butler & Kern, 2016), with the elderly experiencing an age-related decline (Ryff, 2018). By contrast, a US survey using the Dual Continua Model found that older adults are more likely to be flourishing than younger adults (Keyes, 2002). Subjective age also matters: Feeling younger than one's chronological age is associated with higher psychological wellbeing (Ryff, 2013).

Regarding race, ethnicity and religion, Ryff et al. (2003) found no racial differences in psychological wellbeing in the United States. Keyes (2007) reported higher odds of flourishing among Black adults than White adults, despite greater socio-economic disadvantage and discrimination. In contrast, a study applying self-determination needs theory found lower need satisfaction among minority ethnic groups (Su-Russell et al., 2024). Religious affiliation has been linked to improved psychological wellbeing (Ryff, 2013).

Higher socio-economic status is associated with higher wellbeing on Ryff's scale, although effects are modest and shaped by social inequality (Kaplan et al., 2008). Sexual identity has also been linked to psychological wellbeing: Identifying as lesbian, gay or bisexual has been associated with lower psychological wellbeing, likely reflecting discrimination-related pathways (Ryff, 2013).

Education shows a more consistent pattern: Longitudinal evidence suggests that higher educational attainment predicts favourable psychological wellbeing trajectories (Boylan et al., 2025), aligning with evidence that higher education is associated with more flourishing and less languishing (Keyes, 2002).

Personality Traits

Studies have also reported that certain personality traits predict psychological wellbeing (Ryff, 2013): Neuroticism emerges as the strongest negative predictor, whereas extraversion, conscientiousness and agreeableness show moderate positive associations. Openness tends to display a weaker positive relationship.

Parallel patterns have been reported for need fulfilment: Autonomy, competence and relatedness are negatively correlated with neuroticism and positively correlated with extraversion, openness, agreeableness and conscientiousness (Vukasovic Hlupic et al., 2023).

Beyond personality traits, a broad set of psychological resources and skills, including goal orientation, optimism, hope, self-esteem, identity development, self-regulation, self-efficacy, coping, **growth mindset**, life-management strategies, mindfulness, self-compassion, spirituality and gratitude, are associated with higher psychological wellbeing (Ryff, 2013; Lee & Gallagher, 2017; Hanley et al., 2015; Homan, 2016; Simon & Durand-Bush, 2014; Butler & Kern, 2016). In addition, character strengths use has been linked to higher PERMA scores (Wagner et al., 2020).

The Big 5: A personality model that describes personality across five broad traits: Openness, Conscientiousness, Extraversion, Agreeablness and Neuroticism.

Growth mindset: The belief that abilities can be developed through effort, effective strategies, feedback and support, rather than being fixed.

Health

Substantial literature has examined the links between psychological wellbeing and a wide range of physical health conditions. Overall, the evidence points to a bidirectional association: Poor physical health and disability are linked to lower psychological wellbeing, while higher wellbeing appears to predict better health outcomes (Ryff et al., 2015).

Many medical conditions are associated with poor psychological wellbeing and elevated depressive symptoms, including diabetes, coronary heart disease, chronic lung disease, chronic kidney disease, stroke, several types of cancers, and rheumatoid arthritis (Meijer et al., 2011; Satin et al., 2009; Wikman et al., 2011). In older adults, frailty, disability, and long-term conditions are associated with lower wellbeing, although social support may buffer these effects (Ryff, 2013). Sleep is another relevant factor: Insomnia predicts poor psychological wellbeing, whereas optimal sleep is associated with fewer depression and anxiety symptoms (Ryff, 2013). Low weight and positive body image have been linked to improved psychological wellbeing, particularly among young women (Ryff, 2013).

Additionally, high psychological wellbeing predicts improved physical health and vitality, lower cortisol output and stronger immune functioning (Ryff, 2013). Butler and Kern (2016) reported that PERMA score are positively correlated with subjective physical health assessments and negatively associated with fatigue.

Psychological wellbeing is also linked to stronger engagement with health-promoting behaviours, which in turn lead to fewer health problems, lower use of health services and lower mortality risk (Ryff, 2018). Among the chronically ill, psychological wellbeing is linked to better self-care and adjustment (Ryff, 2013).

Longitudinal evidence indicates that thriving (on the Mental Health Continuum Model) predicts lower mortality (Keyes & Simoes, 2012). Likewise, satisfaction of the three basic psychological needs predicts better physical wellbeing and longer life (Ng et al., 2012). Tang et al. (2020) reported that the satisfaction of needs is associated with lower depressive symptoms.

In ageing research, higher psychological wellbeing predicts reduced risk of Alzheimer's disease, lower risk of stroke and myocardial infarction among those with coronary heart disease, and lower overall mortality (Ryff, 2013). Butler and Kern (2016) found that PERMA scores are negatively associated with stress, depression and anxiety.

Work

Varied features of working life can shape psychological wellbeing. These associations are often bidirectional, since mental wellbeing influences how people function at work.

Being employed is associated with better psychological wellbeing (Ryff, 2018), whereas unemployment is linked to poorer psychological wellbeing, higher rates of mental disorder and elevated suicide risk, although the effects are weaker where unemployment is widespread (Huppert, 2009; McKee-Ryan et al., 2005). Employment seems to confer larger psychological wellbeing benefits for men compared to women (Ryff, 2018). Rath and Harter (2010) also reported that wellbeing tends to rebound slowly following extended unemployment.

Psychological wellbeing appears to be associated with better career-related outcomes (Ryff, 2013). As for job satisfaction, many people report low work satisfaction and Gallup data (Rath & Harter, 2010) indicated that thriving in the career wellbeing domain may be relatively uncommon. Work dissatisfaction has been linked to low mental wellbeing among physicians (Kassam et al., 2015).

Work engagement is closely linked to psychological wellbeing, while disengagement is associated with depression (Ryff, 2018). Organisational resources predict higher PERMA scores (Yang et al., 2022), and strengths use, close workplace relationships and **job crafting** are associated with greater mental wellbeing (Kurian et al., 2024; Rath & Harter, 2010). In the tourism industry, **organisational climate** predicts PERMA scores in employees (Shulga et al., 2023).

Conversely, workplace stressors such as high workload, discrimination and harassment predict poor psychological wellbeing (Ryff, 2018). Work–family conflict, especially under caregiving strain, is linked to poorer psychological wellbeing, whereas positive spillover between work and family roles predicts enhanced wellbeing (Ryff, 2013). Notably, valuing occupational prestige is associated with lower psychological wellbeing (Pfund et al., 2024).

Research also indicates that psychological wellbeing can impinge on work. Higher PERMA scores predict better work performance (Jimenez et al., 2023) and high job satisfaction, engagement, resilience and innovative behaviours (Ibrahim et al., 2023; John-Loh, 2025). From a needs perspective, unmet psychological needs are associated with higher role stressors and work–family conflict (Van den Broeck et al., 2016).

Financial Factors

Scarce research has examined the links between personal finances and psychological wellbeing, despite extensive work on money and happiness (see Chapter 4). The main exception is poverty research. Poverty is strongly associated with poorer mental wellbeing, with reviews concluding that deprivation produces toxic, chronic stress with substantial physical and mental health consequences (Breitenbach et al., 2021). People living in poverty face stressors such as violence, overcrowded housing, limited resources, environmental hazards and discrimination (Wadsworth et al., 2011). These intersecting pressures can overwhelm the body's regulatory systems, eroding health, coping capacity and cognitive resources (Mayo et al., 2022). The resulting cumulative wear and tear reduces stress responsivity and increases vulnerability to conditions such as cardiovascular disease, depression and suicidality (Chen et al., 2015; O'Connor & Kirtley, 2017). Financial strain can also erode self-worth, perceived control, independence, and self-determination (Haushofer & Fehr, 2014).

Money problems are also a common source of family conflict, disrupting relationships and weakening social support. Consistent with this, financial difficulties predict lower marital satisfaction, greater marital conflict and higher likelihood of divorce (Papp et al., 2009) which in turn predict low psychological wellbeing.

The Psychology of Poverty framework (Haushofer & Salicath, 2023) indicates that poverty can become self-reinforcing through cognitive depletion, scarcity mindset, chronic stress, learned helplessness, narrow margins for error, stigma, exclusion and diminished self-worth. These mechanisms are linked to financial behaviours that may perpetuate deprivation, including lower **financial literacy**, mistrust of institutions, risk aversion, short-term focus, difficulties with delayed gratification and emotionally driven spending (Shah et al., 2018).

Poverty: A socioeconomic condition marked by a significant dearth of financial resources and material assets. Its key indicator is the insufficient financial means to satisfy essential needs.

Beyond poverty, financial insecurity is associated with poorer psychological need satisfaction (Weinstein & Stone, 2018). Indebtedness is also closely tied to worse mental health (Fitch et al., 2011), with over-indebtedness commonly accompanied by stress, depression, anxiety, shame, hopelessness, loss of control, and reduced self-efficacy (Khan et al., 2024) and linked to greater suicidal intents (Meltzer et al., 2011). Property repossession is associated with particularly high levels of mental health impairment (Cannuscio et al., 2012). Low savings and lack of home ownership have also been associated with stress and depression (Ettman et al., 2023; Simonse et al., 2022).

Research on income and mental wellbeing indicates that higher income is associated with improved psychological wellbeing (Kaplan et al., 2008), and lottery winnings have been found to induce sustained improvements in winners' mental wellbeing (Apouey & Clark, 2015). Beliefs about money also matter: Placing high importance on money has been linked to poorer psychological wellbeing (Pfund et al., 2024), consistent with broader evidence linking materialism to diminished mental wellbeing (Dittmar et al., 2014).

Regarding spending and consumption, there is generally scarce research on its association with mental wellbeing, although some evidence indicates that prosocial spending benefits mental wellbeing more than spending on oneself (Caprariello & Reis, 2021). Finally, higher financial satisfaction has been associated with better psychological wellbeing, even after controlling for financial behaviours and financial literacy (Gerrans et al., 2014).

Social Factors

The association between social life and psychological wellbeing has received substantial attention in the literature. Marriage appears to benefit partners' wellbeing: Married individuals typically report higher psychological wellbeing than those who are single, divorced, or widowed (Ryff, 2013). Among single or widowed adults, women tend to report improved wellbeing than men in comparable circumstances (Ryff, 2018).

Evidence on parenting is mixed. Some studies reported lower mental wellbeing among parents than non-parents, whereas others found similar levels. Parents report greater meaning in life, a key component of psychological wellbeing (Nelson et al., 2014). Nevertheless parenting young children can be demanding, particularly for women, although this tends to ease when parenting adult children, especially when children are well adjusted and living independently (Ryff, 2018). Time with children, family activities and helping others are linked to higher psychological wellbeing across the lifespan (Ryff, 2013). Parents' mental wellbeing also tracks children's adjustment: Perceived child difficulties are associated with poorer parental wellbeing (Ryff, 2013).

Caring for an unwell ageing parent can reduce adult children's wellbeing, with pronounced effects for women. Likewise, having a sibling with mental illness is associated with lower psychological wellbeing and greater distress (Ryff, 2013). Early family environments also matter: Low parental support predict poorer mental wellbeing in adulthood (Ryff, 2013).

Loneliness is negatively associated with PERMA (Butler & Kern, 2016) and positively associated with depression (Lyubomirsky et al., 2005b). Rath and Harter (2010) suggested that people need roughly six hours of social time daily to function optimally. Higher psychological wellbeing is also linked to prosocial behaviours, particularly volunteering and charitable giving (Ryff, 2013).

Finally, major losses and adverse childhood experiences have enduring consequences. The death of a child predicts long-term reductions in psychological wellbeing alongside higher depressive symptoms and health problems, with stronger effects for fathers than mothers (Ryff, 2013). Parental death in childhood has been associated with higher autonomy in adult men but greater depression in adult women (Ryff, 2013). Enduring abuse in childhood predicts poorer mental wellbeing in adulthood (Ryff, 2013). Parental divorce before age 17 is linked to lower self-acceptance, reduced environmental mastery and poorer relationships in midlife (Ryff, 2013).

Country and Culture

Differences between cultures and countries in psychological wellbeing have been scarcely examined. Available evidence suggests that cultural differences in psychological wellbeing are relatively small and nuanced (Ryff, 2013). Butler and Kern (2016) reported broadly comparable PERMA scores across European, Asian and Mediterranean countries, as well as India, Canada, Australia and New Zealand. Scores were slightly higher in the

USA and in South American and African countries, with the highest levels observed in Central America, the Pacific Islands and the Caribbean. Complementing this, European data demonstrated small between-country differences in flourishing (Huppert & So, 2013). Average psychological wellbeing seems to be higher in wealthier countries, where unemployment risk is lower and state-provided safety nets may reduce the likelihood of poverty (Ryff, 2018).

Across this evidence base, several factors show relatively robust associations with mental wellbeing, including personality, physical health, employment, financial insecurity, supportive relationships and prosocial behaviours. At the same time, several commonly examined correlates yield mixed or context-dependent findings, most notably demographic variables, country-level variables and parenting. Findings also vary by model, sample, cultural context and the measure used. These inconsistencies reinforce that mental wellbeing is shaped by intersecting structural and internal conditions.

Although this section includes notable downstream links, the broader literature still appears comparatively weighted towards the predictors of mental wellbeing. This leaves important gaps around causal pathways and boundary conditions. Moreover, psychological wellbeing research has tended to privilege individual-level explanations, leaving environmental determinants under-theorised and empirically underexamined.

Conclusion

In this chapter, wellbeing is positioned as both the organising construct within Positive Psychology and one of its most contested concepts. Beginning from an overarching definition of wellbeing, the chapter offered a scaffold for disentangling commonly conflated facets, while underscoring how frequently these distinctions collapse.

Building on this foundation, the chapter reviewed influential meta-theoretical lenses and then traced how overall wellbeing models typically operationalise multidimensional functioning across life domains, yet frequently leave psychological wellbeing underspecified.

The chapter then narrowed to psychological wellbeing, where needs-based, component-focused and pathway-oriented models have provided widely used accounts of what it means to function well psychologically.

Despite this conceptual plurality, the evidence reviewed on their correlates suggests substantial empirical convergence: Psychological wellbeing tends to correlate with psychological resources, supportive relationships and health, while also being influenced by work and financial security. At the same time, there is limited mapping of psychological wellbeing's downstream consequences and insufficient attention to macro-level determinants. These gaps limit causal inference, comparability and policy translation.

Finally, the critiques reviewed here clarify why debates around wellbeing persist: Wellbeing is central to Positive Psychology's identity and aspirations, and functions as a boundary object whose apparent intuitiveness masks deep normative, philosophical and political commitments, and whose multi-level usage invites category errors, measurement slippage and overextension of models across domains.

The most constructive implication is to tighten the conceptual specifications of wellbeing, improve measurement validity and strengthen interdisciplinary dialogue so that wellbeing research can become more cumulative, integrative and genuinely fit for both explanation and application. Doing so matters not only for scientific coherence but also because wellbeing is socially consequential: Improvements or declines ripple outwards, shaping families, organisations, communities and societies, and thereby linking personal wellbeing to collective outcomes.

References

Adams, T., Bezner, J., & Steinhardt, M. (1997). The conceptualization and measurement of perceived wellness: Integrating balance across and within dimensions. American Journal of Health Promotion, 11(3), 208–218.

Allardt, E. (1976). Dimensions of welfare in a comparative Scandinavian study. Acta Sociologica, 19(3), 227–239.

Allardt, E. (1993). Having, loving, being: An alternative to the Swedish model of welfare research. In M.C. Nussbaum, & A.K. Sen (Eds.), The quality of life (pp. 88–94). Clarendon Press.

Apouey, B., & Clark, A.E. (2015). Winning big but feeling no better? The effect of lottery prizes on physical and mental health. Health Economics, 24(5), 516–538.

Boylan, J.M., Choi, J.H., Kirsch, J.A., & Ryff, C.D. (2025). Educational disparities in 20-year trajectories of psychological well-being in a national sample. Scientific Reports, 15(1), 11437.

Breitenbach, M., Kapferer, E., Sedmak, C., Breitenbach, M., Kapferer, E., & Sedmak, C. (2021). Stress and poverty: An introduction. In M. Breitenbach, E. Kapferer, & C. Sedmak (Eds.), Stress and poverty (pp. 1–19). Springer.

Butler, J., & Kern, M.L. (2016). The PERMA-Profiler: A brief multidimensional measure of flourishing. International Journal of Wellbeing, 6(3), 1–48.

Canadian Index of Wellbeing. (2016). Canadian index of wellbeing. University of Waterloo.

Cannuscio, C.C., Alley, D.E., Pagán, J.A., Soldo, B., Krasny, S., Shardell, M., Asch, D.A., & Lipman, T.H. (2012). Housing strain, mortgage foreclosure, and health. Nursing Outlook, 60(3), 134–142.

Caprariello, P.A., & Reis, H.T. (2021). "This one's on me!": Differential well-being effects of self-centered and recipient-centered motives for spending money on others. Motivation and Emotion, 45(6), 705–727.

Chen, E., Miller, G.E., Brody, G.H., & Lei, M. (2015). Neighbourhood poverty, college attendance, and diverging profiles of substance use and allostatic load in rural African American youth. Clinical Psychological Science, 3(5), 675–685.

Deci, E.L., & Ryan, R.M. (2008). Hedonia, eudaimonia, and well-being: An introduction. Journal of Happiness Studies, 9(1), 1–11.

Dittmar, H., Bond, R., Hurst, M., & Kasser, T. (2014). The relationship between materialism and personal well-being: A meta-analysis. Journal of Personality and Social Psychology, 107(5), 879–924.

Ettman, C.K., Fan, A.Y., Philips, A.P., Adam, G.P., Ringlein, G., Clark, M.A., Wilson, I.B., Vivier, P.M., & Galea, S. (2023). Financial strain and depression in the US: A scoping review. Translational Psychiatry, 13(1), 168.

Fitch, C., Hamilton, S., Bassett, P., & Davey, R. (2011). The relationship between personal debt and mental health: A systematic review. Mental Health Review Journal, 16(4), 153–166.

Franken, K., Lamers, S.M.A., Ten Klooster, P.M., Bohlmeijer, E.T., & Westerhof, G.J. (2018). Validation of the Mental Health Continuum-Short Form and the dual continua model of wellbeing and psychopathology in an adult mental health setting. Journal of Clinical Psychology, 74(12), 2187–2202.

Gallup. (2014). State of global well-being. Gallup.

Gallup. (2024). Global life evaluation index. Gallup.

Gerrans, P., Speelman, C., & Campitelli, G. (2014). The relationship between personal financial wellness and financial wellbeing: A structural equation modelling approach. Journal of Family and Economic Issues, 35(2), 145–160.

Goodman, F., Disabato, D., Kashdan, T., & Kauffman, S. (2017). Measuring well-being: A comparison of subjective wellbeing and PERMA. The Journal of Positive Psychology, 1–12.

Hall, A. (2016). Making good choices: Toward a theory of well-being in medicine. Theoretical Medicine and Bioethics, 37(5), 383–400.

Hanley, A., Warner, A., & Garland, E.L. (2015). Associations between mindfulness, psychological well-being, and subjective well-being with respect to contemplative practice. Journal of Happiness Studies, 16(6), 1423–1436.

Hart, R. (2020). Positive psychology: The basics. Routledge.

Hart, R., & Hart, D. (2026). Cutting through the clutter: Cleaning the lens on work-related wellbeing concepts. Behavioral Sciences, 16(3), 373.

Haushofer, J., & Fehr, E. (2014). On the psychology of poverty. Science, 344(6186), 862–867.

Haushofer, J., & Salicath, D. (2023). The psychology of poverty: Where do we stand? Social Philosophy and Policy, 40(1), 150–184.

Henderson, L.W., & Knight T. (2012). Integrating the hedonic and eudaimonic perspectives to more comprehensively understand wellbeing and pathways to wellbeing. International Journal of Wellbeing, 2(3), 196–221.

Henrich, J., Heine, S.J., & Norenzayan, A. (2010). The weirdest people in the world? Behavioral and Brain Sciences, 33(2–3), 61–135.

Homan, K.J. (2016). Self-compassion and psychological well-being in older adults. Journal of Adult Development, 23(2), 111–119.
Huppert, F.A. (2009). Psychological well-being: Evidence regarding its causes and consequences. Applied Psychology, 1(2), 137–164.
Huppert, F.A. (2014). The state of well-being science: Concepts, measures, interventions, and policies. In F.A. Huppert, & C.L. Cooper (Eds.), Interventions and policies to enhance well-being. Wiley-Blackwell.
Huppert, F.A., & So, T.T.C. (2013). Flourishing across Europe: Application of a new conceptual framework for defining well-being. Social Indicators Research, 110(3), 837–861.
Huta, V. (2016). Eudaimonic and hedonic orientations: Theoretical considerations and research findings. In J. Vitterso (Ed.), Handbook of eudaimonic well-being (pp. 215–231). Springer.
Huta, V., & Waterman, A.S. (2014). Eudaimonia and its distinction from hedonia: Developing a classification and terminology for understanding conceptual and operational definitions. Journal of Happiness Studies, (15), 1425–1456.
Iasiello, M., van Agteren, J., Keyes, C.L.M., & Cochrane, E.M. (2019). Positive mental health as a predictor of recovery from mental illness. Journal of Affective Disorders, 251, 227–230.
Ibrahim, N.F., Sharif, S.M., Saleh, H., Hasan, N.H.M., & Jayiddin, N.F. (2023). PERMA well-being and innovative work behaviour: A systematic literature review. F1000Research, 12, 1338.
Jimenez, W.P., Hu, X., Garden, R., & Zeytonli, A. (2023). The potential and peculiarities of PERMA. Journal of Personnel Psychology, 23(1), 1–58.
John-Loh, F.W. (2025). Modelling employee well-being: A quantitative comparison of the hedonic, eudaimonic, social, JD-R, and PERMA frameworks in occupational settings. International Journal of Innovative Science and Research Technology, 10(6), 1380–1390.
Kaplan, G.A., Shema, S.J., & Leite, C.M.A. (2008). Socioeconomic determinants of psychological well-being: The role of income, income change, and income sources during the course of 29 years. Annals of Epidemiology, 18(7), 531–537.
Kassam, A., Horton, J., Shoimer, I., & Patten, S. (2015). Predictors of well-being in resident physicians: A descriptive and psychometric study. Journal of Graduate Medical Education, 7(1), 70–74.
Keyes, C.L.M. (2002). The mental health continuum: From languishing to flourishing in life. Journal of Health and Social Research, 43, 207–222.
Keyes, C.L.M. (2005). Mental illness and/or mental health? Investigating axioms of the complete state model of health. Journal of Consulting and Clinical Psychology, 73(3), 539–548.
Keyes, C.L.M. (2007). Promoting and protecting mental health as flourishing: A complementary strategy for improving national mental health. American Psychologist, 62(2), 95.
Keyes, C.L.M. (2013). Mental health as a complete state: How the salutogenic perspective completes the picture. In G.F. Bauer, & O. Hämmig (Eds.), Bridging occupational, organizational and public health (pp. 179–192). Springer.

Keyes, C.L.M., & Annas, J. (2009). Feeling good and functioning well: Distinctive concepts in ancient philosophy and contemporary science. The Journal of Positive Psychology, 4(3), 197–201.
Keyes, C.L.M., & Haidt, J. (2010). Flourishing. The Corsini Encyclopaedia of Psychology, 1.
Keyes, C.L.M., & Simoes, E.J. (2012). To flourish or not: Positive mental health and all-cause mortality. American Journal of Public Health, 102(11), 2164–2172.
Khan, M.A., Zummer, A., & Malik, A. (2024). The psychological impact of debt: Stress and its connection to mental health disorders. Review of Education, Administration & Law, 7(4), 319–333.
Kinderman, P., Tai, S., Pontin, E., Schwannauer, M., Jarman, I., & Lisboa, P. (2015). Causal and mediating factors for anxiety, depression and well-being. British Journal of Psychiatry, 206(6), 456–460.
Koltko-Rivera, M.E. (2006). Rediscovering the later version of Maslow's hierarchy of needs: Self-transcendence and opportunities for theory, research, and unification. Review of General Psychology, 10(4), 302–317.
Kurian, A., Patrick, H., Prabakaran, N., & Kumar, A. (2024). The influence of job crafting on employee flourishing: A comprehensive study among IT sector employees in India from the millennial and Gen Z generations. Journal of Information and Optimization Sciences, 45(6), 1487–1499.
Lee, J.Y. & Gallagher, M.W. (2017). Hope and wellbeing. In M.W Gallagher, & S.J. Lopez (Eds.), The Oxford handbook of hope (pp. 287–298). Oxford University Press.
Lomas, T., Hefferon, K., & Ivtzan, I. (2014). Applied positive psychology. Sage.
Lomas, T., Pawelski, J.O., & VanderWeele, T.J. (2024). A flexible map of flourishing: The dynamics and drivers of flourishing, well-being, health, and happiness. International Journal of Wellbeing, 13(4), 3665, 1–38.
Lomas, T., & VanderWeele, T.J. (2023). The mental illness-health matrix and the mental state space matrix: Complementary meta-conceptual frameworks for evaluating psychological states. Journal of Clinical Psychology, 79(8), 1902–1920.
Lyubomirsky, S., King, L., & Diener, E. (2005). The benefits of frequent positive affect: Does happiness lead to success? Psychological Bulletin, (131), 803–855.
Martela, F. (2025). Well-being as having, loving, doing, and being: An integrative organizing framework for employee well-being. Journal of Organizational Behavior, 46(5), 641–661.
Maslow, A.H. (1987). Motivation and personality. Pearson Education.
Mayo, C.O., Pham, H., Patallo, B., Joos, C.M., & Wadsworth, M.E. (2022). Coping with poverty-related stress: A narrative review. Developmental Review, 64, 101024.
McKee-Ryan, F., Song, Z., Wanberg, C.R., & Kinicki, A.J. (2005). Psychological and physical well-being during unemployment: A meta-analytic study. Journal of Applied Psychology, 90(1), 53–76.

Meijer, A., Conradi, H.J., Bos, E.H., Thombs, B.D., van Melle, J.P., & de Jonge, P. (2011). Prognostic association of depression following myocardial infarction with mortality and cardiovascular events: A meta-analysis of 25 years of research. General Hospital Psychiatry, 33(3), 203–216.

Meltzer, H., Bebbington, P., Brugha, T., Jenkins, R., McManus, S., & Dennis, M.S. (2011). Personal debt and suicidal ideation. Psychological Medicine, 41(4), 771–778.

Nelson, S.K., Kushlev, K., & Lyubomirsky, S. (2014). The pains and pleasures of parenting: When, why, and how is parenthood associated with more or less well-being? Psychological Bulletin, 140(3), 846–895.

Ng, J.Y., Ntoumanis, N., Thogersen-Ntoumani, C., Deci, E.L., Ryan, R.M., Duda, J.L., & Williams, G.C. (2012). Self-determination theory applied to health contexts: A meta-analysis. Perspectives on Psychological Science, 7(4), 325–340.

O'Connor, R., & Kirtley, O. (2017). Socioeconomic disadvantage and suicidal behavior: Psychological factors. In S. Platt, S. Stace, & J. Morrissey (Eds.), Socioeconomic disadvantage and suicidal behavior (pp. 92–124). Samaritans.

Papp, L.M., Cummings, E.M., & Goeke-Morey, M.C. (2009). For richer, for poorer: Money as a topic of marital conflict in the home. Family Relations, 58(1), 91–103.

Peterson, C. (2006). A primer in positive psychology. Oxford University Press.

Pfund, G.N., Willroth, E.C., Mroczek, D.K., & Hill, P.L. (2024). Valuing versus having: The contrary roles of valuing and having money and prestige on well-being. Social Psychological and Personality Science, 15(3), 275–287.

Pincus, J.D. (2023). Well-being as need fulfilment: Implications for theory, methods, and practice. Integrative Psychological and Behavioral Science, 1–39.

Rath, T., & Harter, J. (2010). Wellbeing: The five essential elements. Simon and Schuster.

Ryan, R.M., & Deci, E.L. (2017). Self-determination theory. Guilford.

Ryff, C.D. (1989). Happiness is everything, or is it? Explorations on the meaning of psychological well-being. Journal of Personality and Social Psychology, (57), 1069–1081.

Ryff, C.D. (2013). Psychological well-being revisited: Advances in the science and practice of eudaimonia. Psychotherapy and Psychosomatics, 83(1), 10–28.

Ryff, C.D. (2018). Eudaimonic well-being: Highlights from 25 years of inquiry. In K. Shigemasu, S., Kuwano, T., Sato, & T. Matsuzawa (Eds.), Diversity in harmony – Insights from psychology (pp. 375–395). Wiley.

Ryff, C.D., Keyes, C.L.M., & Hughes, D.L. (2003). Status inequalities, perceived discrimination, and eudaimonic well-being: Do the challenges of minority life hone purpose and growth? Journal of Health and Social Behavior, 275–291.

Ryff, C.D., Radler, B.T., & Friedman, E.M. (2015). Persistent psychological well-being predicts improved self-rated health over 9–10 years:

Longitudinal evidence from MIDUS. Health Psychology Open, 2(2), 2055102915601582.
Ryff, C.D., & Singer, B. (1996). Psychological well-being: Meaning, measurement, and implications for psychotherapy research. Psychotherapy and Psychosomatics, 65(1), 14–23.
Satin, J.R., Linden, W., & Phillips, M.J. (2009). Depression as a predictor of disease progression and mortality in cancer patients: A meta-analysis. Cancer, 115(22), 5349–5361.
Seeman, J. (1989). Toward a model of positive health. American Psychologist, 44(8), 1099.
Seligman, M.E.P. (2012). Flourish. Free Press.
Seligman, M.E.P. (2018). PERMA and the building blocks of well-being. The Journal of Positive Psychology, 13(4), 333–335.
Shah, A.K., Zhao, J., Mullainathan, S., & Shafir, E. (2018). Money in the mental lives of the poor. Social Cognition, 36(1), 4–19.
Sheldon, K.M., & Lyubomirsky, S. (2021). Revisiting the sustainable happiness model and pie chart: Can happiness be successfully pursued? The Journal of Positive Psychology, 1–10.
Sheldon, K.M., Elliot, A.J., Kim, Y., & Kasser, T. (2001). What is satisfying about satisfying events? Testing 10 candidate psychological needs. Journal of Personality and Social Psychology, 80(2), 325–339.
Shulga, L.V., Busser, J.A., & Yedlin, J. (2023). Employee engagement on wellbeing: An analysis of PERMA framework. In M. Uysal, & J. Sirgy (Eds.), Handbook of tourism and quality-of-life research (pp. 459–476). Springer.
Simon, C.R., & Durand-Bush, N. (2014). Does self-regulation capacity predict psychological well-being in physicians? Psychology, Health & Medicine, 20(3), 311–321.
Simonse, O., Van Dijk, W.W., Van Dillen, L.F., & Van Dijk, E. (2022). The role of financial stress in mental health changes during COVID-19. NPJ Mental Health Research, 1(1), 15.
Su-Russell, C., Hendricks, M., & Arellanes, J.A. (2024). Latinx college students in a PWI: Perceptions of inclusion, diversity, equity, and access (IDEA), basic psychological needs satisfaction, and access to mentorship. Journal of Underrepresented & Minority Progress, 8(SI-2), 26–49.
Tang, M., Wang, D., & Guerrien, A. (2020). A systematic review and meta-analysis on basic psychological need satisfaction, motivation, and well-being in later life: Contributions of self-determination theory. PsyCh Journal, 9(1), 5–33.
Van den Broeck, A., Ferris, D.L., Chang, C.H., & Rosen, C.C. (2016). A review of self-determination theory's basic psychological needs at work. Journal of Management, 42(5), 1195–1229.
Vukasovic Hlupic, T., Butkovic, A., Pocrnic, M., & Bratko, D. (2023). The relationship between three basic psychological needs and big five personality traits: A meta-analysis. Current Psychology, 42(35), 31559–31578.
Wadsworth, M.E., Raviv, T., Santiago, C.D., & Etter, E.M. (2011). Testing the adaptation to poverty-related stress model: Predicting

psychopathology symptoms in families facing economic hardship. Journal of Clinical Child & Adolescent Psychology, 40(4), 646–657.
Wagner, L., Gander, F., Proyer, R.T., & Ruch, W. (2020). Character strengths and PERMA: Investigating the relationships of character strengths with a multidimensional framework of well-being. Applied Research in Quality of Life, 15(2), 307–328.
Weinstein, N., & Stone, D.N. (2018). Need depriving effects of financial insecurity: Implications for well-being and financial behaviors. Journal of Experimental Psychology: General, 147(10), 1503.
Wijngaards, I., King, O.C., Burger, M.J., & van Exel, J. (2022). Worker well-being: What it is, and how it should be measured. Applied Research in Quality of Life, 17(2), 795–832.
Wikman, A., Wardle, J., & Steptoe, A. (2011). Quality of life and affective well-being in middle-aged and older people with chronic medical illnesses: A cross-sectional population based study. PLoS One, 6(4), e18952.
Yang, C.C., Watanabe, K., & Kawakami, N. (2022). The associations between job strain, workplace PERMA profiler, and work engagement. Journal of Occupational and Environmental Medicine, 64(5), 409–415.

Chapter 4

Happiness

Happiness is one of humanity's most compelling pursuits, invoked in everyday wishes, woven into cultural ideals and chased across the lifespan in ways that are intensely personal and unmistakably shared. Across societies, people talk about wanting to be happy as if it were a place one can finally arrive at: A state promising ease, contentment or that longed-for sense of bliss. The pull of happiness shows up everywhere: In childhood dreams and adult ambitions, in relationships and working lives, in financial pursuits and decisions and in collective visions of what a good life should look like.

Yet happiness has a habit of slipping through our fingers. It is vivid in both its presence and its absence but difficult to sustain, and often begins to recede the moment it becomes a stern requirement for a life well lived. This paradox – yearning for something intensely while finding it so hard to secure – makes happiness a compelling object of scientific enquiry.

Since the launch of Positive Psychology, happiness has become one of the field's signature concerns, so much so that early on the field was dubbed as "happiology" – the science of happiness. At the same time, happiness's rising visibility in political and **public discourse** has prompted some authors to characterise the pursuit of happiness as a modern obsession (Burnett, 2011), and Positive Psychology has been criticised for fuelling this preoccupation (Held, 2005).

Happiology: The science of happiness.

Public discourse: The broader way ideas are discussed in media, policy, education and everyday conversation.

With this critique in mind, this chapter opens by defining happiness and clarifying its relationship to wellbeing. It then reviews key theoretical perspectives that seek to explain the elusiveness of happiness. The chapter concludes by surveying evidence on its predictors and downstream effects. As with the topic of wellbeing (Chapter 3), much of the work examined in this chapter is grounded in Western perspectives.

DOI: 10.4324/9781032663111-6

Conceptualising Happiness

What is happiness? Is it a brief flash of joy, a considered judgement about one's life, an enduring sense of contentment or a personality disposition? Scholars across disciplines have wrestled with these questions for decades.

In much of the academic literature in Positive Psychology, **happiness** is termed *hedonic wellbeing* or *subjective wellbeing*. It is typically understood as comprising two central components (Diener, 2000):

- **Cognitive component:** This facet refers to people's evaluations of their life satisfaction overall or within life domains such as health, relationships, work and finances.
- **Emotional component:** This component captures the frequency with which individuals experience positive emotions (such as excitement, joy and love) and negative emotions (such as fear, anger and disgust) over a specified period.

Subjective wellbeing (SWB): A common academic term for happiness.

Subjective wellbeing is often summarised with the following formula:

SWB = life satisfaction + positive affect – negative affect

Accordingly, individuals with high subjective wellbeing tend to report greater life satisfaction, frequent positive emotions and relatively infrequent negative emotions (Diener, 2000).

Capturing these components of happiness, Hart and Hart (2026) described happiness as a psychological phenomenon that involves an evaluation of one's contentment with life or with a key life domain alongside an emotional response.

Within contemporary wellbeing science, happiness is typically treated as the hedonic component of wellbeing, concerned with how good life feels and is appraised, complementing eudaimonic wellbeing, which focuses on the quality of one's functioning within or across life domains (see Chapter 3).

A common critique in the happiness literature concerns inconsistent terminology. Happiness (or subjective/hedonic wellbeing) is frequently used interchangeably with broader concepts such as overall and mental wellbeing, as well as with its components – *life satisfaction, life evaluation or emotional wellbeing* (Lomas & VanderWeele, 2023c). This lack of distinction creates conceptual ambiguity and complicates how happiness is measured.

Another critique refers to the components of happiness: Should it refer only to emotional experience, to life satisfaction or to both (as seen above), and should it also include other aspects? A further question is whether hedonia (seen as an emotional tone reflecting pleasure or joy) captures the full range of emotional states that people consider as happiness. Lomas and VanderWeele (2023c) argued for a broader account in which happiness encompasses eudaimonic elements and extends beyond hedonic affect, proposing a taxonomy of 16 forms of happiness.

A related empirical puzzle concerns the association between affective and evaluative indicators of subjective wellbeing. If strong, it would suggest that they reflect the same underlying construct. Reported **correlations** vary, averaging around $r = .50$ (Koots-Ausmees et al., 2013). However, an emerging consensus treats these components as distinct, since people can report positive emotional states alongside lower life satisfaction (Knabe et al., 2010), indicating why the use of one component as a proxy for happiness may be misleading.

Most People Are Happy

In an early paper titled "Most People are Happy," Diener and Diener (1996) reviewed a large body of evidence showing that in most nations, a clear majority of people (over 70%) report positive levels of happiness. Average happiness is 6.7 on a 0–10 scale, and these levels seem to be stable over several decades. On this basis, the authors concluded that "most people are mildly happy and satisfied" (Biswas-Diener et al., 2005, p. 205).

Two decades on, Diener and colleagues (2018b) updated these conclusions. They suggested that in economically developed countries, average happiness remains positive, but in contexts where basic needs are not met, both life satisfaction and emotional experience are adversely affected. Once basic needs are secured, individual circumstances (ranging from illness to income) tend to show modest associations with happiness, and these tend to fade over time.

Theoretical Perspectives on Happiness

This section reviews major theoretical perspectives on happiness, showing how different frameworks illuminate distinct facets of the construct. Some theories link overall happiness to happiness in specific domains, while others focus on the function of positive emotions and their downstream benefits. Complementing these accounts, several perspectives examine the determinants of happiness. Others shift from explanation to optimisation, considering how individuals can best pursue happiness. Together, these approaches span multiple levels of analysis, offering diverse yet complementary lenses for conceptualising, explaining and cultivating happiness.

Happiness Overall and Within Life Domains: Bottom-Up, Top-Down and Bi-Directional Theory

Happiness can refer to specific domains (work, health, relationships) or to overall life contentment and emotional experience. Early research viewed global life satisfaction as the sum of satisfaction across key domains. This is known as the **bottom-up theory** (Diener, 1984). From this perspective, external circumstances (such as secure employment or supportive relationships) accumulate to produce overall happiness, informing policy and economic efforts to enhance happiness through improved living conditions. However, empirical findings challenged this account: Income and marital status explain only a modest share of variation in happiness, and even substantial life events often have limited long-term effects (Lyubomirsky et al., 2005a).

In response, **top-down theory** proposed that overall happiness shapes how people interpret and evaluate specific life domains. Happier individuals may appraise their circumstances more positively, thus "colouring" domain judgements through a more optimistic lens. This view aligns with claims that happiness is partly heritable and relatively stable over time despite changing circumstances (Lyubomirsky et al., 2005a).

Taken together, these perspectives suggest two routes to enhancing happiness: Improving external conditions (bottom-up) and shifting internal dispositions and interpretations (top-down). In practice, both matter, with research evidence supporting a **bidirectional model** in which domain satisfaction and global life satisfaction mutually influence one another (Malvaso & Kang, 2022).

Happiness Set-Point Theory

Set-Point Theory proposes that individuals have a relatively stable baseline of subjective wellbeing, reflecting their typical level of happiness.

Lyubomirsky et al. (2005a) argued that the set-point is "genetically determined and is assumed to be fixed, stable over time, and immune to influence or control" (p. 13). These genetic imprints are expressed through enduring characteristics such as temperament and personality traits. Crucially, while life events can produce short-term changes, most people tend to drift back towards their set-point over time.

Happiness set-point: A person's typical level of happiness, which is partially genetically determined.

The theory has been tested using longitudinal panel studies tracking happiness before and after major life events, alongside twin studies (especially twins raised apart to minimise shared environmental explanations) (Lykken & Tellegen, 1996; Fujita & Diener, 2005). Genetic research has also suggested that genetic factors account for 20–40% of the variance in happiness (Nes & Roysamb, 2015, 2017), while emphasising gene–environment interplay.

These findings sparked debates, partly because they imply that pursuing greater happiness is futile. However, contradictory evidence suggested that set-points can shift across the life course, and that some individuals do not return to baseline, particularly after traumatic events (Diener et al., 2018a). Moreover, intentional practices such as meditation have been linked to sustained increases in happiness (Zeng et al., 2015).

Despite these points of contention, Set-Point Theory remains influential. It suggests that happiness is often stable, with most life changes producing meagre long-term effects, with the exception of specific life-changing events and intentional activities that can alter a person's set-point. It also informed two related theories – hedonic adaptation and the Sustainable Happiness Model, discussed next.

The Sustainable Happiness Model

A long-standing question is what determines happiness, and what explains individual differences in happiness? Lyubomirsky et al. (2005a) proposed the Sustainable Happiness Model to outline the principal determinants of happiness. Later work (Diener et al., 2018a; Nes & Roysamb, 2015; Sheldon & Lyubomirsky, 2021) revisited the model, supporting some elements while challenging others. The summary below presents the original model and key recent refinements.

According to Lyubomirsky et al.'s (2005a) model (known as the **Happiness Pie**), three core factors account for individuals' levels of happiness:

- **Genetics and personality:** Consistent with Set-Point Theory, genetic influences explain a meaningful share of variation in happiness.

Current estimates suggest that genetic influences can explain 20–40% of happiness (Nes & Roysamb, 2017), which is lower than the original model's proposition (around 50%). These influences can be difficult to shift since they are expressed through happiness-relevant traits such as affective style, temperament, extraversion, optimism, hope and neuroticism.

The Happiness Pie model: Also known as the Sustainable Happiness Model, it proposes that happiness is determined by three key factors: genetics and personality, life circumstances and intentional activities.

- **Life circumstances**: Lyubomirsky et al.'s (2005a) original model suggested that life circumstances account for a relatively small share of happiness (around 10% on average, with substantial variability). Circumstances include demographic factors, personal history and life events, basic needs fulfilment and wider socio-cultural contexts, as well as partly controllable conditions such as health, education, marital status, work, income and lifestyle. While these factors matter, their modest contribution implies that common goals (such as a pay rise, relocating to a warmer climate, getting married or having a child) may not yield the lasting increases in happiness that people expect. This mismatch spurred further research, with hedonic adaptation considered a leading explanation for the limited long-term effects of circumstances (discussed later).
- **Intentional activities:** The final component of Lyubomirsky et al.'s (2005a) model concerns day-to-day choices in thoughts, emotions and behaviours. The authors claimed this is "arguably the most promising means of altering one's happiness level" (p. 15), since these are largely under individual control. The term *intentional* implies that such activities involve will, deliberate effort and commitment. Behavioural examples include exercising, socialising and engaging with nature. Cognitive examples include goal-setting and cultivating optimism or gratitude. Emotional examples include practising mindfulness and reducing social comparison. Many have been tested as Positive Psychology interventions, yielding moderate improvements in happiness (see Chapter 5). The original model suggested that intentional activities might explain around 40% of the variance in happiness, though Sheldon and Lyubomirsky (2021) proposed a lower figure (around 15% albeit with substantial variability).

Lyubomirsky et al.'s (2005a) analysis reported population averages, with substantial variation around these estimates. Although the model has been critiqued on statistical and conceptual grounds (Brown & Rohrer, 2020), a more consequential issue is that the figures are often treated as uniformly applicable to individuals, reflecting an ecological fallacy (Lomas & VanderWeele, 2023a). This has encouraged a discourse that downplays context while centring academic and popular attention on intentional activities. A recent review (Lomas & VanderWeele, 2023a) suggested that environmental factors exert a larger influence than the original model implied. Moreover, the three domains are interdependent: They interact, and people can also shape aspects of their environment through intentional actions.

A key critique of this model is the notion that people are, to some degree, responsible for their own happiness (Held, 2002). This framing implies that unhappiness reflects personal failure rather than adverse circumstances. Coyne and Tennen (2010) warned that it can promote a "blame the victim" ethos in which people are held responsible for their suffering. A counterpoint to this critique is that Positive Psychology is not unique in emphasising agency over mental states. Cognitive Behavioural Therapy (CBT) similarly teaches clients to notice and challenge negative automatic thoughts and develop more realistic, adaptive interpretations (Beck, 2021), implying that mental health is partly open to personal influence. In this sense, happiness research aligns with a broader cognitive – behavioural tradition, while avoiding blame and acknowledging constraints beyond individual control.

Hedonic Adaptation

Hedonic adaptation (or habituation) refers to the tendency for positive or negative life events to produce only temporary shifts in happiness. After a positive event, people typically experience an initial boost in happiness; after a negative event, they may experience a temporary dip in happiness. Over time, however, individuals often become accustomed to the new circumstances and gradually drift back towards their happiness set-point, such that the emotional impact of the event diminishes. Research suggests that "hedonic adaptation is faster and more likely to be 'complete' in response to positive than negative experiences" (Lyubomirsky, 2011, p. 203).

The phenomenon of habituation helps explain why life circumstances often have only a modest impact on long-term happiness. It has also fuelled pessimism about interventions that can produce enduring gains in subjective wellbeing:

Hedonic adaptation: The tendency for the emotional effects of positive or negative life changes to fade over time as people get used to them.

Hedonic treadmill: The idea that people keep chasing new sources of happiness because gains in happiness often fade through adaptation.

"The notion of an individual fighting against the effects of adaptation brings to mind an image of a pedestrian walking up a descending escalator. Although the improving circumstances of her life may propel her upwards towards ever greater happiness, the process of adaptation forces her back to her initial state" (Layous et al., 2015, p. 186). This dynamic can encourage an ongoing pursuit of the next short-lived boost to happiness, commonly described as the **hedonic treadmill.**

Notably, hedonic adaptation is not inherently negative, as it can support recovery after setbacks. However, it challenges the assumption that major achievements produce lasting happiness, since their emotional benefits fade as they become routine.

As with Set-Point Theory, the universality of hedonic adaptation has been questioned, since adaptation rates vary across events. Some positive changes show relatively rapid adjustment (marriage, income increases, lifestyle changes), whereas others involve slower adaptation (immigration, cosmetic surgery) (Lyubomirsky, 2012). Some adverse experiences, such as disability onset or widowhood, can have enduring negative effects, implying incomplete or prolonged adaptation (Luhmann et al., 2012). Unemployment appears particularly damaging, with evidence of a "scarring" effect that may persist after re-employment (Lucas et al., 2004). Individuals also differ in how they appraise events and in their propensity to adapt over time (Lyubomirsky, 2012).

Taken together, the literature indicates that hedonic adaptation is a powerful but conditional process: It helps explain why changes in circumstances often yield only transient boosts in happiness, while showing that long-term outcomes depend on the event and the individual's response. It therefore cautions against overestimating the lasting impact of positive changes and supports interventions that build ongoing happiness-**boosting** habits.

The Broaden-and-Build Theory of Positive Emotions

The Broaden and Build Theory of Positive Emotions: A theory that explains the key functions of positive emotions.

Positive emotions undeniably feel good, but do they also serve a function? Over the past decades, research has grown markedly, with evidence that positive emotions yield meaningful advantages. The Broaden-and-Build Theory of Positive Emotions (Fredrickson, 2001) was developed to clarify what positive emotions do and why they matter.

Since positive emotions are central to happiness, the theory also speaks to a pivotal issue: Does happiness generate benefits beyond feeling good? Pavot and Diener (2004) argued this is a crucial point, since happiness is a less compelling life goal if it is not linked to meaningful outcomes.

Drawing on theory and a substantial empirical literature, the Broaden-and-Build framework proposes that positive emotions are adaptive: They broaden momentary thought–action repertoires, build enduring resources and help undo the physiological and psychological after-effects of negative emotions, supporting affective balance.

These findings gave rise to what Fredrickson and Cohn (2008) described as **the paradox of positive emotions**: "How is it that fleeting experiences of joy, interest, or love – which can be so easily squelched or dismissed – produce lasting gains in strengths and wellbeing?" (p. 777). The theory explains how brief positive emotional episodes can trigger processes that extend beyond the moment and, over time, accumulate into durable psychological and social resources.

The theory presents six key assertions:

- **The contrasting functions of positive and negative emotions:** The Broaden-and-Build Theory aims to clarify what is distinctive about positive emotions and to move beyond models developed mainly for negative emotions. It proposes that "positive emotions broaden people's momentary thought–action repertoires and lead to actions that build enduring personal resources" (Fredrickson & Cohn, 2008, p. 782). By contrast, negative emotions constrict thought–action repertoires and orient individuals towards action-ready responses (fight, flight or freeze), which supports swift action under threat. Fredrickson and Joiner (2018) noted that, "just as negative emotions both characterise depression and promote it . . . positive emotions appear to both characterise optimal functioning and promote it" (p. 196).
- **The broadening function:** According to the theory, positive emotions broaden people's momentary thought–action repertoires, fostering a "big picture" perspective. Empirical studies link this broadening effect to more flexible and inclusive thinking, greater creativity, problem-solving, reasoned decision-making, perseverance and engagement with challenging tasks. These shifts typically, though not universally, translate into improved performance. Socially, broadening is reflected in greater attentiveness to others, increased self–other overlap, higher trust and reduced intergroup tension (Fredrickson, 2013).
- **The building function:** A substantial evidence base links positive emotions to benefits across multiple life domains. Research suggests that they foster intellectual resources (problem-solving, learning, resourcefulness, openness), physical resources (cardiovascular health, immune functioning, healthier lifestyles), social resources (interaction,

play, trust-building, prosocial behaviour) and psychological resources (coping, resilience, goal pursuit). These findings imply that positive emotions help build resources that later enhance physical and psychological wellbeing, longevity, performance and relationships (Fredrickson, 2013). Crucially, these resources can be durable, outlasting the transient emotional states that helped generate them, allowing individuals to draw upon them later, including in contexts characterised by different emotional experiences.

- **The upwards spiral:** As individuals accumulate resources, upwards spirals can emerge: New capacities and assets elicit further positive emotions, which broaden thought–action repertoires and build additional resources, creating self-reinforcing cycles of growth. Recent support for this account comes from studies using the theory to explain how positive emotions can drive gradual, sustained improvements in health behaviours (Fredrickson & Joiner, 2018).
- **The undoing function:** The undoing hypothesis proposes that positive emotions can counteract the psychological and physiological aftereffects of negative states such as anger, anxiety, sadness or stress. In the context of chronic stress, positive emotions "clearly stood out in their ability to 'undo' lingering cardiovascular activation" (Fredrickson, 2013, p. 10). Positive emotions are also linked to lower pain and better resistance to, or faster recovery from, illness or injury by offsetting the negative emotions that often accompany these experiences (Fredrickson & Cohn, 2008). They also help restore self-regulatory capacity after depletion. In the clinical domain, depression often involves downwards spirals in which low mood and pessimistic thinking reinforce one another. Fredrickson (2013) suggested positive emotions may disrupt these spirals and help initiate upwards spirals. Finally, even in highly adverse contexts that can trigger trauma, positive emotions have been linked to posttraumatic growth.
- **The positivity ratio:** The undoing effect suggests that positive emotions can offset negative ones, yet Baumeister et al. (2001) argued that negative psychological phenomena tend to be more potent than positive ones: Losses, negative information and relationship difficulties typically have stronger effects than equivalent gains. They attributed this asymmetry to evolutionary processes: For our ancestors, rapidly detecting and responding to threats was essential for survival. The authors contended that "when equal measures of good and bad are present . . . the psychological effects of bad ones outweigh those

> **Bad is stronger than good:** negative experiences typically have a greater psychological impact than equally intense positive experiences.

of the good ones . . . This is not to say that bad will always triumph over good . . . Rather, good may prevail over bad by superior force of numbers: Many good events can overcome the psychological effects of a single bad one." (Baumeister et al., 2001, p. 323). In this spirit, Fredrickson and Losada (2005) proposed the idea of a positivity ratio: A quantitative index intended to capture an optimal balance between positive and negative emotions that can bring about an affective equilibrium (3:1) or serve as an indicator of flourishing (up to 12:1). Following critiques of the mathematical model underpinning the positivity ratios (Brown et al., 2013), the numerical values were withdrawn, although the broader principle was retained (Fredrickson & Losada, 2013).

The Broaden-and-Build framework positions positive emotions as consequential processes rather than merely pleasant experiences. By broadening attention and cognition in the moment, positive emotions build durable resources over time, while also helping to restore balance after adversity. Acknowledging that negative experiences can carry disproportionate psychological weight, the theory highlights how positive emotions can offset their effects, tipping trajectories towards resilience, growth and flourishing. Overall, it offers an evidence-informed account of why cultivating positive emotions matters for functioning well across numerous life domains.

Frameworks for Optimising the Pursuit of Happiness

Building on the Sustainable Happiness Model and decades of research showing that happiness can be promoted through intentional activities, Sheldon and Lyubomirsky (2021) outlined several models that explain these strategies:

- **The Eudaimonic Activity Model:** This model maintains that happiness can emerge as a by-product of intentionally engaging in eudaimonic activities. Such activities support basic psychological needs and promote wellbeing through optimal functioning. Examples include pursuing personally valued goals, undertaking meaningful projects, nurturing social connections and choosing activities that foster growth.
- **The Positive Activity Model:** This framework advocates the use of evidence-based interventions shown to reliably raise happiness and offers guidance on how to select and implement them effectively. It also introduces the person–activity fit diagnostic, a tool for identifying which interventions are most likely to suit a particular individual (see Chapter 5).
- **Hedonic Adaptation Prevention Model:** This model challenges the idea that hedonic adaptation is unavoidable. It suggests that adaptation can be slowed by continuing to actively engage with positive changes and by appreciating and **savouring** new circumstances. It also emphasises reducing social comparison and resisting the urge to continually upgrade what one has, which can fuel the hedonic treadmill.

- **Prioritising Positivity:** A further approach to embedding intentional happiness practices involves prioritising positivity (Catalino et al., 2014). This model proposes that people can structure daily life to create frequent, natural opportunities for positive emotion, for example, by making time for enjoyable activities such as walking, gardening or socialising, and by considering the likely emotional consequences in everyday decisions. Catalino and colleagues (2014) found that individuals who pursue happiness in this way report greater happiness than those who do not, suggesting that integrating happiness-promoting activities into daily routines is a worthwhile strategy.

These models emphasise that happiness is best supported when people adopt intentional, values-consistent activities, choose strategies that fit their preferences and context and structure daily life to sustain positive emotion while limiting adaptation. Rather than prescribing a single route to wellbeing, they offer a practical toolkit for building sustainable habits and environments that keep happiness-enhancing practices active over time.

A major critique of this line of research is that it can create social pressure to remain happy regardless of circumstances. Held (2002) described this as the "**tyranny of positivity**," arguing that research findings, particularly on happiness interventions, are often conveyed in the media in a prescriptive tone: "We must think positive thoughts, we must cultivate positive emotions and attitudes" (Held, 2004, p. 12). This framing implies that unhappiness is intolerable, socially unacceptable and even harmful. In response, Linley and Joseph (2004) maintained that accounts of "the good life" and "valued subjective experiences" inevitably rest on value commitments, but argued that taking a value position need not mean prescribing how individuals should live their lives.

> **Tyranny of positivity:** The criticism that people may be pressured to stay positive and happy regardless of difficult circumstances.

Common Pitfalls in the Pursuit of Happiness

The pursuit of happiness is often presented as an unequivocally desirable aim, yet growing evidence suggests that deliberate attempts to increase happiness can be counterproductive. Several impediments can derail the pursuit of happiness, suggesting that well-intentioned efforts may inadvertently undermine the outcomes they seek:

- **Striving for happiness can backfire:** Mauss et al. (2014) argued that striving for happiness can be counterproductive. One explanation is the goal-striving dynamic: Aspirational goals prompt continual progress monitoring, which can heighten disappointment when the goal feels unmet. When happiness becomes the goal, this evaluation may intensify dissatisfaction and push people further from the desired state. Consistent with this, valuing happiness is linked to greater depressive symptoms (Ford & Mauss, 2014). In contrast, Catalino et al. (2014) found that prioritising happiness-promoting activities can increase happiness, suggesting happiness is better pursued indirectly, through engagement in practices that cultivate positive emotions, rather than as an explicit target. A further issue is how people relate to negative emotions: Judging them as unacceptable or trying to avoid them is associated with lower happiness (Dejonckheere et al., 2017), whereas valuing negative emotions can buffer their impact (Luong et al., 2016).

- **Social comparison:** This phenomenon, often described as "keeping up with the Joneses," is widespread and embedded in how people evaluate life events and circumstances (Gerber et al., 2018). Individuals may compare their present situation with past experiences or evaluate themselves against others across domains such as health, relationships, income and lifestyle. Upwards social comparison involves comparing oneself with those who seem better off, whereas downwards comparison involves comparing oneself with those perceived to be worse off. Some upwards comparison can be constructive by motivating ambitious goals, but frequent or persistent upwards comparison can be counterproductive, contributing to poorer self-evaluations, negative emotions (envy, anxiety, depression), feelings of inadequacy and reduced happiness. Consistent with this, happier individuals tend to engage more often in downwards comparisons (Gerber et al., 2018).

Social comparison: Comparing oneself with other people.

- **Affective forecasting errors:** Wilson and Gilbert (2005) argued that people often misjudge which experiences will make them happy or unhappy. Research on affective forecasting shows that individuals often attempt to predict the emotional consequences of future events, yet these forecasts are often off the mark: People typically recover from negative experiences sooner than expected, and positive experiences deliver less happiness than anticipated. This increases the risk that the pursuit of happiness becomes misdirected.

Affective forecasting: Predicting how happy or unhappy future events will make a person feel.

Together, these models suggest that pursuing happiness is most likely to backfire when it becomes overly effortful, evaluative and based on flawed assumptions about what produces happiness. Monitoring happiness too closely, rejecting negative emotions, engaging in frequent upwards comparisons and relying on inaccurate affective forecasts can distort priorities and interpretations. A more fruitful approach is to treat happiness less as a direct target and more as a by-product of meaningful activities, supportive relationships and holding a flexible, accepting stance towards the full range of emotional life.

Measures of Happiness

Research into happiness frequently employs self-report questionnaires to measure the two components of subjective wellbeing – satisfaction with life and emotional experiences.

- **Life satisfaction measures:** Two scales are commonly used to assess life satisfaction:
    - **The Cantril Self-Anchoring Scale:** Developed by Cantril (1965) and commonly presented as a ladder, this measure uses a single life-satisfaction item: "Overall, how satisfied are you with your life nowadays?" Responses are recorded on a 0–10 scale. It is widely used in large-scale surveys, such as the World Happiness Report (Helliwell et al., 2025).
    - **The Satisfaction with Life Scale (SWLS):** This measure (Diener et al., 1985) is commonly used in academic research. It consists of five items.
- **Emotions measures:** To assess participants' emotional experiences, researchers commonly use the following questionnaires:
    - **The Positive and Negative Affect Schedule (PANAS):** This measure (Watson et al., 1988) invites participants to indicate the extent to which they experienced ten positive and ten negative emotions over a specified time frame.
    - **The Scale of Positive and Negative Experience (SPANE):** This measure assesses 12 broad categories of positive and negative experience (Diener et al., 2010).

For both measures, items are summed separately to produce positive and negative affect scores. An overall affect balance score can also be derived by subtracting negative affect from positive affect.

A central limitation of these subjective wellbeing measures is that life satisfaction and emotional indicators do not easily integrate into a single composite score and therefore are analysed separately. In practice, the burden of administering multiple instruments often leads researchers to use one component as a proxy for happiness. This shortcut has fuelled conceptual ambiguity: When a study claims to examine happiness but measures only positive affect, it becomes unclear what the findings reflect. This tendency may also explain why the terms subjective wellbeing, positive emotions and life satisfaction are often used interchangeably. This limitation has motivated the development of additional measures intended to generate a more unified happiness score.

- **Combined happiness measures:**
  - **The UK Census item:** This single-item measure assesses happiness with the question, "Overall, how happy did you feel yesterday?" Responses are scored on a 0–10 scale (ONS, 2023).
  - **The Subjective Happiness Questionnaire:** This scale (Lyubomirsky & Lepper, 1999), includes four items beginning with the prompt: "In general, I consider myself . . . . " A mean score is typically computed across items.
  - **The Oxford Happiness Questionnaire:** This questionnaire (Hills & Argyle, 2002) includes 29 items. A mean score is computed to represent overall happiness.
  - **The Australian Unity (2021) Wellbeing Index:** This measure assesses satisfaction across seven life domains: Health, relationships, standard of living, achievements, community connectedness, personal safety and future security (covering employment, health, the environment and other factors). Items include: "How satisfied are you with your standard of living?" Score are then combined to produce an overall Index score.
- **Other methods**:
  - **Experience Sampling Methodology (ESM):** A useful alternative to standard questionnaires is ESM (Pavot, 2018). Participants are prompted at random moments to record their thoughts and emotions via a mobile device, allowing researchers to compute an individual's average happiness and to examine how it varies across time, settings and circumstances.
  - **Other methodologies:** Happiness can also be assessed using interviews, physiological indicators (brain activity and hormone levels) and coding emotional experiences from facial expressions (Diener et al., 2018a).

These measures are used widely and show strong psychometric performance (Pavot, 2018). It is worth noting that the measures reviewed here represent only a small sample of the many instruments used to assess happiness. This proliferation of questionnaires hinders comparison across studies and impedes the development of more coherent, robust theory.

Happiness: Key Predictors and Outcomes

A substantial body of research has examined the antecedents and consequences of happiness. Whereas work on overall and psychological wellbeing (see Chapter 3) tends to prioritise predictors, happiness research has been more evenly split between causes and effects. Researchers have focused particularly on its downstream consequences, since demonstrating tangible benefits strengthens the case for pursuing happiness.

A particularly compelling question in this body of literature concerns directionality: Does happiness follow from success, or can it also help generate it (Lyubomirsky et al., 2005b)? Although lay intuition often assumes that success produces happiness, evidence suggests a more generative role.

Alongside this outcomes-focused work, a substantial literature has identified key predictors of happiness, many of which align with the "circumstances" and "intentional activities" components in Lyubomirsky et al.'s (2005a) happiness pie. Drawing on several reviews, this section summarises six widely studied correlates of happiness.

Given that happiness is a central component of wellbeing, many findings on its antecedents and consequences overlap with those discussed in Chapter 3. To avoid repetition, several points are summarised more briefly below.

Demographic Factors

Happiness is shaped by a wide range of demographic factors, some of which interact with one another and intersect with cultural context, country-level indicators or personality characteristics (see below). However, research on these influences remains relatively underdeveloped.

Evidence on the association between age and happiness is often interpreted as indicating a U-shaped trajectory across the lifespan, particularly for life satisfaction (Lomas & VanderWeele, 2023b). Recent US data, however, suggested that younger cohorts may be faring less well than previous generations. Some researchers also contested the U-shaped trajectory, arguing that it appears mainly in Western countries, whereas elsewhere subjective wellbeing may decline with age (Lomas & VanderWeele, 2023b).

Research findings indicated that gender differences in happiness are minute (Lomas & VanderWeele, 2023b). Some work, however, found gender variation in affective wellbeing, with women reporting greater emotional intensity at both positive and negative ends of the spectrum compared to men (Kahneman & Deaton, 2010). Interpretation is complicated by gendered socialisation: Men may be encouraged to constrain emotional expression, while women are socialised to articulate emotions (Lomas & VanderWeele, 2023b). Gender gaps also appear contingent on macro sociocultural conditions, particularly gender equality, with more gender-equal countries showing smaller disparities (Zuckerman & Diener, 2017).

Relatively modest research has examined the links between race, ethnicity and happiness. In the United States, White Americans typically report higher happiness than Black and Hispanic Americans, though this gap appears to have narrowed in recent decades (Lomas & VanderWeele, 2023b). Much of the association is explained by differences in socioeconomic status, health, social ties and experiences of discrimination (Barger et al., 2009). Tang et al. (2019) however described a "race paradox" showing that among older adults, Black participants were at least as satisfied as White counterparts when social resources and health were held constant. For Black Americans, spiritual or religious experiences are particularly important for life satisfaction, potentially buffering socioeconomic and health-related disadvantages (Brown & Patterson, 2021).

Research on immigrants suggests that happiness varies by host-country context: Where immigrants face negative public attitudes, their happiness declines. Length of residence moderates this association, as it is strongest among recent arrivals and tends to weaken with more time in the destination country (Sedovic, 2023).

Regarding religious affiliation and religiosity, US research suggests that, compared with Protestants, Catholics and Jews report lower happiness (Sander, 2017). Tay et al. (2014), however, found that affiliation with each of the four major religions is associated with higher happiness, particularly in poorer countries. Nonreligious individuals tend to report lower happiness than religious peers, especially in religious contexts (Sholihin et al., 2022). Specific facets may underpin these links: Spirituality appears more strongly related to happiness than other components of religiosity (Yaden et al., 2022), and religious beliefs, prayer, service attendance and the belonging and social support that religious communities offer have also been associated with happiness (Hackney & Sanders, 2003).

Education

A substantial body of work suggests that education is positively associated with happiness (Lawless & Lucas, 2011), though this relationship remains debated (Lomas & VanderWeele, 2023b). Some scholars argued that education has little direct effect, instead influencing life satisfaction indirectly by expanding occupational, financial and social opportunities. Others suggested that higher education may increase ambition and aspirations, potentially lowering life satisfaction when these are difficult to realise (Nikolaev, 2018). Education may also operate differently across racial groups: The Minorities' Diminished Returns perspective proposes that educational attainment yields smaller happiness gains for non-White than for White Americans (Assari, 2019).

Personality

Research examining the links between the Big Five personality traits and happiness has produced mixed findings. A meta-analysis found that neuroticism is strongly and negatively associated with happiness, while extraversion, agreeableness and conscientiousness show positive but weaker associations (Busseri & Erb, 2023). Other studies, however, reported a strong extraversion–happiness link (Lyubomirsky et al., 2005b). Openness appears positively related only to the emotional component of happiness. Evidence using the HEXACO (Big 6) model broadly mirrors these findings, with no association observed between honesty–humility and happiness (Pilch, 2023).

The Big 6 (HEXACO) model: a personality framework comprising six broad traits—Honesty–Humility, Emotionality, Extraversion, Agreeableness, Conscientiousness, and Openness to Experience.

A range of other personality characteristics are linked to happiness, including an upbeat temperament, high self-esteem, confidence and self-efficacy and lower self-criticism (Lyubomirsky et al., 2005b). These dispositions translate into distinctive outlooks and behavioural patterns, indicating that happier people set more ambitious goals and pursue them with greater optimism, competence, self-control, creativity and a stronger sense of mastery, control and perseverance (Lyubomirsky et al., 2005b). They also tend to make more effective decisions, often "satisficing" (selecting a good enough option) rather than "maximising" (striving for the best outcome), evaluate their performance more favourably and are more likely to experience gratitude and savour everyday pleasures (Lyubomirsky et al., 2005b). When confronted with

Satisficing: choosing the first option that is "good enough" rather than continuing to search for the best choice.

Maximising: searching extensively for the best possible option.

adversity, they typically show greater resilience and lower stress levels, exhibit more adaptive coping, convey hope and interpret events more positively, suggesting that happiness is not associated with denial or maladjustment in difficult circumstances (Lyubomirsky et al., 2005b; Luhmann et al., 2012).

Physical and Mental Health

The relationship between happiness and health appears bidirectional, reflecting the interdependence of mind and body. Compared with less happy individuals, happier people report better overall health, fewer physical complaints, fewer medical appointments and hospital visits, reduced medication use and fewer days of sickness absence (Lyubomirsky et al., 2005b). They also tend to be more health-conscious, more physically active, less likely to engage in unhealthy behaviours and more likely to follow health guidance and adhere to medications (Lyubomirsky et al., 2005b). These patterns are linked to better quality of life and functioning, stronger immune functioning, higher energy and longevity. Positive affect has also been associated with better quality of life in cancer patients and, in some studies, longer survival (Lyubomirsky et al., 2005b).

At the same time, claims that happiness predicts health outcomes have been contested (Coyne & Tennen, 2010) and criticised for their potential to imply personal blame for illness by suggesting that individuals are partly responsible because they are "not happy enough" (Ehrenreich, 2010). Happiness research in the health domain has also been criticised for advancing claims that outstrip the strength or scope of the underlying evidence, at times amounting to what Coyne and Tennen (2010) described as "bad science."

Considering the reverse direction of influence, many people assume that health should be a major determinant of happiness, yet research suggests that the health–happiness association is most evident among those in poor health. For individuals who are healthy, good health may be taken for granted and thus play a smaller role in happiness appraisals (Lomas & VanderWeele, 2023b). One notable exception is sleep quality, which shows a strong association with happiness (Lyubomirsky et al., 2005b).

In relation to mental health, since many psychological disorders (such as depression and anxiety) involve sustained negative emotions, enduring subjective wellbeing is often taken to signal the absence of mental illness. In a study of very happy individuals, Diener et al. (2018b) reported that this group exhibits few symptoms of psychopathology and described feeling well-rested, experiencing personal growth and autonomy and having more free time.

Does meeting key psychological needs (autonomy, relatedness and competence) promote happiness? Stanley et al. (2021) found that higher need satisfaction is linked to more frequent positive emotions and fewer negative emotions, while Tang et al. (2020) reported that it is positively associated with life satisfaction.

Employment and Work

Employment robustly predicts happiness: On average, employed people report higher happiness than unemployed people (Argyle, 2013). Lucas et al. (2004) reported that the happiness costs of job loss can persist for years, with many failing to return to pre-loss levels, suggesting a "scarring effect" that may shift the happiness set point. Unemployment distress can also spill over to significant others. However, unemployed individuals who are healthier, wealthier, better socially supported and less strongly motivated to work tend to report higher happiness than other unemployed people (Lucas et al., 2004).

> **The scarring effect of unemployment:** the lasting negative impact of experiencing job loss and unemployment on happiness, even after returning to work.

While good-quality, meaningful work can foster happiness, there is also evidence of the reverse direction of influence: Happiness shapes work outcomes. During job searches, happier individuals apply for more jobs, receive more interview invitations and obtain higher-paying and more prestigious roles than less happy job seekers. Once employed, they often perform better (though not across all task types), showing greater engagement, effort and productivity and more often exceeding role requirements. They also demonstrate stronger decision-making, creativity and flexibility, experience more flow, persist in long-term goals and show greater resilience when facing obstacles (Walsh et al., 2018). Happier employees engage less in counterproductive or retaliatory behaviour and show higher work standards. Consequently, they are evaluated more favourably, receive more support, are less likely to lose their jobs and report higher job satisfaction, lower burnout and absenteeism and lower turnover intentions (Walsh et al., 2018).

Happiness also appears to shape workplace relationships. Happier employees are more likely to show goodwill, organisational citizenship and prosocial behaviours. They also report greater cohesion and trust and fewer conflicts (Walsh et al., 2018).

At the leadership level, happier managers are typically rated more positively by their followers, who also view their workplace climate more favourably and report better health and happiness than those led by unhappy managers.

There is also evidence that organisations with happier employees achieve higher profitability (Walsh et al., 2018). These findings underpin the Happy – Productive Employee model (see Chapter 8), suggesting that investing in employee happiness can benefit both employee performance and organisational outcomes (Cropanzano & Wright, 2001).

Financial Factors

Can money buy happiness? Many assume a strong link, treating money as a primary route to subjective wellbeing. Lyubomirsky (2014) argued that this belief is a myth, but does the evidence support this view? Research on this topic, known as Happiness Economics, has yielded several key insights over time.

At the lower end of the financial spectrum, being unable to meet basic needs and obligations is linked to enduring unhappiness (Haushofer & Fehr, 2014). Accordingly, at lower income levels, rises in income tend to produce marked gains in happiness, largely because additional monetary resources allow people to secure life's essentials. Yet once a basic threshold is reached, the incremental benefit of higher income for happiness becomes progressively smaller. This pattern, described as the diminishing marginal utility of income, implies that after basic needs and reasonable comforts are met, further income adds relatively little to subjective wellbeing (Kahneman & Deaton, 2010). Higher income is also linked to a lower prevalence of negative emotions, although this association likewise weakens after a basic income threshold has been attained (Tay et al., 2018).

Satiation point: the income level beyond which further increases in income no longer produce meaningful gains in happiness.

The diminishing marginal utility of income: after basic needs and comforts are met, additional income contributes progressively less to happiness.

Having immediately accessible money appears to be a distinct predictor of happiness. Ruberton et al. (2016) found that "cash-on-hand" is positively related to life satisfaction, suggesting that perceived financial control may matter more for happiness than income or wealth. However, the association shows

Income: the flow of money received over a period of time, such as earnings from work, investments, or benefits.

Wealth: the total value of accumulated assets a person owns minus their debts and liabilities.

diminishing returns: Increases from \$0 to \$1,000 correspond with happiness gains, highlighting the value of maintaining a modest emergency buffer, whereas raising assets from \$1,000 to \$10,000 yields much smaller gains in happiness (Ruberton et al., 2016).

Much of the research on money and happiness focuses on income, but a fuller account should also consider wealth, defined as the total of assets, savings and investments, net of debt. Research indicates that higher wealth is positively associated with life satisfaction (Schroder et al., 2020). Greater assets are linked to higher happiness, and an investment portfolio ownership has been associated with improved happiness, whereas debt is associated with lower happiness (Jantsch et al., 2024; Rao & Wang, 2016). Wealth may also buffer adversity, attenuating declines in happiness following illness or disability (Smith et al., 2005).

Studies of lottery winnings report mixed results. Brickman et al. (1978) found an initial surge in happiness but no long-term difference from comparison groups, attributing this to hedonic adaptation. More recent evidence is inconsistent: Some studies suggested that windfall benefits fade over time (Kuhn et al., 2011), while others reported enduring improvements in life satisfaction (Lindqvist et al., 2020). Effects also seem to depend on how winnings are used: When they reduce financial strain and increase security, life satisfaction rises (Apouey & Clark, 2015), whereas poor financial management, heightened social comparison, excessive consumption and relationship changes may erode gains.

Although financial gains tend to show diminishing returns for happiness, research on financial losses indicates that these typically have a greater negative effect on happiness than equivalent income gains (Tay et al., 2018). This pattern aligns with the concept of loss aversion (Kahneman et al., 1991), which suggests that individuals experience losses as more psychologically impactful than comparable gains.

> **Loss aversion:** the tendency for losses to feel more psychologically impactful than equivalent gains.

The literature also highlights several caveats. Economic inequality and perceptions of relative income or wealth are central to the money – happiness link. When individuals perceive substantial disadvantages compared to others, this can generate feelings of relative deprivation and lower life satisfaction (Oishi et al., 2011). Conversely, being better off relative to others is associated with higher life satisfaction (Boyce et al., 2010). Within couples, Kapelle et al. (2022) reported no association between relative wealth and happiness, whereas Hutker et al. (2020) found that women's life satisfaction increases when they are the wealthier partner, while men's did not. The income – happiness association is therefore shaped by broader cultural and societal contexts, particularly inequality (see section on country and culture) (Diener et al., 2003).

Higher levels of income and wealth are often linked to spending more time working or managing assets, leaving less time for activities that enhance happiness, such as socialising (Kahneman et al., 2006). Research also indicates that money can heighten self-focused behaviours, undermine prosocial behaviours (Vohs et al., 2008), and weaken social connection, and these in turn undermine happiness (see below).

Greater financial resources can also expand the range of options available, creating a sense of choice and flexibility, yet research indicates that an overabundance of options can reduce happiness (Iyengar & Lepper, 2000).

> **The paradox of choice:** while having choice can increase autonomy and satisfaction, too many options can make decisions more difficult and reduce satisfaction with the choice made.

Finally, Nickerson et al. (2003) found that prioritising the pursuit of money can dampen life satisfaction. This point is linked to materialism, defined as the belief that acquiring material possessions is a primary route to happiness (Richins & Dawson, 1992). A meta-analysis by Dittmar et al. (2014) found that materialistic values are associated with lower happiness. Similarly, Diener and Oishi (2000) reported that placing greater importance on wealth is negatively related to life satisfaction.

> **Materialism:** the tendency to place high importance on acquiring money, possessions, and material goods as a source of success and happiness.

As in many life domains, hedonic adaptation occurs in the financial and lifestyle contexts. After a pay rise, people typically experience a short-term uplift in happiness but often adjust quickly. As income increases, consumption also tends to rise (Tay et al., 2018).

To counteract adaptation, researchers recommend spending money in ways less prone to habituation, suggesting that happiness depends more on *how* money is spent than on *how much* one has. Spending on others is more strongly associated with happiness than spending on oneself (Aknin et al., 2012). Likewise, spending on experiences tends to be more beneficial to happiness than spending on possessions (Gilovich & Gallo, 2020). Another pathway is buying time: Outsourcing tasks to reduce time pressure is linked to greater life satisfaction (Whillans et al., 2017). Lyubomirsky (2014) argued that purchases that meet basic needs or reduce discomfort are likely to yield more happiness than luxury consumption, and that happiness may rely more on savouring everyday pleasures than expensive "highs." Consistent with this, prudent money management, especially living within one's means and maintaining financial security, shows a stronger relationship with happiness than income or consumption (Spuhlera & Dew, 2019).

Although the bulk of research has focused on whether money predicts happiness, considerably less attention has been paid to the reverse direction. The available evidence indicates that happier individuals are more likely to meet their financial needs and fare better financially than their less happy peers (Lyubomirsky et al., 2005b). Longitudinal studies also indicated that happier young adults achieve higher incomes decades later. This association may be partly attributed to their stronger work ethic and performance, which enhance employability and contribute to more favourable career trajectories (Walsh et al., 2018).

Social Ties

Do happier people enjoy better social relationships than their less happy peers? The literature suggests a bidirectional association: Social relationships shape happiness, and happier dispositions in turn predict stronger ties and more constructive social interactions.

Multiple dimensions of social connectedness have been linked to happiness, including relationship type, network size, the number of organisational affiliations, time spent socialising, level of engagement, relationship quality and closeness, perceived support, relationship satisfaction, and a sense of belonging or affiliation (Lyubomirsky et al., 2005b). Studies on the happiest individuals revealed that they typically report close, supportive social networks and spend a substantial proportion of their time engaged in social activities (Diener et al., 2018a). Consistent with these observations, loneliness is negatively associated with happiness (Lyubomirsky et al., 2005b).

Longitudinal evidence on marriage indicates that newlyweds show an initial boost in happiness, but on average return to their happiness baseline within two years, consistent with hedonic adaptation (Lyubomirsky et al., 2005b). Even with this attenuation, findings on marriage and happiness are robust: Individuals in happy marriages report higher subjective wellbeing than those who are unmarried, divorced or separated, and this pattern appears across age groups, educational levels, racial groups and cultures. Moreover, happier individuals are more likely to report satisfying, high-quality marriages, whereas those who characterise their marriages as unhappy tend to report the lowest happiness levels, indicating that marital quality is a key determinant of subjective wellbeing (Lyubomirsky et al., 2005b).

Happiness commonly declines around the age of 30–40 (see section on age above), but this decrease is typically steeper among single adults, suggesting that marriage may buffer against the age-associated declines (Grover & Helliwell, 2019). In Western countries, the marriage – happiness association has weakened in recent decades, a trend attributed to declining marriage rates and rising cohabitation. However, cohabitation is associated with smaller gains in happiness compared to marriage (Mikucka, 2016).

Notably, higher levels of happiness at earlier time points appear to be linked to a greater likelihood of marrying and experiencing a happier marriage later in life (Lyubomirsky et al., 2005b). Harker and Keltner (2001) found that the amount of positive affect expressed in college year book photos at the age 21 predicted marital satisfaction 31 years later.

Children are often experienced as a profound source of joy, yet they can also bring significant sorrow. How, then, is parenthood associated with happiness? The evidence is mixed, with some studies reporting that parents are slightly happier than non-parents, while others found no meaningful differences (Nelson et al., 2014). More nuanced work indicated that happiness often increases in the period leading up to the birth of a first child, but it returns to baseline shortly afterwards. Other studies reported declines in happiness following the birth of each child, with the lowest levels commonly experienced during children's adolescence. This is followed by improvements in parents' happiness once children have left home (Nelson et al., 2014). These patterns are attributed to the strains of parenting, such as sleep deprivation, increased worry and reductions in marital satisfaction. Consistent with these findings, Kahneman et al. (2004) found that working mothers reported fewer positive emotions and rated childcare as slightly more enjoyable than commuting and housework.

Further work indicated that parents' happiness varies with the child's characteristics (particularly temperament). Factors such as the parent's age, gender, attachment style, socioeconomic circumstances and the availability of social support also predict parents' happiness (Nelson et al., 2014).

Research on friendship shows a strong association with happiness (Lyubomirsky et al., 2005b). However, as with other close relationships, the quality of friendships matters more than the number of friends one has (Demir & Weitekamp, 2007). Happier individuals also report greater satisfaction with their friendships and social activities, and tend to experience lower levels of jealousy towards others (Lyubomirsky et al., 2005b).

Rath and Harter (2010) suggested that happiness spreads within social networks: A person's likelihood of being happy rises by 15% when their friends are happy, and increases even more when those friends are themselves embedded in happy friendship circles. The authors argued that access to a happy social network may exert a stronger influence on happiness than a $10,000 pay rise!

Contrary to a common myth, happier individuals are not selfish. Rather, they tend to be more engaged with current affairs, hold prosocial outlooks, and are more likely to behave cooperatively, altruistically and compassionately compared to their less happy counterparts (Lyubomirsky et al., 2005b). Further findings indicated that happier people contribute more than unhappy individuals to their communities through volunteering and involvement in charity and community services (Lyubomirsky et al., 2005b). This pattern has been described as the "feel good, do good" phenomenon or the "glow of goodwill" (Lyubomirsky et al., 2005b). Scholars have highlighted the bidirectional relationship between positive affect and prosocial attitudes and behaviours, whereby positive emotional states motivate prosocial action, and engaging in prosocial behaviour, in turn, heightens positive emotion (Aknin et al., 2018).

Is there any truth to the idea that happy people are disliked for being shallow or overly cheerful? **Cross-sectional analyses** suggested the opposite pattern (Lyubomirsky et al., 2005b): Happier individuals tend to be perceived as more physically attractive and intelligent, socially skilled, competent, confident, friendly, warm, assertive and more moral.

Macro Level Factors: Country and Culture

Over the past two decades, national and cultural variation have become central to happiness research (Diener et al., 2018a), supported by large-scale national and international surveys that measure happiness. Culture shapes how happiness is defined, the values people hold, the expectations they bring to life and how emotions are expressed. Nations also differ in their capacity to provide services and support, hence influencing citizens' priorities and lifestyles.

Cross-national studies of happiness reported that people are happier in wealthier, more economically developed countries than in less developed nations (Diener et al., 2018a). This pattern may reflect societal factors such as stronger rule of law, lower corruption and crime, less discrimination and unemployment, higher government effectiveness and equality, progressive taxation, robust health and welfare systems, higher educational attainment, stronger social bonds and trust, and greater freedom, autonomy, choice, modernity and environmental protections (Lomas & VanderWeele, 2023b; Diener et al., 2018a). However, a common view is that the association between individuals' happiness and the wealth of their countries reaches a satiation point, weakening at higher levels of wealth (Lomas & VanderWeele, 2023b). Inequality and social comparison may help explain these dynamics (Oishi et al., 2011), and there is evidence that many countries are becoming more unequal (Lomas & VanderWeele, 2023b).

Individualism: a cultural orientation that emphasises personal autonomy, independence, and individual goals.

Collectivism: a cultural orientation that emphasises interdependence, group harmony, and shared goals.

Turning to culture, relationships and community sit within a wider context of shared values, ideologies and traditions that appear to shape happiness (Lomas, 2015). A key cultural dimension in happiness research is individualism – collectivism (Triandis, 2001), with individualism often linked to Western societies and collectivism to Eastern cultures. These orientations can influence happiness: Collectivism may support happiness by fostering social capital, but can also constrain it by limiting autonomy (Lomas & VanderWeele, 2023b), while the opposite pattern may occur in individualistic cultures.

Finally, studying happiness across cultures presents distinct challenges. Language, for instance, is deeply embedded in culture, and societies differ in the terms and concepts they use to describe happiness, often attaching different meanings to similar expressions (Lomas, 2018). Additionally, in some cultures happiness is expressed through low-arousal positive emotions, which may be missed in cross-cultural research (Uchida & Kitayama, 2009).

The Easterlin Paradox

The Easterlin Paradox: A series of studies indicating that a country's economic growth over time does not lead to increases in average happiness.

The Easterlin Paradox describes an apparent disconnect between a country's economic growth and people's happiness. The original question was whether economic growth increases life satisfaction, and the intention was to inform policy on whether raising GDP should be treated as a primary route to greater happiness (Easterlin & O'Connor, 2022). Easterlin's (1974, 2014) studies suggested that although life satisfaction is positively associated with GDP per capita at a given point in time, it does not rise as a country becomes wealthier over time. The paradox therefore reflects a tension between cross-sectional patterns and time-series evidence (Easterlin &

O'Connor, 2022). This view implies that economic growth alone is insufficient to improve life contentment.

Easterlin and O'Connor (2022) argued that social comparison offers a plausible explanation. When an economy grows, incomes tend to rise broadly, meaning that reference groups' incomes rise in parallel. As a result, relative standing may remain stable, leaving average life satisfaction unchanged. By contrast, large individual income gains (such as lottery wins) can increase happiness, though the logic suggests that if everyone experienced the same windfall, the gains would dissipate and happiness would plateau (Oswald & Winkelmann, 2019). Recessions, however, tend to reduce life satisfaction because people compare their income to their pre-recession baseline, making it harder to sustain accustomed living standards and repay debts (De Neve et al., 2018). As incomes recover, life satisfaction often gradually returns to earlier levels. Across both economic expansions and downturns, social comparison appears to be a key **mechanism** shaping experienced happiness.

Gross Domestic Product (GDP): the total monetary value of all goods and services produced within a country over a specific period.

Reference group: a group of people used as a standard for comparing and evaluating one's own attitudes, behaviour, achievements, or circumstances.

It is noteworthy that the paradox has been contested, with some scholars arguing that the association between national wealth and life satisfaction is well established, noting that many of the world's richest countries also rank among the happiest (Sacks et al., 2010). Others have challenged the paradox by presenting evidence that economic growth is associated with rising subjective wellbeing (Stevenson & Wolfers, 2008).

In sum, research on the correlates of happiness suggests that it is both an outcome to be explained and a resource that generates further desirable outcomes. Across domains, the pattern is consistent: Happiness is linked to better health, stronger relationships and more favourable work and economic trajectories, while also being shaped by demographic, personality, social, health, economic and contextual conditions. Evidence also points to dynamic processes: Hedonic adaptation, social comparison, people's behaviours and interactions between factors highlight the complex dynamics of happiness and its pursuit. Identifying predictors therefore requires attention to feedback loops, whereby happier people behave in ways that further consolidate subjective wellbeing over time.

These findings clarify why happiness is a legitimate target not only for individually driven applied practices, but also for public policy interventions that improve people's life conditions. The goal is typically not to maximise happiness, but to raise it when low, support recovery after adverse events and restore emotional equilibrium. Effective interventions should therefore be calibrated, context-sensitive and focused on alleviating suffering and strengthening adaptive functioning rather than pursuing ever-higher happiness levels. This balanced approach highlights both the promise and limits of happiness as a scientific and applied target (Lyubomirsky et al., 2005a).

Conclusion

Since the emergence of Positive Psychology, happiness research has expanded dramatically, shifting from a largely philosophical concern to a substantial empirical enterprise that informs interventions, organisational practice and public policy. As this chapter has shown, happiness is more than a fleeting pleasant feeling: It is linked to a wide range of desirable outcomes and can help generate success across multiple life domains.

At the same time, the research reviewed here converges on three broad determinants of happiness: Genetic influences, life circumstances and volitional activities. These foundations have fuelled a debate about whether pursuing happiness is worthwhile, or whether it is "as futile as trying to become taller" (Lykken & Tellegen, 1996, p. 189). Some scholars argued that explicitly striving for happiness can backfire, suggesting that accepting one's happiness levels may be a wiser strategy (Gruber et al., 2011).

In contrast, other authors argued that although happiness shows meaningful stability, it is not fixed. Sheldon and Lyubomirsky (2021) contended that sustained gains are possible when people attend to cognitive habits, make deliberate choices about how they spend their time and engage in activities that fit their values and circumstances – an intentional, indirect and sustainable route to happiness.

Finally, any account of happiness should also address sustained critiques of the field. As discussed, ambiguous terminology, incompatible measures and unresolved questions about happiness' downstream effects complicate cumulative knowledge-building. Concerns about the tyranny of positivity also caution against communicating findings in prescriptive ways. Yet these critiques need not diminish the field's value; rather, they sharpen it by underscoring conceptual precision, methodological rigour and ethical **reflexivity**. In that spirit, the pursuit of happiness can be framed as an evidence-informed commitment to living well, illuminating pathways for individuals and societies alike.

References

Aknin, L.B., Dunn, E.W., & Norton, M.I. (2012). Happiness runs in a circular motion: Evidence for a positive feedback loop between prosocial spending and happiness. Journal of Happiness Studies, 13(2), 347–355.

Aknin, L.B., Van de Vondervoort, J.W., & Hamlin, J.K. (2018). Positive feelings reward and promote prosocial behavior. Current Opinion in Psychology, 20, 55–59.

Apouey, B., & Clark, A.E. (2015). Winning big but feeling no better? The effect of lottery prizes on physical and mental health. Health Economics, 24(5), 516–538.

Argyle, M. (2013). The psychology of happiness. Routledge.

Assari, S. (2019). Race, education attainment, and happiness in the United States. International Journal of Epidemiologic Research, 6(2), 76.

Australian Unity. (2021). 20th anniversary Australian unity wellbeing index. Australian Unity and Deakin University.

Barger, S.D., Donoho, C.J., & Wayment, H.A. (2009). The relative contributions of race/ethnicity, socioeconomic status, health, and social relationships to life satisfaction in the United States. Quality of Life Research, 18(2), 179–189.

Baumeister, R.F., Bratslavsky, E., Finkenauer, C., & Vohs, K.D. (2001). Bad is stronger than good. Review of General Psychology, (5), 323–370.

Beck, J. (2021). Cognitive behavior therapy. Guildford.

Biswas-Diener, R., Vittersø, J., & Diener, E. (2005). Most people are pretty happy, but there is cultural variation: The Inughuit, the Amish, and the Maasai. Journal of Happiness Studies, 6(3), 205–226.

Boyce, C.J., Brown, G.D.A., & Moore, S.C. (2010). Money and happiness: Rank of income, not income, affects life satisfaction. Psychological Science, 21(4), 471–475.

Brickman, P., Coates, D., & Janoff-Bulman, R. (1978). Lottery winners and accident victims: Is happiness relative? Journal of Personality and Social Psychology, (36), 917–927.

Brown, M.J., & Patterson, R. (2021). Gendered racial differences and similarities in subjective cognitive decline and life satisfaction: Results from a population-based sample. Aging & Mental Health, 25(9), 1636–1641.

Brown, N.J.L., & Rohrer, J.M. (2020). Easy as (happiness) pie? A critical evaluation of a popular model of the determinants of well-being. Journal of Happiness Studies, 21(4), 1285–1301.

Brown, N.J.L., Sokal, A.D., & Friedman, H.L. (2013). The complex dynamics of wishful thinking: The critical positivity ratio. American Psychologist, 68(9), 801–813.

Burnett, S. (2011). The happiness agenda. Springer.

Busseri, M.A., & Erb, E.M. (2023). The happy personality revisited: Re-examining associations between big five personality traits and subjective

well-being using meta-analytic structural equation modelling. Journal of Personality, 92(4), 968–984.
Cantril, H. (1965). The pattern of human concerns. Rutgers University Press.
Catalino, L.I., Algoe, S.B., & Fredrickson, B.L. (2014). Prioritizing positivity: An effective approach to pursuing happiness? Emotion, 14(6), 1155–1161.
Coyne, J.C., & Tennen, H. (2010). Positive psychology in cancer care: Bad science, exaggerated claims, and unproven medicine. Annals of Behavioral Medicine, 39(1), 16–26.
Cropanzano, R., & Wright, T.A. (2001). When a "happy" worker is really a "productive" worker: A review and further refinement of the happy-productive worker thesis. Consulting Psychology Journal, 53(3), 182.
De Neve, J.E., Ward, G., De Keulenaer, F., Van Landeghem, B., Kavetsos, G., & Norton, M.I. (2018). The asymmetric experience of positive and negative economic growth: Global evidence using subjective well-being data. Review of Economics and Statistics, 100(2), 362–375.
Dejonckheere, E., Bastian, B., Fried, E., Murphy, S., & Kuppens, P. (2017). Perceiving social pressure not to feel negative predicts depressive symptoms in daily life. Depression and Anxiety, 34(9), 836–44.
Demir, M., & Weitekamp, L.A. (2007). I am so happy 'cause today I found my friend: Friendship and personality as predictors of happiness. Journal of Happiness Studies, 8(2), 181–211.
Diener, E. (1984). Subjective well-being. Psychological Bulletin, 95(3), 542.
Diener, E. (2000). Subjective well-being: The science of happiness and a proposal for a national index. American Psychologist, 55(1), 34–43.
Diener, E., & Diener, C. (1996). Most people are happy. Psychological Science, 7, 181–185.
Diener, E., Diener, C., Choi, H., & Oishi, S. (2018b). Revisiting "most people are happy" – and discovering when they are not. Perspectives on Psychological Science, 13(2), 166–170.
Diener, E., Emmons, R.A., Larsen, R.J., & Griffen, S. (1985). The satisfaction with life scale. Journal of Personality Assessment, 49, 71–75.
Diener, E., Lucas, R.E., & Oishi, S. (2018a). Advances and open questions in the science of subjective well-being. Collabra: Psychology, 4(1), 15–19.
Diener, E., & Oishi, S. (2000). Money and happiness: Income and subjective well-being across nations. In E. Diener, & E.M. Suh (Eds.), Culture and subjective well-being (pp. 185–218). MIT Press.
Diener, E., Oishi, S., & Lucas, R.E. (2003). Personality, culture, and subjective well-being: Emotional and cognitive evaluations of life. Annual Review of Psychology, 54(1), 403–425.
Diener, E., Wirtz, D., Tov, W., Kim-Prieto, C., Choi, D.W., Oishi, S., & Biswas-Diener, R. (2010). New wellbeing measures: Short scales to assess flourishing and positive and negative feelings. Social Indicators Research, 97, 143–156.
Dittmar, H., Bond, R., Hurst, M., & Kasser, T. (2014). The relationship between materialism and personal well-being: A meta-analysis. Journal of Personality and Social Psychology, 107(5), 879–924.

Easterlin, R.A. (1974). Does economic growth improve the human lot? Some empirical evidence. In: P.A. David, & W.R. Melvin (Eds.), Nations and households in economic growth (98–125). Stanford University Press.
Easterlin, R.A. (2014). Happiness and economic growth – the evidence. In W. Glatzer, L. Camfield, V. Moller, & M. Rojas (Eds.), Global handbook of quality of life (pp. 283–299). Springer.
Easterlin, R.A., & O'Connor, K.J. (2022). The Easterlin paradox. In K.F. Zimmermann (Ed.), Handbook of labor, human resources and population economics (pp. 1–25). Springer.
Ehrenreich, B. (2010). Smile or die. Granta Books.
Ford, B.Q., & Mauss, I.B. (2014). The paradoxical effects of pursuing positive emotion: When and why wanting to feel happy backfires. In J. Gruber, & J.T. Moskowitz (Eds.), Positive emotion (pp. 363–381). Oxford University Press.
Fredrickson, B.L. (2001). The role of positive emotions in positive psychology: The broaden-and build theory of positive motions. The American Psychologist, 56(3), 218–226.
Fredrickson, B.L. (2013). Positive emotions broaden and build. In P. Devine, & A. Plant (Eds.), Advances in experimental social psychology (Vol. 47, pp. 1–53). Academic Press.
Fredrickson, B.L., & Cohn, M.A. (2008). Positive emotions. In M. Lewis, J. Haviland-Jones, & L.F. Barrett (Eds.), Handbook of emotion (pp. 777–796). Guilford.
Fredrickson, B.L., & Joiner, T. (2018). Reflections on positive emotions and upward spirals. Perspectives on Psychological Science, 13(2), 194–199.
Fredrickson, B.L., & Losada, M.F. (2005). Positive affect and the complex dynamics of human flourishing. American Psychologist, 60(7), 678–686.
Fredrickson, B.L., & Losada, M.F. (2013). Positive affect and the complex dynamics of human flourishing: Correction to Fredrickson and Losada (2005). American Psychologist, 68(9), 822.
Fujita, F., & Diener, E. (2005). Life satisfaction set point: Stability and change. Journal of Personality and Social Psychology, 88, 158–164.
Gerber, J.P., Wheeler, L., & Suls, J. (2018). A social comparison theory meta-analysis 60+ years on. Psychological Bulletin, 144(2), 177–197.
Gilovich, T., & Gallo, I. (2020). Consumers' pursuit of material and experiential purchases: A review. Consumer Psychology Review, 3(1), 20–33.
Grover, S., & Helliwell, J.F. (2019). How's life at home? New evidence on marriage and the set point for happiness. Journal of Happiness Studies, 20(2), 373–390.
Gruber, J., Mauss, I.B., & Tamir, M. (2011). A dark side of happiness? How, when, and why happiness is not always good. Perspectives on Psychological Science, 6(3), 222–233.
Hackney, C.H., & Sanders, G.S. (2003). Religiosity and mental health: A meta-analysis of recent studies. Journal for the Scientific Study of Religion, (42), 43–55.
Harker, L., & Keltner, D. (2001). Expressions of positive emotion in women's college yearbook pictures and their relationship to personality and life outcomes across adulthood. Journal of Personality and Social Psychology, (80), 112–124.

Hart, R., & Hart, D. (2026). Cutting through the clutter: Cleaning the lens on work-related wellbeing concepts. Behavioral Sciences, 16(3), 373.
Haushofer, J., & Fehr, E. (2014). On the psychology of poverty. Science, 344(6186), 862–867.
Held, B.S. (2002). The tyranny of the positive attitude in America: Observation and speculation. Journal of Clinical Psychology, 58(9), 965–991.
Held, B.S. (2004). The negative side of positive psychology. Journal of Humanistic Psychology, (44), 9–46.
Held, B.S. (2005). The "virtues" of positive psychology. Journal of Theoretical and Philosophical Psychology, 25(1), 1–34.
Helliwell, J.F., Layard, R., Sachs, J.D., De Neve, J.E., Aknin, L.B., & Wang, S. (2025). World happiness report. Gallup.
Hills, P., & Argyle, M. (2002). The Oxford happiness questionnaire: A compact scale for the measurement of psychological well-being. Personality and Individual Differences, 33(7), 1073–1082.
Hutker, H., Rainer, H., & Siedler, T. (2020). My gain or your loss? Changes in within-couple relative wealth and partners' life satisfaction. European Sociological Review, 36(6), 853–869.
Iyengar, S.S., & Lepper, M.R. (2000). When choice is demotivating: Can one desire too much of a good thing? Journal of Personality and Social Psychology, 79(6), 995.
Jantsch, A., Le Blanc, J., & Schmidt, T. (2024). Beyond income: Exploring the role of household wealth for subjective well-being in Germany. Journal of Happiness Studies, 25(7), 101.
Kahneman, D., & Deaton, A. (2010). High income improves evaluation of life but not emotional well-being. Proceedings of the National Academy of Sciences, 107(38), 16489–16493.
Kahneman, D., Knetsch, J.L., & Thaler, R.H. (1991). Anomalies: The endowment effect, loss aversion, and status quo bias. Journal of Economic Perspectives, 5(1), 193–206.
Kahneman, D., Krueger, A.B., Schkade, D.A., Schwarz, N., & Stone, A.A. (2004). A survey method for characterizing daily life experience: The day reconstruction method. Science, 306, 1776–1780.
Kahneman, D., Krueger, A.B., Schkade, D.A., Schwarz, N., & Stone, A.A. (2006). Would you be happier if you were richer? A focusing illusion. Science, 312, 1908–1910.
Kapelle, N., Nutz, T., Tisch, D., Schechtl, M., Lersch, P.M., & Struffolino, E. (2022). My wealth,(y) our life satisfaction? Sole and joint wealth ownership and life satisfaction in marriage. European Journal of Population, 38(4), 811–834.
Knabe, A., Rätzel, S., Schöb, R., & Weimann, J. (2010). Dissatisfied with life but having a good day: Time-use and well-being of the unemployed. The Economic Journal, 120(547), 867–889.
Koots-Ausmees, L., Realo, A., & Allik, J. (2013). The relationship between life satisfaction and emotional experience in 21 European countries. Journal of Cross-Cultural Psychology, 44(2), 223–244.
Kuhn, P., Kooreman, P., Soetevent, A., & Kapteyn, A. (2011). The effects of lottery prizes on winners and their neighbors: Evidence from

the Dutch postcode lottery. American Economic Review, 101(5), 2226–2247.
Lawless, N.M., & Lucas, R.E. (2011). Predictors of regional well-being: A county level analysis. Social Indicators Research, 101, 341–357.
Layous, K., Sheldon, K.M., & Lyubomirsky, S. (2015). The prospects, practices, and prescriptions for the pursuit of happiness. In P.A. Linley, & S. Joseph (Eds.), Positive psychology in practice (pp. 183–206). Wiley.
Lindqvist, E., Östling, R., & Cesarini, D. (2020). Long-run effects of lottery wealth on psychological well-being. The Review of Economic Studies, 87(6), 2703–2726.
Linley, P.A., & Joseph, S. (2004). Applied positive psychology: A new perspective for professional practice. In P.A. Linley, & S. Joseph (Eds.), Positive psychology in practice (pp. 3–12). Wiley.
Lomas, T. (2015). Positive cross-cultural psychology: Exploring similarity and difference in constructions and experiences of wellbeing. International Journal of Wellbeing, 5(4), 4.
Lomas, T. (2018). Experiential cartography and the significance of "untranslatable" words. Theory & Psychology, 28(4), 476–495.
Lomas, T., & VanderWeele, T.J. (2023a). The mental illness-health matrix and the mental state space matrix: Complementary meta-conceptual frameworks for evaluating psychological states. Journal of Clinical Psychology, 79(8), 1902–1920.
Lomas, T., & VanderWeele, T.J. (2023b). The complex creation of happiness: Multidimensional conditionality in the drivers of happy people and societies. The Journal of Positive Psychology, 18(1), 15–33.
Lomas, T., & VanderWeele, T.J. (2023c). Toward an expanded taxonomy of happiness: A conceptual analysis of 16 distinct forms of mental wellbeing. Journal of Humanistic Psychology, 00221678231155512.
Lucas, R.E., Clark, A.E., Georgellis, Y., & Diener, E. (2004). Unemployment alters the set point for life satisfaction. Psychological Science, 15, 8–13.
Luhmann, M., Hofmann, W., Eid, M., & Lucas, R.E. (2012). Subjective well-being and adaptation to life events: A meta-analysis. Journal of Personality and Social Psychology, 102, 592–615.
Luong, G., Wrzus, C., Wagner, G.G., & Riediger, M. (2016). When bad moods may not be so bad: Valuing negative affect is associated with weakened affect – health links. Emotion, 16(3), 387.
Lykken, D., & Tellegen, A. (1996). Happiness is a stochastic phenomenon. Psychological Science, 7(3), 186–189.
Lyubomirsky, S. (2011). The how of happiness. Penguin.
Lyubomirsky, S. (2012). Hedonic adaptation to positive and negative experiences. In S. Folkman (Ed.), The Oxford handbook of stress, health, and coping (pp. 200–224). Oxford University Press.
Lyubomirsky, S. (2014). The myths of happiness. Penguin.
Lyubomirsky, S., King, L., & Diener, E. (2005b). The benefits of frequent positive affect: Does happiness lead to success? Psychological Bulletin, (131), 803–855.

Lyubomirsky, S., & Lepper, H.S. (1999). A measure of subjective happiness: Preliminary reliability and construct validation. Social Indicators Research, (46), 137–155.
Lyubomirsky, S., Sheldon, K.M., & Schkade, D. (2005a). Pursuing happiness: The architecture of sustainable change. Review of General Psychology, 9(2), 111–131.
Malvaso, A., & Kang, W. (2022). The relationship between areas of life satisfaction, personality, and overall life satisfaction: An integrated account. Frontiers in Psychology, 13, 894610.
Mauss, I.B., Floerke, V.A., & Gruber, J. (2014). Desperately seeking happiness: Valuing happiness is associated with symptoms and diagnosis of depression. Journal of Social and Clinical Psychology, 33(10), 890–905.
Mikucka, M. (2016). The life satisfaction advantage of being married and gender specialization. Journal of Marriage and Family, 78(3), 759–779.
Nelson, S.K., Kushlev, K., & Lyubomirsky, S. (2014). The pains and pleasures of parenting: When, why, and how is parenthood associated with more or less well-being? Psychological Bulletin, 140(3), 846–895.
Nes, R.B., & Roysamb, E. (2015). The heritability of subjective well-being: Review and meta-analysis. In M. Pluess (Ed.), The genetics of psychological well-being (pp. 75–96). Oxford University Press.
Nes, R.B., & Roysamb, E. (2017). Happiness in behaviour genetics: An update on heritability and changeability. Journal of Happiness Studies, 18(5), 1533–1552.
Nickerson, C., Schwarz, N., Diener, E., & Kahneman, D. (2003). Zeroing in on the dark side of the American dream: A closer look at the negative consequences of the goal for financial success. Psychological Science, 14(6), 531–536.
Nikolaev, B. (2018). Does higher education increase hedonic and eudaimonic happiness? Journal of Happiness Studies, 19(2), 483–504.
Oishi, S., Kesebir, S., & Diener, E. (2011). Income inequality and happiness. Psychological Science, 22(9), 1095–1100.
ONS. (2023). Personal well-being in the UK. Office of National Statistics.
Oswald, A.J., & Winkelmann, R. (2019). Lottery wins and satisfaction: Overturning Brickman in modern longitudinal data on Germany. In M. Rojas (Ed.), The economics of happiness (pp. 57–84). Springer.
Pavot, W. (2018). The cornerstone of research on subjective well-being: Valid assessment methodology. In E. Diener, S. Oishi, & L. Tay (Eds.), Handbook of well-being. DEF Publishers.
Pavot, W., & Diener, E. (2004). Findings on subjective well-being: Applications to public policy, clinical interventions, and education. In A.P. Linley, & S. Joseph (Eds.), Positive psychology in practice (pp. 679–692). Wiley.
Pilch, I. (2023). Comparison of the big five and the HEXACO models of personality in the prediction of emotional wellbeing: An experience sampling study. Trends in Psychology, 1–17.
Rao, Y., & Wang, C. (2016). Happiness and stock-market participation: Empirical evidence from China. Journal of Happiness Studies, 17(1), 271–293.
Rath, T., & Harter, J. (2010). Wellbeing. Simon and Schuster.

Richins, M.L., & Dawson, S. (1992). A consumer values orientation for materialism and its measurement: Scale development and validation. Journal of Consumer Research, 19(3), 303–316.

Ruberton, P.M., Gladstone, J., & Lyubomirsky, S. (2016). How your bank balance buys happiness: The importance of "cash on hand" to life satisfaction. Emotion, 16(5), 575–580.

Sacks, D.W., Stevenson, B., & Wolfers, J. (2010). Subjective well-being, income, economic development and growth (No. w16441). National Bureau of Economic Research.

Sander, W. (2017). Religion, religiosity, and happiness. Review of Religious Research, 59(2), 251–262.

Schroder, C., Bartels, C., Göbler, K., Grabka, M.M., & König, J. (2020). Millionaires under the microscope: Data gap on top wealth holders closed; wealth concentration higher than presumed. DIW Weekly Report, 10, 313–322.

Sedovic, M. (2023). Do attitudes towards immigrants matter? The subjective wellbeing of immigrants in England and Wales and their exposure to non-migrants. European Journal of Population, 39(1), 38.

Sheldon, K.M., & Lyubomirsky, S. (2021). Revisiting the sustainable happiness model and pie chart: Can happiness be successfully pursued? The Journal of Positive Psychology, 1–10.

Sholihin, M., Hardivizon, H., Wanto, D., & Saputra, H. (2022). The effect of religiosity on life satisfaction: A meta-analysis. HTS Theological Studies, 78(4), 7172.

Smith, D.M., Langa, K.M., Kabeto, M.U., & Ubel, P.A. (2005). Health, wealth, and happiness: Financial resources buffer subjective well-being after the onset of a disability. Psychology and Aging, 20(2), 200–206.

Spuhlera, B.K., & Dew, J. (2019). Sound financial management and happiness: Economic pressure and relationship satisfaction as mediators. Journal of Financial Counseling and Planning, 30(2), 157–174.

Stanley, P.J., Schutte, N.S., & Phillips, W.J. (2021). A meta analytic investigation of the relationship between basic psychological need satisfaction and affect. Journal of Positive School Psychology, 5(1), 1–16.

Stevenson, B., & Wolfers, J. (2008). Economic growth and subjective well-being: Reassessing the easterlin paradox (No. w14282). National Bureau of Economic Research.

Tang, F., Jang, H., Rauktis, M.B., Musa, D., & Beach, S. (2019). The race paradox in subjective wellbeing among older Americans. Ageing & Society, 39(3), 568–589.

Tang, M., Wang, D., & Guerrien, A. (2020). A systematic review and meta-analysis on basic psychological need satisfaction, motivation, and well-being in later life: Contributions of self-determination theory. PsyCh Journal, 9, 5–33.

Tay, L., Li, M., Myers, D., & Diener, E. (2014). Religiosity and subjective well-being: An international perspective. In C. Kim-Prieto (Ed.), Religion and spirituality across cultures (pp. 163–175). Springer.

Tay, L., Zyphur, M., & Batz, C.L. (2018). Income and subjective well-being: Review, synthesis, and future research. In E. Diener, S. Oishi, & L. Tay (Eds.), Handbook of well-being. DEF Publishers.

Triandis, H.C. (2001). Individualism and collectivism: Past, present, and future. In D. Matsumoto (Ed.), The handbook of culture and psychology (pp. 35–50). Oxford University Press.

Uchida, Y., & Kitayama, S. (2009). Happiness and unhappiness in east and west: Themes and variations. Emotion, 9(4), 441.

Vohs, K.D., Mead, N.L., & Goode, M.R. (2008). Merely activating the concept of money changes personal and interpersonal behavior. Current Directions in Psychological Science, 17(3), 208–212.

Walsh, L.C., Boehm, J.K., & Lyubomirsky, S. (2018). Does happiness promote career success? Revisiting the evidence. Journal of Career Assessment, 26(2), 199–219.

Watson, D., Clark, L.A., & Tellegen, A. (1988). Development and validation of brief measures of positive and negative affect: The PANAS Scales. Journal of Personality and Social Psychology, 54, 1063–1070.

Whillans, A.V., Dunn, E.W., Smeets, P., Bekkers, R., & Norton, M.I. (2017). Buying time promotes happiness. Proceedings of the National Academy of Sciences, 114(32), 8523–8527.

Wilson, T.D., & Gilbert, D.T. (2005). Affective forecasting: Knowing what to want. Current Directions in Psychological Science, 14(3), 131–134.

Yaden, D.B., Batz-Barbarich, C.L., Ng, V., Vaziri, H., Gladstone, J.N., Pawelski, J.O., & Tay, L. (2022). A meta-analysis of religion/spirituality and life satisfaction. Journal of Happiness Studies, 23(8), 4147–4163.

Zeng, X., Chiu, C.P., Wang, R., Oei, T.P., & Leung, F.Y. (2015). The effect of loving-kindness meditation on positive emotions: A meta-analytic review. Frontiers in Psychology, 6, 1693.

Zuckerman, M., Li, C., & Diener, E. (2017). Societal conditions and the gender differences in well-being: Testing a 3-stage model. Personality and Social Psychology Bulletin, (43), 329–336.

Section 3

Key Applications

This Section in Summary

Chapter 5: Positive Psychology Interventions

- Positive Psychology Interventions are treatment methods or intentional activities geared to cultivate positive emotions, cognitions or behaviours, by activating a positive mechanism.
- Multi-component programmes incorporate multiple topics, modules, or sessions, typically combining several activities whereas single-component activities are designed to foster specific positive states or outcomes through brief exercises.
- Their effectiveness depends on how they are delivered, including timing, frequency, variation, delivery mode, participant motivation, autonomy and social support.
- No intervention works for everyone, and they are more effective when adapted to fit individual needs and contexts.
- Ethical guidelines have been developed to support high quality, evidence-based practice, and protect the public from potential harm.
- The evidence base on their impact is broadly favourable, with many interventions showing small-to-moderate benefits.
- Limitations include methodological weaknesses, limited cultural diversity, unclear mechanisms of change, and the need for more realistic expectations about what brief activities can achieve.

Chapter 6: Applied Interdisciplinary Domains

- Positive Psychology is increasingly being embedded within established applied traditions, expanding the focus of practice beyond symptom reduction to include wellbeing and other positive outcomes.
- Six prominent interdisciplinary domains are reviewed: Positive Psychology Coaching, Positive Psychotherapy, Wellbeing Therapy, Quality of Life Therapy, Positive CBT, and Positive Psychiatry.

DOI: 10.4324/9781032663111-7

- Evidence base of their efficacy is limited but encouraging.
- Despite their promise, these approaches face recurring challenges including limited and uneven evidence bases, methodologically weak studies and unclear mechanisms of change.

Chapter 5

Positive Psychology Interventions

Positive Psychology scholarship, spanning theory development and a growing body of empirical research, suggests that happiness, wellbeing, performance, resilience and other desirable psychological states can be strengthened through intentional engagement in positive activities. Such activities include, for example, expressing gratitude, performing acts of kindness, identifying and deploying character strengths, setting personally meaningful goals and practising mindfulness. Since the field's emergence, experimental research on Positive Psychology interventions has expanded substantially, becoming a cornerstone of the discipline and providing a robust evidence base for its applied aims and practices.

This chapter offers an overview of the theory and research on Positive Psychology Interventions (PPIs). It begins by defining what constitutes a positive activity and outlining key forms that these interventions can take. The chapter then examines the conditions that support effective delivery. Lastly, the chapter synthesises the principal findings on intervention outcomes and their broader implications.

Conceptualising Interventions

An intervention is a deliberate action undertaken to enhance the wellbeing or functioning of an individual, group or organisation. Interventions can be implemented with the aim of:

Intervention: A structured activity, programme or technique designed to improve a person's or a group's condition or produce positive change.

DOI: 10.4324/9781032663111-8

- Preventing harm, injury or illness;
- Healing or decreasing the severity or duration of an existing condition;
- Restoring diminished functions;
- Building capacity or fostering growth.

Interventions span virtually all professional fields, from healthcare to social services, and are customised according to the context, client needs and the professionals delivering them. Interventions can be implemented at individual, organisational, community or national scales. They are often (but not always) introduced by a professional in a client-facing setting.

In Psychology, interventions are frequently categorised by their domain, which reflects the specific approach employed by the practitioner. Examples include psychiatric treatment, clinical or counselling psychology interventions, couple or family therapy and numerous others.

Historically, psychological interventions were categorised according to client condition severity, associated risks to the patient or others and the complexity of the intervention (Gelder et al., 2001):

- Severe, persistent, and complicated mental health conditions often require **psychiatric interventions** involving hospitalisation, medication or prolonged remedial therapy.
- Less severe to moderately complex disorders are frequently managed through diverse **therapeutic interventions**, such as clinical or counselling psychology or alternative approaches.
- Interventions aimed at prevention or growth promotion often serve non-clinical clients and are classified as coaching or Positive Psychology Interventions (Parks & Biswas-Diener, 2013).

In the past two decades, however, the boundaries between these categories have become less distinct. Psychological practitioners often operate within interdisciplinary teams comprising practitioners from various specialisations

Interdisciplinary teams: groups of professionals from psychology and other disciplines who combine their expertise to understand problems and develop more comprehensive solutions.

Integrative approach: an approach in psychology that combines theories, concepts, and methods from different perspectives to provide a more comprehensive understanding of behaviour and mental processes.

(Tang, 2019). Moreover, many psychology practitioners adopt an integrative approach that transcends disciplinary boundaries (Wood et al., 2019) and incorporate Positive Psychology and coaching interventions (Ruini, 2017).

Defining Positive Psychology Interventions

> Sin and Lyubomirsky (2009) defined **Positive Psychology Interventions** (also termed positive activities) as "treatment methods or intentional activities that aim to cultivate positive feelings, behaviours, or cognitions" (p. 468).

Parks and Biswas-Diener (2013) proposed that positive activities should meet the following criteria:

- The intervention's central aim is to enhance a positive outcome;
- The activity should operate a positive mechanism;
- The intervention should be evidence-based;
- The activity should be implemented optimally, responsibly and ethically, tailored to the needs of the target population and designed to avoid harm;
- The intervention should prioritise the cultivation of positive processes and outcomes rather than the remediation of flaws, deficits or pathology.

Types of Positive Psychology Interventions

Scholars often distinguish between two broad types of interventions:

- **Multi-component programmes** incorporate multiple topics, modules or sessions, typically combining several activities. Illustrative examples include the Penn Resilience Programme (Gillham et al., 2013), The Sound Relationship House Model, developed by Gottman (2018), and the Mindfulness-Based Stress Reduction (MBSR) programme (Kabat-Zinn, 2003). These approaches are manualised and commonly delivered by a trained facilitator. They vary in format (group or individual), mode (online, face-to-face or hybrid) and target population (including programmes designed for adults, children, couples or particular target audiences).
- **Single-component positive activities** are designed to foster specific positive states or outcomes, such as wellbeing, engagement, optimism, performance and relationship satisfaction. These exercises are typically brief, focused and straightforward to implement, and most do not require specialised settings or equipment. Examples include goal-setting,

keeping a gratitude diary, identifying and using strengths and performing acts of kindness. Some are intended as one-off activities, whereas others require repetition to optimise impact. Many are now widely accessible through books, websites and phone applications, enabling self-administration, with a minority requiring delivery by a coach or therapist.

Multi-Component Programmes

A selection of empirically supported, multi-component programmes incorporating Positive Psychology interventions for adults is outlined next.

The Fundamentals for Happiness Programme

The Fundamentals for Happiness Programme (Fordyce, 1983) is widely regarded as the earliest structured happiness programme grounded in principles now associated with Positive Psychology. It focuses on 14 fundamental principles designed to foster and sustain happiness. Typically delivered over around 10–20 weeks, it involves teaching and practising these principles, with participants encouraged to apply them consistently and integrate them into everyday routines. The principles were derived from observed characteristics of naturally happy individuals. Examples include: Spend more time socialising; be productive at meaningful work; make plans and organise; don't worry needlessly; develop positive, optimistic thinking; focus on today; nurture close relationships.

The intervention has been implemented in group formats or incorporated into individual therapeutic work, and research following its implementation reported significant improvements in happiness and psychological wellbeing among participants (Fordyce, 1983).

The Happy Life: Voyages to Wellbeing

The Voyages to Wellbeing programme (Cloninger, 2006) is a psychoeducational intervention for individuals recovering from mental illness, aiming to support a return to normative functioning while enhancing psychological wellbeing. It integrates elements of Cognitive Behavioural Therapy and mindfulness, with improved self-awareness as its central mechanism of change. It can be delivered either in groups

Psycho-education: providing individuals with psychological knowledge and practical information to help them better understand and manage their symptoms or difficulties.

Mechanism: The process through which an intervention is thought to bring about change.

or on an individual basis by a therapist, and participants are expected to practise the exercises routinely.

The programme comprises 15 sessions, with sample topics including recognising what brings joy, understanding thinking traps, observing and elevating thoughts, cultivating relationships, reducing stress and raising awareness.

Research on the programme (Cloninger, 2006) indicated that it is associated with increased happiness and psychological wellbeing, alongside reductions in mental illness.

The Penn Resiliency Programme

The Penn Resiliency Programme (PRP) is a preventative intervention for children and adults, designed to strengthen resilience and reduce risk of developing mental illness (Gillham et al., 2013). In adult contexts, it is most often delivered in groups by a trained facilitator. Grounded in cognitive-behavioural principles, PRP targets a range of resilience-related skills, including emotional understanding, self-regulation, coping, problem-solving, decision-making, cognitive flexibility, social awareness, relationship skills, self-efficacy and optimism. It combines psychoeducation with structured exercises, helping participants identify unhelpful interpretations of events, evaluate and dispute these appraisals and develop more adaptive thinking. Social support is treated as a key protective resource, and PRP incorporates the development of social skills.

The programme has been implemented across varied settings, including the US army and a range of organisational contexts, and is one of the most widely disseminated resilience education programmes globally.

Reviews of the evaluation literature link adult PRP to improved resilience and mental health, enhanced performance and reduced stress, with similar patterns reported for school-based programmes (Gillham et al., 2013).

The Mindfulness-Based Stress Reduction Programme

The Mindfulness-Based Stress Reduction (MBSR) was developed in the late 1970s by Kabat-Zinn (2003), initially for individuals living with chronic pain. It was later examined across a range of physical and psychological presentations, including stress, and has since been widely disseminated.

Mindfulness: Paying attention to present-moment experience intentionally and non-judgementally.

Mindfulness is defined as paying attention to present-moment experiences, intentionally and non-judgementally. As a practice, it cultivates self-awareness, clarity and acceptance, enabling people to observe thoughts and emotions with greater perspective and reduced reactivity.

This attentional engagement and emotional decentring can support calmness and self-regulation under pressure.

MBSR is delivered in groups and typically involves eight to ten weekly sessions alongside one or two days of silent retreat, though self-guided formats (including online, app-based and book-based programmes) also exist. The programme combines psychoeducation on stress and mindfulness with skills training, including formal meditation, informal mindfulness practices, yoga and reflective group discussions, with daily practice typically expected.

Silent retreat: a period of intentional silence, often combined with meditation and reflection, designed to reduce distractions and promote greater self-awareness and mental clarity.

There is a substantial research literature on mindfulness programmes. Research findings indicate that mindfulness training can influence brain activity and is associated with functional and structural changes in brain regions linked to attention, emotion regulation, self-awareness, memory and sensory processing (Chiesa & Serretti, 2010; Marchand, 2012). It has also been linked to physiological markers of rest and to enhanced immune function (Marchand, 2012; Witek-Janusek et al., 2008). In applied settings, mindfulness training has been associated with improved learning-related skills (attention, memory, cognitive flexibility and creativity). Some trials also reported benefits for specific health outcomes such as pain, psoriasis, sleep and fatigue (Kabat-Zinn et al., 1992, 1998; Shapiro et al., 2003; Marchand, 2012). In psychological domains, mindfulness interventions are associated with reductions in a broad range of distress symptoms (anxiety, depression, stress, rumination, post traumatic stress disorder and substance misuse) and show promise across several clinical presentations (Keng et al., 2011; Williams et al., 2008; Kristeller & Wolever, 2010; Chadwick, 2014; Zerubavel & Messman-Moore, 2013). Reported psychological wellbeing gains also include higher positive affect, life satisfaction, self-compassion, self-regulation, resilience, empathy and improved relationships (Keng et al., 2011; Robins et al., 2012; Friese et al., 2012).

In parallel, a number of related mindfulness programmes have been adapted for particular populations, often following a similar structure. One prominent example is Mindfulness-Based Cognitive Therapy (MBCT), which integrates mindfulness practice with cognitive-behavioural techniques to treat depression (Segal & Teasdale, 2018).

The 7 Humour Habits Programme

McGhee (2010) developed the 7 Humour Habits Programme (7HHP), a structured humour intervention designed to strengthen core humour habits and related skills. It aims to demonstrate that humour can be learned, increase humour use, raise positive emotions, reduce negative emotions and build resilience and coping under stress.

The programme begins with practising habits on "good days" and then supports transfer to stressful contexts. It is typically delivered in groups over eight weekly sessions. Core habits include surrounding oneself with humour, cultivating playfulness, laughing more, creating verbal humour, noticing everyday humour, taking oneself lightly and finding humour during stress. The programme includes home practice and humour log reflections.

A review by Ruch and McGhee (2014) concluded that the programme enhances subjective wellbeing, with additional gains in playfulness, cheerfulness, optimism, self-efficacy and perceived control, alongside reductions in seriousness, negative mood, depression, anxiety and stress. Several studies reported long-term benefits. In clinical samples, improvements were observed in pleasure capacity and emotional balance, with some individuals showing meaningful reductions in depression and anxiety.

The Sound Relationship House Model

The Sound Relationship House model, developed by Gottman (2018), is a seven-step programme intended to help couples cultivate relationships that are healthy, intimate and enduring. The steps include:

- **Building love maps:** Developing a detailed understanding of each other's inner world through open-ended questions that deepen familiarity and connection.
- **Nurturing fondness and admiration**: Regularly expressing affection, appreciation and respect in everyday interactions can buffer against negativity and reduce the likelihood of escalation during conflict.
- **Turning towards each other:** Strengthening connection by engaging in small talk, responding positively to bids for attention or support and communicating areas of agreement.
- **Facilitating partners' influence:** Listening carefully to each other's perspectives, acknowledging what is valid and responding with respect, even when disagreeing.
- **Managing solvable problems:** Gently raising concerns and making or accepting repair attempts when tension rises. These skills prevent conflict from spiralling.
- **Overcoming gridlock:** Working on persistent "stuck" issues by exploring the underlying needs driving each person's position.
- **Creating shared meaning:** Building a sense of shared purpose through rituals of connection and support, and by clarifying and pursuing shared goals and values.

Findings from a limited number of studies that tested the intervention indicated that it enhances relationship functioning, quality, intimacy and satisfaction, strengthens trust and reduces conflict (Gottman, 2018).

Single-Component Interventions

Boniwell's (2017) ACTIONS model groups key single-component evidence-based positive activities into seven categories, organised by their primary aims and underlying mechanisms:

- **Active interventions:** Primarily physical activities, such as yoga, aerobic exercise, dance, tai chi and group walking.
- **Calming activities:** Self-soothing practices largely drawn from mindfulness and related contemplative approaches, including present-moment awareness, mindfulness meditation, prayer, non-judgemental acceptance and breathing exercises.
- **Thinking exercises:** Reflective activities intended to support meaning-making, typically involving writing about or discussing life experiences. Examples include benefit-finding, expressive writing, creativity exercises, replaying positive experiences, cognitive reframing and keeping a gratitude diary.
- **Identity interventions:** Mainly cognitive exercises designed to increase self-awareness, clarify identity and promote personal development, such as identifying and using character strengths, the best possible self exercise, values clarification, job crafting and wisdom-based practices.
- **Optimising exercises:** Activities aimed at improving behavioural regulation and goal-directed action, including goal setting and pursuit, cultivating hope, practising optimistic thinking, building resilience, developing psychological capital, the life journey exercise, satisficing, fostering flow and strengthening courage and patience.
- **Nourishing interventions:** Practices that promote self-care, restoration and pleasure, such as taking "me time" for enjoyable activities, savouring small pleasures, using humour, engaging with nature and practising self-compassion.
- **Social activities:** Relationship- and community-focused exercises, including socialising, acts of kindness, practising forgiveness, capitalisation, active listening and cultivating empathy or compassion.

A selection of evidence-based single-component interventions is outlined below.

Gratitude Interventions

Emmons and Shelton (2002, p. 460) defined gratitude as "a felt sense of wonder, thankfulness, and appreciation for life. It can be expressed towards others, as well as towards impersonal (nature) or nonhuman sources (God, animals)." Gratitude interventions are activities intended to enhance positive cognitions and emotions by inviting participants to express gratitude in different ways.

A number of gratitude-based exercises have been examined empirically (Lomas et al., 2014):

- **Gratitude diary/counting blessings:** In this exercise, participants are invited to reflect on three good things in their lives for which they feel grateful and record them in a diary. The activity is typically repeated daily over several weeks.

> **Gratitude:** the feeling and expression of appreciation for positive experiences, benefits, or kindness received from others.

- **Gratitude letter or visit**: In this intervention, participants write a letter of gratitude to someone, expressing appreciation for something that the person has done. The letter may be delivered in person or sent. Evidence suggests, however, that delivery is not necessary for the activity to produce wellbeing benefits.

Several reviews indicated that gratitude interventions are used widely across psychological, workplace and health contexts, and with both children and adults. They produce small-to-medium improvements in happiness and psychological wellbeing (Kirca et al., 2023; Garg, 2024), as well as reducing anxiety and depression in clinical populations (Kerr et al., 2015), and have also been shown to improve physical aspects, such as blood pressure, sleep quality, asthma and eating behaviours (Boggiss et al., 2020).

Acts of Kindness

In this intervention, participants are instructed to carry out five acts of kindness for others within a single day (Lyubomirsky et al., 2005). These acts may be minor or substantial, and the recipient may or may not be aware that kindness has been shown.

Research evaluating this exercise suggested that completing all five acts on the same day is particularly effective, whereas distributing the five acts across a week does not appear to yield the same benefits (Lyubomirsky et al., 2005).

Several **meta-analyses** reported small-to-medium effects of kindness interventions on happiness and psychological wellbeing (Curry et al., 2018), and on health outcomes among patient groups (increased uptake of tests or vaccines, greater physical activity and improvements in biomarkers) (Byrne et al., 2023). Further work suggested that even recalling one's kind acts can enhance wellbeing (Ko et al., 2021).

The Best Possible Self Intervention

The Best Possible Self is a brief, evidence-based activity designed to cultivate optimism and enhance happiness. In this exercise, participants are offered the following guidance: "Think about your life in the future. Imagine that everything has gone as well as it possibly could. You have worked hard and succeeded at accomplishing all of your life goals. Think of this as the realisation of all of your life dreams" (King, 2001, p. 801). They are then asked to describe this imagined future in writing. Delivery is typically group-based and face-to-face, with guidance from a trained facilitator, although some programmes are delivered online.

A meta-analysis indicated that the intervention produces moderate improvements in psychological wellbeing, optimism, depressive symptoms and positive and negative affect (Carrillo et al., 2019).

Goal-Setting Interventions

Nearly five decades of research indicates that goal setting is among the most effective activities for enhancing psychological wellbeing and happiness (Locke & Latham, 2013). Typically, participants are guided to reflect on what they want to accomplish in the near or more distant future and write these goals down. The intervention often includes developing a plan for pursuing these goals and deciding which goals should take priority. Some interventions begin by helping participants take stock of their current circumstances.

Goal-setting interventions may be delivered periodically and can focus on a single domain (career, health, finances or relationships) or invite participants to set goals across multiple domains. They can be implemented individually or in groups, with or without support from a coach or therapist, delivered face-to-face or online, and are also widely available through books and digital tools.

Building on extensive research, scholars reported that goal-setting improves performance and goal attainment (Locke & Latham, 2013), leads to moderate increases in happiness (Klug & Maier, 2014), psychological wellbeing, need satisfaction, resilience and relationship satisfaction, as well as reductions in stress and depression (Liversage et al., 2023). Within work settings, benefits have been reported for work motivation, engagement and job satisfaction, while in sports contexts, goal setting has been linked to enhanced team cohesion (Liversage et al., 2023). Goal setting also appears to support behavioural change. Epton et al. (2017) also found that goal-setting interventions seem to produce stronger effects when change goals are difficult and set publicly. Research on group goals reported that setting shared goals leads to higher group performance (Kleingeld et al., 2011).

Self-Regulation Interventions

> **Self-regulation:** The ability to manage one's thoughts, emotions and behaviour in order to pursue goals and respond effectively to situations.

A substantial body of experimental research suggests that self-regulation capacity can be strengthened through exercises that involve repeated, consistent practice of self-control. These interventions are often likened to building muscle through regular physical training (Baumeister & Vohs, 2016).

The exercises used in these interventions are highly varied. Examples include improving posture, modifying study routines, practising financial restraint, resisting tempting foods, monitoring and regulating speech, engaging in a fitness programme and other comparable activities. Typically, these exercises are practised consistently over a period of several weeks.

The findings indicate that these interventions can lead to meaningful gains in self-regulatory capacities which in turn increases performance and perseverance on tasks (Baumeister et al., 2007). In addition, mindfulness training has been associated with improvements in self-regulation, suggesting another promising route for enhancing regulatory skills (Hart et al., 2013).

The VIA Strengths Intervention

The Values in Action (VIA) classification comprises 24 character strengths organised into six overarching virtues (see Chapter 2). The associated intervention enables participants to assess their strengths profiles, increases strengths awareness and encourages more effective strengths use. The interventions can be delivered individually or in groups, face-to-face or online, and can range from a brief exercise to multi-session programmes for adults and children (Niemiec, 2017).

Niemiec's (2017) review synthesised evidence from experimental research, which revealed that strengths spotting and deployment are associated with improved psychological wellbeing and happiness, increased sense of purpose and meaning, optimism, confidence, vitality, resilience, self-esteem, problem solving, creativity, positive relationships and lower stress and depression. In work settings, strengths use has been associated with higher engagement, productivity, **organisational citizenship behaviours**, greater job satisfaction, reduced turnover intentions and a stronger sense of work as a calling. In education, strengths use is linked to psychological wellbeing, engagement and enjoyment, and academic attainment.

In recent years, two programmes have been introduced that integrate VIA character strengths work with other approaches. The Mindfulness-Based Strengths Practice (MBSP) (Niemiec, 2023) is a structured, **manualised intervention**, typically delivered across eight sessions, that combines mindfulness training with the VIA intervention to promote flourishing. In The Strengths-Based Workbook for Stress Relief, Niemiec (2019) presented a structured strengths-focused programme aimed at alleviating stress by supporting individuals to identify, apply and embed their VIA character strengths as habitual coping resources.

> **Manualised programme/intervention:** A structured intervention delivered according to a set guide or manual, often with defined sessions and procedures.

Active–Constructive Responding

When we share good news with family or friends, how they respond mattes. Gable et al. (2006) argued that others' reactions can either amplify or dampen our happiness. Reactions can range from enthusiastic congratulations to indifference or signals of a lack of interest.

Active–Constructive Responding (also termed capitalisation) refers to those excited, engaged and affirming reactions to someone else's positive news. Such responses tend to heighten the sharer's positive feelings and strengthen relationships by fostering a sense of closeness (Reis et al., 2010).

Evidence indicates that practising active–constructive responding can improve relationship quality, intimacy, trust and satisfaction for both people involved, while also reducing conflict (Reis et al., 2010). These benefits occur partly because the interaction generates additional positive emotion, which intensifies the impact of the original event. It also boosts the recipient's self-esteem (Reis et al., 2010; Lambert et al., 2012).

Perspective Taking

Empathy is defined as the capacity to understand or share another person's emotional state. One widely used approach for cultivating empathy is **perspective taking** (Davis & Begovic, 2014). It can be delivered in two ways:

> **Empathy:** the ability to understand and share another person's emotions.
>
> **Perspective taking:** the ability to consider a situation from another person's point of view.

- **Direct perspective taking** involves role-play, where a person adopts another's role and responds within a comparable situation.
- **Indirect perspective taking** encourages individuals to imagine another person's thoughts, feelings and experiences in a specific circumstance.

A review by Todd and Galinsky (2014) revealed that perspective taking increases empathy and sympathy, strengthens rapport and enhances willingness to forgive. It is also associated with reduced social bias, supporting more positive intergroup evaluations. There is also evidence that changes in evaluation can translate into behaviour: Taking the perspective of a group member may increase approach-oriented responses and reduce avoidance towards that group, contributing to smoother interactions and greater helping behaviour. Although these shifts appear robust in the short term, it remains unclear how consistently they persist beyond the initial session.

Forgiveness

Forgiveness is often discussed as a relational process and is associated with reconciliation. As a psychological intervention, however, it is conceptualised primarily as an **intra-personal** process. Following a transgression, the injured person works towards accepting the event and releasing the negative emotions tied to the wrongdoing and the offender (Worthington et al., 2014). While this may sometimes lead to changes in the relationship with the transgressor, it does not necessarily do so. Accordingly, the literature tends to emphasise **emotional forgiveness**, given evidence that persisting in blame and associated distress can be detrimental to one's health.

> **Forgiveness:** the process of reducing resentment, anger, or desire for revenge towards someone who has caused harm.

The **REACH model** is a structured, multi-step method commonly delivered in therapeutic settings (Worthington et al., 2014). It involves:

- **Recalling** the transgression;
- **Empathising** with the offender;

- **Altruistic framing** of forgiveness as a generous, morally meaningful act;
- **Committing** to forgiving;
- **Holding** on to forgiveness over time.

Importantly, forgiveness is not universally appropriate. In some situations, encouraging forgiveness may increase risk and could contribute to the escalation or perpetuation of harm (Sinclair et al., 2020).

Meta-analytic reviews of these interventions (Lundahl et al., 2008; Akhtar & Barlow, 2018; Lahiri & Padmakumari, 2025) indicated that these programmes increase forgiveness, positive affect, psychological and spiritual wellbeing, self-esteem, hope and meaning in life. They also reduce anger, hostility, rumination, stress, anxiety, depression and post-traumatic stress symptoms. Studies also reported improvements in relationships with the offender and better interpersonal functioning, with gains often maintained at follow-up.

Savouring

> **Savouring:** Deliberately noticing, attending to and appreciating positive experiences in order to enhance or prolong them.

Savouring refers to the capacity to notice, attend to and appreciate positive experiences (Bryant & Veroff, 2017). It involves deliberately focusing on past, present or anticipated positive future events and actively engaging with the thoughts, feelings and meanings associated with them. The aim is to rekindle, amplify or extend the pleasure derived from these experiences. Savouring can take multiple forms: It may be purely cognitive (mentally revisiting a moment), expressed through writing, shared by recounting the experience to others or supported by activities such as taking photographs to capture positive moments.

A review of the research on savouring (Bryant, 2021) indicated that these interventions are associated with increases in happiness, resilience, optimism and functioning, alongside benefits for health (reduced pain and increases in health-promoting behaviours). Within relationships, savouring has been linked with healthier relationships, stronger family functioning and greater relationship satisfaction. In education, savouring appears to enhance students' creativity, engagement and learning, while reducing teacher burnout. In leisure settings, it tends to heighten enjoyment. In workplace research, savouring has been associated with reduced work – family conflict, improved performance and organisational commitment. It has also been linked to higher customer satisfaction. In clinical contexts, savouring interventions have been found to reduce depression, hopelessness, anxiety, schizophrenia, anhedonia and rumination, as well as improve coping with stressors (Bryant, 2021).

Environmental-Engagement Interventions

Nature-based interventions encourage people to engage with nature, either briefly or on a regular basis, and research indicates that these interventions can yield meaningful benefits (Capaldi et al., 2015). In a review of nature-engagement interventions, Capaldi et al. (2015) documented improvements in positive affect, and reduced negative affect, anxiety and depression. Studies also reported gains in psychological wellbeing and related outcomes – meaning in life, autonomy, authenticity, personal growth, self-esteem, self-regulation, vitality, feelings of awe, inspiration and spiritual uplift. Cognitive benefits have also been observed, including improved concentration and attention. Physiologically, nature exposure is linked to reduced stress and improved immune functioning. Nature-based interventions also support social functioning, enhancing social competence, connectedness, caring and closeness.

Technologically mediated exposure (viewing nature images or videos) is generally associated with increased **hedonic wellbeing**, although direct contact with nature tends to produce larger improvements. While longer-term effects have been less studied, evidence suggests that living near green spaces is linked to lower psychological distress and greater life satisfaction (Capaldi et al., 2015).

Expressive Writing

Early research on expressive writing focused on the potential benefits of self-disclosure. In these studies, participants are instructed to write about an emotionally significant upheaval for three to four consecutive days, for up to 30 minutes per day. Findings from this body of research suggest that writing can be beneficial, demonstrating meaningful improvements in physical outcomes (Pennebaker & Chung, 2011). Building on these results, expressive writing has been incorporated into psychological interventions for a range of health conditions, including AIDS, cancer and diabetes (Pennebaker & Chung, 2011).

Researchers later examined whether writing about positive content might yield comparable benefits (Burton & King, 2009). Studies on writing about personal goals, positive experiences or positive meaning derived from adverse events revealed that these practices can enhance psychological wellbeing, optimism and happiness. However, effects appear less consistent for negative affect, stress, anxiety and physical health indicators (Hoult et al., 2025).

Optimising the Application of Positive Activities

Scholars have attempted to identify key conditions that enhance the impact of positive activities (Layous & Lyubomirsky, 2014):

- **Activity features – timing, frequency, variation, and delivery methods:** The manner in which positive activities are implemented substantially shapes their effectiveness. Research indicates that key features, including timing, frequency and variation, play crucial roles in outcomes. For example, participants who counted blessings weekly for six weeks showed greater wellbeing gains than those doing so three times weekly over the same period (Lyubomirsky et al., 2005). The higher-frequency group reported the task as tedious, which undermined its benefits.

  Intervention duration also matters. Layous and Lyubomirsky (2014) proposed a curvilinear relationship: Brief interventions may not endure, while prolonged repetition of the same activity can produce boredom and reduced efficacy. They therefore recommend rotating among multiple activities rather than relying on a single approach.

  Delivery formats vary widely: Activities may be embedded in individual, family or group therapy, coaching or training workshops, or self-administered via books, websites or apps. While digital and print formats increase accessibility, self-help interventions tend to yield smaller effects than face-to-face engagement (Bolier & Abello, 2014).
- **Individual characteristics – motivation, beliefs, and effort:** Positive interventions have been implemented across diverse populations: Healthy individuals and those facing physical or psychological challenges, children and adults and people from varied cultural backgrounds.

  Several factors shape the success of positive activities: Motivation to participate, belief that the intervention will help achieve valued goals and the effort invested. Individuals high on these factors tend to benefit more. In experimental research, it is especially important that participants opt in voluntarily and receive clear information about what the intervention involves and its intended purpose. One exception concerns happiness-focused activities: Strong motivation to become happier can reduce impact. Participants are therefore encouraged to focus on the activity and its procedures rather than on the outcome of being happier.

  Other person-level influences include culture, age and baseline wellbeing. Cultural relevance is crucial. Age-related research shows that older adults often gain more than younger participants. Regarding wellbeing status: Because most activities target healthy individuals, those with diminished wellbeing may find some exercises too demanding to complete. Therefore, trained clinicians should supervise delivery for individuals with lower wellbeing. Overall, Layous and

Lyubomirsky (2014) argued that effectiveness depends on both appropriate motivation (will) and correct application (proper way).

- **Social support:** The presence or absence of social support can shape both the implementation and effectiveness of positive interventions. Group-based approaches such as Alcoholics Anonymous and Weight Watchers illustrate how social groups can facilitate behavioural change. However, the form of support also matters: Support perceived as patronising, pestering or invasive can undermine intervention effectiveness.

The body of research on the optimisation of positive activities therefore suggests that these activities can backfire when pursued too frequently, experienced as inauthentic, undertaken out of obligation, poorly matched to the person or context, or driven by rigid "I must be happy" goals. This underscores the importance of fit, autonomy, and contextual sensitivity, discussed next.

Person-Activity Fit

Individuals vary in their preferences for positive activities, and no single intervention benefits everyone. The Positive Activity Model proposes that people gain more when interventions fit their preferences and lifestyle (Layous & Lyubomirsky, 2014). The person–activity fit research shows that those who prefer specific activities tend to adhere more, engage more deeply, sustain practice for longer and consequently report greater improvements in the desired outcomes. Preference may reflect greater enjoyment, perceived value or benefit, intuitiveness or ease of execution.

The Person-Activity Fit Diagnostic

This questionnaire (Lyubomirsky, 2011) helps participants choose activities that match their preferences. It covers 12 activities and participants rate how natural, enjoyable, and valued each activity feels, or whether it is done out of guilt or necessity. Scores then indicate which activities are likely to be the best fit.

The Elements Model

While positive activities offer numerous benefits, further evidence is needed to determine which activities are effective for specific individuals and under what circumstances. Pawelski (2020) contended that off-the-shelf interventions have limited capacity to generate lasting change. To optimise effectiveness, Pawelski proposed the Elements Model as a means of enabling individuals to design and implement new interventions by deconstructing existing interventions into fundamental elements and then recombining them according to individual needs.

The model identifies five key elements:

- **The activity:** The specific task the exercise requires an individual to perform;
- **The active ingredient**: The core component of the exercise that produces the intended change;
- **The target system:** The behavioural, affective or cognitive system being addressed;
- **The target focus**: The intended shift within the target system;
- **The desired outcome**: The ultimate goal or end state.

By disaggregating interventions into these elements, customised activities can be developed that prove more effective. In line with the model, Ciarrochi et al. (2022) also argued that attempting to validate packaged interventions is ineffective and advocated shifting from evidence-based composite interventions towards evidence-based elements.

Ethical Guidelines for Positive Psychology Practice

Ethical frameworks are essential in Psychology since they translate core professional values into practical guidance for day-to-day decisions in complex, high-stakes contexts. They help practitioners balance competing responsibilities, manage power asymmetries in helping relationships and reduce harm linked to boundary issues, bias, cultural insensitivity or misapplied interventions. They also promote accountability by clarifying standards for competence, informed consent, record-keeping and evidence-based practice, thereby strengthening public trust and professional legitimacy.

A key critique of positive activities has been that they can be co-opted as tools to produce more productive or compliant workers and citizens, shifting responsibility for wellbeing from institutions to individuals and obscuring **structural determinants of wellbeing** such as power and inequality (Van Zyl & Rothmann, 2022).

> **Structural determinants of wellbeing:** Social, economic, political and institutional conditions that shape people's wellbeing.

Another critique is that Positive Psychology remains largely unregulated and unaccredited as a field of practice, with few agreed standards for training and competence. As a result, interventions and training can be delivered by anyone and via almost any medium, with the quality of delivery varying considerably. As the field matures, calls to professionalise practice through ethical regulation and accreditation have intensified (see also Chapter 13).

In response to these critiques Jarden et al. (2021) formed a committee of leaders, researchers and practitioners who worked together to create guiding principles for practitioners to support high-quality, evidence-based practice and protect the public from potential harm, whether deliberate or unintended. The guidelines aim to strengthen ethical decision-making and clarify what ethically informed Positive Psychology practice entails for professionals delivering interventions or applying Positive Psychology knowledge. Their overarching purpose is to promote optimal practice.

The document highlights several core values that should be actively considered and enacted in client-facing settings:

- Defending the welfare of clients and others;
- Easing distress and misery;
- Safeguarding the integrity of the practitioner–client relationship;
- Understanding the diversity of human experience and culture;
- Nurturing a sense of self that is meaningful to the individual(s) involved;
- Developing professional knowledge and its application;
- Improving the quality of relationships between people;
- Enhancing individual effectiveness;
- Striving for the fair and appropriate provision of counselling, psychotherapy, coaching and wellbeing services;

It also identifies key ethical principles that should guide practice:

- **Beneficence:** Promoting clients' wellbeing and mitigating harm;
- **Responsible caring:** Maintaining concern for clients' wellbeing while recognising one's professional limits;
- **Respect for rights and dignity:** Valuing clients, safeguarding their rights, and demonstrating cultural and social sensitivity;
- **Trustworthiness:** Acting in line with agreements and promises, and ensuring confidentiality;
- **Justice:** Ensuring fair treatment, supporting equality of opportunity and avoiding discrimination;
- **Autonomy:** Respecting clients' independence and supporting self-direction.

Beneficence: The ethical principle of promoting clients' wellbeing and working to prevent or reduce harm.

Justice: The ethical principle of ensuring fair treatment, equality of opportunity and non-discrimination.

These values and principles position ethical practice as both outcomes-oriented and process-sensitive. In doing so, they provide a practical ethical foundation for applying the science of wellbeing with care, integrity and accountability.

The Efficacy of Positive Activities

The earlier sections demonstrated that some interventions are delivered as multi-component programmes. These are typically trainer-facilitated and include multiple topics, practices and home exercises, engaging participants in sustained behavioural change and habituation. Research across clinical and non-clinical samples, diverse health conditions, child and adult populations and multiple countries consistently reports small-to-medium effects on outcomes such as wellbeing, happiness, resilience, relationship quality, depression, anxiety and stress. Where follow-up data are available, gains are often maintained months later (Hendriks et al., 2020; Carr et al., 2024).

Similarly, Hobbs et al. (2022) meta-analytically reviewed university-based Positive Psychology courses and found that they improve students' happiness and psychological wellbeing, with effect sizes comparable to multi-component interventions.

A key question is what can realistically be expected when positive interventions are delivered as standalone exercises, without psychoeducation, structured skill development, extended habituation or expert facilitation. Many such activities are brief, low-effort and completed only a few times over a short period. On that basis, one might assume they would not produce substantial or enduring improvements in wellbeing, happiness, relationships, health, coping or other outcomes. Yet, surprisingly, the evidence suggests otherwise. Most of these interventions show moderate effects, a minority show small effects, several demonstrate larger effects, and some yield benefits that persist over time across healthy and clinical populations (Sin & Lyubomirsky, 2009; Bolier et al., 2013; Koydemir et al., 2020)

Reviews and meta-analyses synthesising diverse interventions and outcomes report broadly similar findings. Sin and Lyubomirsky (2009) concluded that positive interventions can enhance wellbeing and reduce depression, with effects varying between small to large effect sizes. Later meta-analyses reached comparable conclusions. Koydemir et al. (2020), found predominantly moderate effects on wellbeing, with some weaker and stronger results. Other reviews, varying in scope and emphasis, reported similar effect sizes, albeit with some variation (Meyers et al., 2013; Bolier et al., 2013; Weiss et al., 2016; Donaldson et al., 2019; Tonis et al., 2023). However, White et al. (2019) reported notably weaker effects on wellbeing and depression than earlier publications, though still statistically significant.

A key consideration in interpreting intervention effects is the nature of experimental research. Sheldon and Lyubomirsky (2021) argued that experiments may be a suboptimal way to assess such activities. Many studies occur in laboratory contexts where participants may not fully understand the intervention or feel motivated to invest the effort and commitment needed for short- or long-term benefits. This differs from real-world contexts, where people typically choose to pursue behavioural change and therefore bring greater motivation and sustained commitment. However, real-world settings often do not readily allow the methodological conditions required for **experimental designs**.

Layous and Lyubomirsky (2014) proposed that a key benefit of positive interventions is the learning they generate. Through practising positive activities, individuals gain knowledge and experience with techniques they can later use to enhance wellbeing or related states.

Positive Psychology Interventions are central to the field's scholarly and applied ambitions, providing the primary means of translating theory and research into measurable improvements in desired outcomes. Precisely because they are so central and widely disseminated across education, healthcare, workplaces and self-help contexts, their evidence base and real-world use have attracted fierce critique.

Reviews of experimental studies testing interventions' efficacy have identified recurring limitations, including small sample sizes, inadequate control conditions, selective and insufficient transparency in reporting (Carr et al., 2024; Koydemir et al., 2020; White et al., 2019). These limitations reduce confidence in the reported effects and make it harder to determine what works, for whom and in which contexts.

Additionally, many interventions have been developed and tested in Western contexts and with healthy participants, and are often exported with limited contextual adaptation, leaving questions about transferability to diverse groups and clinical populations unresolved.

> **Placebo effects:** improvements in symptoms that occur because of a person's expectations or beliefs about a treatment rather than its specific active effects.

Another limitation is that intervention studies can demonstrate that change occurs between measurement points, but they often cannot establish that the intervention itself is the primary cause or explain how change occurred. This limits mechanism-based understanding and raises concerns that some observed improvements may be driven by placebo effects, whereby anticipating benefit, helps to produce it (Colloca & Benedetti, 2005).

Research attention has also been uneven: Some interventions have been studied extensively, whereas others remain under-examined, limiting the field's ability to make balanced comparative claims about efficacy, boundaries and mechanisms.

Lastly, a key critique refers to their small-to-moderate effects, reinforcing longer-standing concerns that some claims in the field have been overstated (Coyne & Tennen, 2010). However, a counter-argument is that expectations of these interventions, particularly brief activities, are unrealistic. When results are short-lived or modest, authors may frame this as disappointment rather than as evidence that expectations were inflated. This suggests a need to align intervention aims with more realistic assumptions about their outcomes.

These critiques do not reject the value of these interventions. Rather, they underscore the need for greater methodological rigour, clearer mechanisms, more realistic claims and stronger ethical and professional standards.

Conclusion

The examination of positive activities and their outcomes conveys a compelling message: Individuals can exert some influence over their happiness, wellbeing, performance and success across many life domains, including health, relationships, employment and finances. Although other forces, such as genetic endowment and life circumstances, can constrain these outcomes, the central point is that people are self-determined, autonomous and capable of shaping their lives, and that what they choose to think and do meaningfully affects their desired life outcomes.

A second message emerging from the wide range of interventions is that positive activities vary substantially in the time, motivation and effort required to implement them. Some may take only a few minutes and demand relatively modest effort. People are often surprised by the difference that such small practices can make. Others typically involve an initial course followed by sustained daily practice, requiring time, effort and persistence. Nonetheless, all positive activities depend on intention, drive and motivation, and they are unlikely to be effective when imposed on others.

A third message from recent research is that no single intervention is optimal for everyone. The activities reviewed in this chapter therefore need to be selected with care, taking into account their fit with individuals' personalities and lifestyle preferences.

References

Akhtar, S., & Barlow, J. (2018). Forgiveness therapy for the promotion of mental well-being: A systematic review and meta-analysis. Trauma, Violence, & Abuse, 19(1), 107–122.

Baumeister, R.F., Schmeichel, B.J., & Vohs, K.D. (2007). Self-regulation and the executive function: The self as controlling agent. In A.W. Kruglanski, & E.T. Higgins (Eds.), Social psychology (pp. 516–539). Guilford.
Baumeister, R.F., & Vohs, K.D. (2016). Strength model of self-regulation as limited resource: Assessment, controversies, update. In M.O. James, & P.Z. Mark (Eds.), Advances in experimental social psychology (pp. 67–127). Academic Press.
Boggiss, A.L., Consedine, N.S., Brenton-Peters, J.M., Hofman, P.L., & Serlachius, A.S. (2020). A systematic review of gratitude interventions: Effects on physical health and health behaviors. Journal of Psychosomatic Research, 135, 110165.
Bolier, L., & Abello, K.M. (2014). State of the art and future directions. In A.C. Parks, & S. Schueller (Eds.), The Wiley Blackwell handbook of positive psychological interventions (pp. 286–309). Wiley.
Bolier, L., Haverman, M., Westerhof, G., Riper, H., Smit, F., & Bohlmeijer, E. (2013). Positive psychology interventions: A meta-analysis of randomized controlled studies. BMC Public Health, (13), 119.
Boniwell, I. (2017). Positive actions: Evidence based positive psychology intervention cards. Positron.
Bryant, F.B. (2021). Current progress and future directions for theory and research on savoring. Frontiers in Psychology, 12, 771698.
Bryant, F.B., & Veroff, J. (2017). Savoring: A new model of positive experience. Psychology Press.
Burton, C.M., & King, L.A. (2009). The health benefits of writing about positive experiences: The role of broadened cognition. Psychology and Health, 24(8), 867–879.
Byrne, M., Tan, R.K.J., Wu, D., Marley, G., Hlatshwako, T.G., Tao, Y., Bissram, J. Nachman, S., Tang, W., Ramaswamy, R., & Tucker, J.D. (2023). Prosocial interventions and health outcomes: A systematic review and meta-analysis. JAMA Network Open, 6(12), e2346789-e2346789.
Capaldi, C.A., Passmore, H.A., Nisbet, E.K., Zelenski, J.M., & Dopko, R.L. (2015).Flourishing in nature: A review of the benefits of connecting with nature and its application as a wellbeing intervention. International Journal of Wellbeing, 5(4), 1–16.
Carr, A., Finneran, L., Boyd, C., Shirey, C., Canning, C., Stafford, O., Lyons, J. Cullen, K., Predergast, C., Corbett, C., Drumm, C., & Burke, T. (2024). The evidence-base for positive psychology interventions: A mega-analysis of meta-analyses. The Journal of Positive Psychology, 19(2), 191–205.
Carrillo, A., Rubio-Aparicio, M., Molinari, G., Enrique, Á., Sánchez-Meca, J., & Banos, R.M. (2019). Effects of the best possible self intervention: A systematic review and meta-analysis. PloS One, 14(9), e0222386.
Chadwick, P. (2014). Mindfulness for psychosis. The British Journal of Psychiatry, 204, 333–334.
Chiesa, A., & Serretti, A. (2010). A systematic review of neurobiological and clinical features of mindfulness meditations. Psychological Medicine, 40, 1239–1252.

Ciarrochi, J., Hayes, S.C., Oades, L.G., & Hofmann, S.G. (2022). Toward a unified framework for positive psychology interventions: Evidence-based processes of change in coaching, prevention, and training. Frontiers in Psychology, 12, 809362.
Cloninger, C.R. (2006). The science of well-being: An integrated approach to mental health and its disorders. World Psychiatry, 5(2), 71–76.
Colloca, L., & Benedetti, F. (2005). Placebos and painkillers: Is mind as real as matter? Nature Reviews Neuroscience, 6(7), 545–552.
Coyne, J.C., & Tennen, H. (2010). Positive psychology in cancer care: Bad science, exaggerated claims, and unproven medicine. Annals of Behavioral Medicine, 39(1), 16–26.
Curry, O.S., Rowland, L.A., Van Lissa, C.J., Zlotowitz, S., McAlaney, J., & Whitehouse, H. (2018). Happy to help? A systematic review and meta-analysis of the effects of performing acts of kindness on the well-being of the actor. Journal of Experimental Social Psychology, 76, 320–329.
Davis, M.H., & Begovic, E. (2014). Empathy-related interventions. In A.C. Parks, & S. Schueller (Eds.), The Wiley Blackwell handbook of positive psychological interventions (pp. 111–134). Wiley.
Donaldson, S.I., Lee, J.Y., & Donaldson, S.I. (2019). Evaluating positive psychology interventions at work: A systematic review and meta-analysis. International Journal of Applied Positive Psychology, 4(3), 113–134.
Emmons, R.A., & Shelton, C.M. (2002). Gratitude and the science of positive psychology. In C.R. Snyder, & S.J. Lopez (Eds.), Handbook of positive psychology (pp. 459–471). Oxford University Press.
Epton, T., Currie, S., & Armitage, C.J. (2017). Unique effects of setting goals on behavior change: Systematic review and meta-analysis. Journal of Consulting and Clinical Psychology, 85(12), 1182.
Fordyce, M.W. (1983). A program to increase happiness: Further studies. Journal of Counseling Psychology, 30(4), 483–498.
Friese, M. Messner, C., & Schaffner, Y. (2012). Mindfulness meditation counteracts self-control depletion. Consciousness and Cognition, 21, 1016–1022.
Gable, S.L., Gonzaga, G.C., & Strachman, A. (2006). Will you be there for me when things go right? Supportive responses to positive event disclosures. Journal of Personality and Social Psychology, 91(5), 904.
Garg, N. (2024). Gratitude research: Review and future agenda using bibliometric analysis of the studies published in the last 20 years. Asian Journal of Social Psychology, 27(4), 639–656.
Gelder, M.G., Mayou, R., & Cowen, P. (2001). Shorter Oxford textbook of psychiatry (Vol. 4). Oxford University Press.
Gillham, J.E., Abenavoli, R.M., Brunwasser, S.M., Linkins, M., Reivich, K.J., & Seligman, M.E.P. (2013). Resilience education. In S.A. David, I. Boniwell, & A.C. Ayers (Eds.), The Oxford handbook of happiness (pp. 609–630). Oxford University Press.
Gottman, J.M. (2018). The seven principles for making marriage work. Hachette.

Hart, R., Ivtzan, I., & Hart, D. (2013). Mind the gap in mindfulness research: A comparative account of the leading schools of thought. Review of General Psychology, 17(4), 453–466.
Hendriks, T., Schotanus-Dijkstra, M., Hassankhan, A., De Jong, J., & Bohlmeijer, E. (2020). The efficacy of multi-component positive psychology interventions: A systematic review and meta-analysis of randomized controlled trials. Journal of Happiness Studies, 21(1), 357–390.
Hobbs, C., Armitage, J., Hood, B., & Jelbert, S. (2022). A systematic review of the effect of university positive psychology courses on student psychological wellbeing. Frontiers in Psychology, 13, 1023140.
Hoult, L.M., Wetherell, M.A., Edginton, T., & Smith, M.A. (2025). Positive expressive writing interventions, subjective health and wellbeing in non-clinical populations: A systematic review. PLoS One, 20(5), e0308928.
Jarden, A., Rashid, T., Roache, A., & Lomas, T. (2021). Ethical guidelines for positive psychology practice (version 2.0: English). International Journal of Wellbeing, 11(3), 1–38.
Kabat-Zinn, J. (2003). Mindfulness-based interventions in context: Past, present, and future. Clinical Psychology, 10(2), 144–156.
Kabat-Zinn, J., Massion, A.O., Kristeller, J., Peterson, L.G., Fletcher, K., Fletcher, K.E., Pbert, L., Lenderking, W.R., & Santorelli, S.F. (1992). Effectiveness of a meditation based stress reduction program in the treatment of anxiety disorders. The American Journal of Psychiatry, 149, 936–943.
Kabat-Zinn, J., Wheeler, E., & Light, T. (1998). Influence of a mindfulness meditation based stress reduction intervention on rates on skin clearing in patients. Psychosomatic Medicine, 60, 625–632.
Kerr, S.L., O'Donovan, A., & Pepping, C.A. (2015). Can gratitude and kindness interventions enhance well-being in a clinical sample? Journal of Happiness Studies, 16, 17–36.
Keng, S.L., Smoski, M.J., & Robins, C.J. (2011). Effects of mindfulness on psychological health: A review of empirical studies. Clinical Psychology Review, 31, 1041–1056.
King, L.A. (2001). The health benefits of writing about life goals. Personality and Social Psychology Bulletin, (27), 798–807.
Kirca, A., M. Malouff, J., & Meynadier, J. (2023). The effect of expressed gratitude interventions on psychological wellbeing: A meta-analysis of randomised controlled studies. International Journal of Applied Positive Psychology, 8(1), 63–86.
Kleingeld, A., van Mierlo, H., & Arends, L. (2011). The effect of goal setting on group performance: A meta-analysis. Journal of Applied Psychology, 96(6), 1289–1304.
Klug, H.J., & Maier, G.W. (2014). Linking goal progress and subjective well-being: A meta-analysis. Journal of Happiness Studies, 16(1), 37–65.
Ko, K., Margolis, S., Revord, J., & Lyubomirsky, S. (2021). Comparing the effects of performing and recalling acts of kindness. The Journal of Positive Psychology, 16(1), 73–81.
Koydemir, S., Sökmez, A.B., & Schütz, A. (2020). A Meta-Analysis of the effectiveness of randomized controlled positive psychological

interventions on subjective and psychological well-being. Applied Research in Quality of Life, 1–41.

Kristeller, J.L., & Wolever, R.Q. (2010). Mindfulness-based eating awareness training for treating binge eating disorder: The conceptual foundation. Eating Disorders, 19(1), 49–61.

Lahiri, A., & Padmakumari, P. (2025). Beyond apologies: A systematic review of forgiveness in different relationship contexts. Current Psychology, 44(18), 15351–15368.

Lambert, N.M., Gwinn, A.M., Baumeister, R.F., Strachman, A., Washburn, I.J., Gable, S.L., & Fincham, F.D. (2012). A boost of positive affect: The perks of sharing positive experiences. Journal of Social and Personal Relationships, 30(1), 24–43.

Layous, K., & Lyubomirsky, S. (2014). The how, why, what, when, and who of happiness. In J. Gruber, & J.T. Moskowitz (Eds.), Positive emotion (pp. 473–495). Oxford University Press.

Liversage, C., Wissing, M.P., & Schutte, L. (2023). Promotion of well-being in work and interpersonal relationships: A scoping review of goals and meaning interventions. International Journal of Wellbeing, 13(3), 94–110.

Locke, E.A., & Latham, G.P. (2013). Goal-setting theory: The current state. In E.A. Locke, & G.P Latham (Eds.), New developments in goal setting and task performance (pp. 623–630). Routledge.

Lomas, T., Froh, J.J., Emmons, R.A., Mishra, A., & Bono, G. (2014). Gratitude interventions. In A.C. Parks, A.C., & S. Schueller (Eds.), The Wiley Blackwell handbook of positive psychological interventions (pp. 3–19). Wiley.

Lundahl, B.W., Taylor, M.J., Stevenson, R., & Roberts, K.D. (2008). Process-based forgiveness interventions: A meta-analytic review. Research on Social Work Practice, 18(5), 465–478.

Lyubomirsky, S. (2011). The how of happiness. Penguin.

Lyubomirsky, S., Sheldon, K.M., & Schkade, D. (2005). Pursuing happiness: The architecture of sustainable change. Review of General Psychology, 9(2), 111–131.

Marchand, W.R. (2012). MBSR, Mindfulness-based cognitive therapy, and Zen meditation for depression, anxiety, pain, and psychological distress. Journal of Psychiatric Practice, 18, 233–252.

McGhee, P.E. (2010). Humor as survival training for a stressed-out world. Author House.

Meyers, M.C., van Woerkom, M., & Bakker, A.B. (2013). The added value of the positive: A literature review of positive psychology interventions in organizations. European Journal of Work and Organizational Psychology, 22(5), 618–632.

Niemiec, R.M. (2017). Character strengths interventions. Hogrefe.

Niemiec, R.M. (2019). The strengths-based workbook for stress relief. New Harbinger.

Niemiec, R.M. (2023). The mindfulness and character strengths workbook. Hogrefe.

Parks, A.C., & Biswas-Diener, R. (2013). Positive interventions: Past, present and future. In T.B. Kashdan, & J.V. Ciarrochi (Eds.), Mindfulness, acceptance, and positive psychology (pp. 140–165). New Harbinger.

Pawelski, J.O. (2020). The elements model: Toward a new generation of positive psychology interventions. The Journal of Positive Psychology, 15(5), 675–679.
Pennebaker, J.W., & Chung, C.K. (2011). Expressive writing: Connections to physical and mental health. In H.S. Friedman (Ed.), Oxford handbook of health psychology (pp. 417–437). Oxford University Press.
Reis, H.T., Smith, S.M., Carmichael, C.L., Caprariello, P.A., Tsai, F.F., Rodrigues, A., & Maniaci, M.R. (2010). Are you happy for me? How sharing positive events with others provides personal and interpersonal benefits. Journal of Personality and Social Psychology, 99(2), 311–329.
Robins, C.J., Keng, S.L. Ekblad, A.G., & Brantley, J.G. (2012). Effects of mindfulness-based stress reduction on emotional experience and expression: A randomized controlled trial. Journal of Clinical Psychology, 68, 117–131.
Ruch, W., & McGhee, P.E. (2014). Humor intervention programs. In A.C. Parks, & S.M. Schueller (Eds.), The Wiley Blackwell handbook of positive psychological interventions (pp. 179–193). Wiley.
Ruini, C. (2017). Positive psychology in the clinical domains. Springer.
Segal, Z.V., & Teasdale, J. (2018). Mindfulness-based cognitive therapy for depression. Guilford.
Shapiro, S.L., Walsh, R., & Britton, W.B. (2003). An analysis of recent meditation research and suggestions for future directions. Journal for Meditation and Meditation Research, 3, 69–90.
Sheldon, K.M., & Lyubomirsky, S. (2021). Revisiting the sustainable happiness model and pie chart: Can happiness be successfully pursued? The Journal of Positive Psychology, 1–10.
Sin, N.L., & Lyubomirsky, S. (2009). Enhancing well-being and alleviating depressive symptoms with positive psychology interventions: A practice-friendly meta-analysis. Journal of Clinical Psychology, 65(5), 467–487.
Sinclair, E., Hart, R., & Lomas, T. (2020). Can positivity be counterproductive when suffering domestic abuse? A narrative review. International Journal of Wellbeing, 10(1), 26–53.
Tang, M. (2019). Fostering creativity in intercultural and interdisciplinary teams: The victory model. Frontiers in Psychology, 10, 2020.
Todd, A.R., & Galinsky, A.D. (2014). Perspective-taking as a strategy for improving intergroup relations: Evidence, mechanisms, and qualifications. Social and Personality Psychology Compass, 8(7), 374–387.
Tonis, K.J., Kraiss, J.T., Linssen, G.C., & Bohlmeijer, E.T. (2023). The effects of positive psychology interventions on well-being and distress in patients with cardiovascular diseases: A systematic review and Meta-analysis. Journal of Psychosomatic Research, 170, 111328.
Van Zyl, L.E., & Rothmann, S. (2022). Grand challenges for positive psychology: Future perspectives and opportunities. Frontiers in Psychology, 13, 833057.
Weiss, L.A., Westerhof, G.J., & Bohlmeijer, E.T. (2016). Can we increase psychological well-being? The effects of interventions on psychological well being: A meta-analysis of randomized controlled trials. PloS One, 11(6).
White, C.A., Uttl, B., & Holder, M.D. (2019). Meta-analyses of positive psychology interventions: The effects are much smaller than previously reported. PloS One, 14(5), e0216588.

Williams, J.M.G., Alatiq, Y., Crane, C., Barnhofer, T., Fennell, M.J.V., Duggan, D.S., Hepburn, S., & Goodwin, G.M. (2008). Mindfulness-based cognitive therapy (MBCT) in bipolar disorder. Journal of Affective Disorders, 107, 275–279.

Witek-Janusek, L., Albuquerque, K., Rambo Chroniak, K., Chroniak, C., Durazo-Arvizu, R., & Mathews, H. (2008). Effect of mindfulness-based stress reduction on immune function, quality of life and coping in women newly diagnosed with early stage breast cancer. Brain, Behavior, and Immunity, 22, 969–981.

Wood, L., Williams, C., Billings, J., & Johnson, S. (2019). The role of psychology in a multidisciplinary psychiatric inpatient setting: Perspective from the multidisciplinary team. Psychology and Psychotherapy, 92(4), 554–564.

Worthington Jr, E.L., Wade, N.G., & Hoyt, W.T. (2014). Positive psychological interventions for promoting forgiveness: History, present status, and future prospects. In A.C. Parks, & S. Schueller (Eds.), The Wiley Blackwell handbook of positive psychological interventions (pp. 20–41). Wiley.

Zerubavel, N., & Messman-Moore, T.L. (2013). Staying present: Incorporating mindfulness into therapy for dissociation. Mindfulness, 1–12.

Chapter 6

Applied Interdisciplinary Domains

This chapter examines **applied interdisciplinary domains** that have emerged at the intersection of Positive Psychology and adjacent professional traditions. These domains illustrate how Positive Psychology has been incorporated into Coaching, Psychotherapy, Psychiatry and related therapeutic approaches, each with its own epistemological commitments, professional standards and intervention traditions. Across these integrations, a shared emphasis is evident: Building **positive psychological resources** alongside, and sometimes in service of, symptom reduction, functioning and recovery. At the same time, the interdisciplinary character of these approaches raises questions about mechanism, evidence standards, practitioner training and ethical practice, particularly when models are manualised, exported across contexts or delivered outside regulated professional pathways.

> **Applied interdisciplinary domains:** Areas of practice that combine Positive Psychology with neighbouring professional fields such as Coaching, Psychotherapy, CBT and Psychiatry.
>
> **Positive psychological resources:** Helpful internal capacities such as strengths, hope, optimism, resilience, meaning or self-compassion that support wellbeing and functioning.

The chapter aims to map the conceptual foundations, core processes and empirical support for a set of prominent applied integrated domains. In doing so, it provides a framework for understanding how wellbeing-oriented practice is evolving across disciplines, and where future development is needed to strengthen credibility, cultural relevance and responsible implementation.

DOI: 10.4324/9781032663111-9

Positive Psychology Coaching

Positive Psychology Coaching is an applied practice that integrates **Coaching Psychology** principles and methods with Positive Psychology concepts and interventions (Biswas-Diener, 2020). Coaching Psychology is a branch of Applied Psychology concerned with the systematic application of psychological theory and evidence-based methods to enhance life experience, work performance, personal or professional development and wellbeing in **non-clinical populations**. It is conceptualised as a collaborative, goal-focused, solution-oriented process that supports self-awareness, personal responsibility and sustainable change in clients' personal and professional lives (Grant & Atad, 2022). Its key aim is to enhance wellbeing and performance across life and work domains (Palmer & Whybrow, 2006).

Positive Psychology Coaching: A coaching approach that integrates Positive Psychology concepts and interventions to help clients build strengths, wellbeing and optimal functioning.

Coaching Psychology: A branch of Applied Psychology that uses psychological theory and evidence-based methods to support development, wellbeing and performance in non-clinical populations.

Non-clinical population: People who are not identified as having a clinical disorder.

Several authors argued that the link between Positive Psychology and Coaching Psychology is both conceptual and methodological. Conceptually, Coaching Psychology aligns with Positive Psychology's philosophical emphasis on wellbeing and strengths. Methodologically, Coaching Psychology provides a structured, goal-directed conversational framework within which Positive Psychology interventions can be embedded (Van Nieuwerburgh & Biswas-Diener, 2020). There is also a strong match in the target audience of both fields, with an emphasis on non-clinical populations seeking growth and improved functioning (Boniwell et al., 2014).

Drawing on these points, **Positive Psychology Coaching** has been defined as a professional, collaborative relationship aimed at identifying, utilising, optimising and developing clients' strengths and personal resources to enhance positive states, traits and behaviours, and to facilitate personal growth, optimal functioning, enhanced wellbeing and the actualisation of potential (Van Zyl et al., 2020).

In client-facing practice, this integration is reflected through strengths-focused assessment and dialogue, goal setting around self-concordant and values-aligned goals, and the use of evidence-based interventions within a structured coaching process (Biswas-Diener, 2020). Within sessions, the coach maintains a collaborative stance that supports clients' self-reflection and experimentation. Between sessions, clients implement tasks that are designed to build psychological resources and move them towards their desired outcomes (Biswas-Diener, 2020).

A key distinction between Positive Psychology Coaching and Coaching Psychology is that the former represents a specific strengths- and wellbeing-focused approach, while Coaching Psychology can draw on multiple psychological traditions. Positive Psychology Coaching is theory-bound to Positive Psychology and systematically incorporates constructs such as strengths, hope, optimism, engagement, meaning and flourishing as its primary lens. This is also manifested in setting explicitly positive goals and defining successful outcomes in terms of enhanced positive states, traits and behaviours (Van Zyl et al., 2020).

According to Van Zyl et al. (2020), the processes involved in Positive Psychology Coaching are underpinned by eight core principles:

- **Working with well-adjusted clients** largely free from severe psychopathology, and referring clinical concerns to other practitioners where appropriate.
- **Prioritising strengths development and optimisation,** focusing on building what is strong rather than fixing what is wrong.
- **Maintaining a balanced view** of strengths and developmental areas, using strengths to address growth edges.
- **Adopting a holistic approach,** drawing on resources across domains and systems (work, family and social networks).
- **Assuming an inherent capacity for growth and development**, cultivating a growth mindset and clients' sense of agency.
- **Empowering clients to take ownership** of the change process, positioning them as active agents rather than passive recipients.
- **Grounding development in an ideal-self vision,** translating a preferred future self into clear goals and concrete actions.
- **Coaching through deep active listening and ongoing support,** attending to unrecognised strengths while encouraging and sustaining progress.

Ideal-self: A positive and personally meaningful picture of the person one hopes to become in the future.

Positive Psychology Coaching is also described as a structured process (Van Zyl et al., 2020):

- **Phase 1 – creating the relationship:** Involves building trust and psychological safety, establishing rapport and aligning expectations through a clear working agreement.
- **Phase 2 – strengths profiling and feedback:** Identifying the client's key strengths and resources, providing strengths-based feedback, and clarifying priority themes for development.
- **Phase 3 – developing an ideal-self vision:** Crafting a compelling best possible self picture that stretches the client's potential and reflects what they genuinely value and desire.
- **Phase 4 – setting goals, strategising and executing:** Translating the vision into realistic, strengths-led goals and an actionable plan, and supporting implementation via accountability, feedback and adaptive problem-solving.
- **Phase 5 – conclusion and re-contracting:** Evaluating progress and impact, celebrating gains and closing the engagement or renegotiating priorities for a further cycle of work.

These components position Positive Psychology Coaching as a sequenced developmental journey and a flexible, iterative process, where progress is reinforced through practice, monitoring and empowerment.

Positive Psychology Coaching integrates Positive Psychology tools and interventions within this phased model, including goal-based exercises, strengths work, gratitude, savouring, hope, optimism, meaning and purpose, values clarification, mindfulness, self-compassion, and acts of kindness (Van Zyl et al., 2020; Richter et al., 2021). It also frequently incorporates self-administered exercises between sessions to support the transfer of insights into everyday life and increase the sustainability of behaviour change (Richter et al., 2021). In addition, coaches often use **psychometric assessments** (such as strengths profiling, wellbeing measures, work preferences and personality-related instruments) to support structured self-reflection and inform developmental goals (Van Zyl et al., 2020).

Empirical evidence indicates that Positive Psychology Coaching enhances wellbeing, resilience, psychological resources, goal attainment and performance, thereby benefiting both individuals and organisations (Pelaez Zuberbuhler et al., 2024).

Positive Psychotherapy

Positive Psychotherapy (PPT) is an applied practice that integrates Positive Psychology principles and interventions with the applied practices of Psychotherapy (Rashid & Seligman, 2018)

Psychotherapy can be defined as a collaborative, purposeful and ethically governed psychological treatment that uses a therapeutic relationship and structured psychological methods to alleviate distress, reduce impairment and support adaptive functioning and change over time. It involves the systematic application of defined methods in the treatment of psychic suffering and psychosomatic complaints, as well as life crises. The basis for treatment is the relationship of the psychotherapist to the patient (McLeod, 2025).

Positive Psychotherapy (PPT): A therapy that combines Positive Psychology principles with Psychotherapy in order to reduce distress while also building wellbeing, strengths and positive functioning.

Psychotherapy: A collaborative and ethically governed psychological treatment that uses structured methods and a therapeutic relationship to reduce distress and support change.

Positive Psychotherapy (Rashid & Seligman, 2018) is designed to increase mental wellbeing and alleviate psychopathology in people who are unwell by focusing on symptoms alongside strengths, risks alongside resources and misgivings alongside hopes, to build a more **balanced formulation** of the person and their difficulties.

Balanced formulation: An understanding of a client that includes both difficulties and resources, rather than focusing only on symptoms or deficits.

The model is organised around Seligman's (2012) PERMA mental wellbeing framework (see Chapter 3), which entails five pathways to wellbeing: Positive emotion, engagement, relationships, meaning and accomplishment. These components are treated as measurable, actionable therapeutic targets.

Rashid (2015) outlined its three core assumptions:

- **Psychopathology reflects thwarted growth and diminished wellbeing**, emerging from person–environment interactions that restrict capacities for fulfilment. Interventions should aim not only to reduce distress but to revitalise growth via strengths-building.

- **Positive emotions and strengths are clinically meaningful**. Symptom remission is not assumed to automatically enhance wellbeing, whereas strengths amplification may both enhance fulfilment and buffer against relapse.
- **Therapeutic bonds can be built through positive contents**, with careful attention to strengths and positive experiences used to foster trust, hope and engagement, without playing down suffering.

PPT is a manualised, structured intervention delivered by a trained therapist. It can be provided individually or in groups, used as a standalone treatment, adapted to client needs or integrated into other therapies. One of its defining features is that sessions involve positive activities and homework practice.

Rashid (2015) described three phases of the therapy:

- **Phase 1: Balanced narrative, strengths assessment and goal setting:** The therapy begins with a positive introduction, in which clients write a narrative showing them at their best and then identify strengths expressed in that narrative. Clients then identify their strengths, analyse their use and gather strengths feedback from others. These strengths are then translated into goals tied to symptom reduction and wellbeing gains.
- **Phase 2: Cultivating positive emotion while working with negative memories:** PPT uses structured practices to increase positive emotion (such as gratitude or savouring interventions) while also addressing painful memories. Negative experiences are approached with balance, attending to pain while exploring possibilities for meaning and growth when clinically appropriate.
- **Phase 3: Relationships, meaning, and purposeful action:** These sessions emphasise building positive relationships and enhancing meaning and purpose, including orienting signature strengths towards something beyond the self.

Across phases, the therapist helps clients identify, own and practise strengths while maintaining clinical realism. Sessions include topics such as forgiveness, choice, gratitude, optimism, posttraumatic growth, meaning in life, relationships and wisdom.

The evidence base on PPT is promising but limited (Rashid & Seligman, 2018). Across studies, it has been applied to depression, anxiety, stress, psychosis, borderline personality disorder and smoking cessation. These studies reported reductions in symptoms and increases in psychological wellbeing, some with medium-to-large effect sizes, though the authors noted the limitations of small samples and the need for larger, multi-site trials.

Wellbeing Therapy

Fava (2016) developed Wellbeing Therapy (WBT) as a **relapse-prevention** approach for people in recovery from clinical depression and anxiety.

Relapse prevention: Strategies designed to reduce the risk that a previous psychological difficulty or disorder will return.

Informed by Cognitive Behavioural Therapy (CBT) (Beck, 2011) and Ryff's (1989) model of psychological wellbeing (see Chapter 3), WBT seeks to strengthen each wellbeing domain (purpose in life, autonomy, personal growth, environmental mastery, positive relationships and self-acceptance) to promote sustained wellbeing.

CBT (Beck, 2011) is a structured, time-limited, and collaborative approach in which therapist and client jointly develop a shared formulation connecting situations, cognitions, emotions, physiological responses and behaviour. The therapy is goal-focused and is delivered within a collaborative therapeutic relationship, and it commonly includes graded task assignments, guided discovery and relapse-prevention planning. It integrates behavioural and cognitive strategies, with a strong emphasis on building skills so that clients can apply strategies independently through practice and guided discovery. CBT targets negative automatic thoughts, cognitive distortions and more enduring dysfunctional assumptions and core beliefs that bias attention, interpretation and recall in ways that sustain low mood.

WBT is manualised, delivered by a trained therapist and can be provided individually or in groups. It is typically delivered across eight sessions organised into three phases:

- Increasing awareness of triggers by keeping a diary of wellbeing episodes and experiences that influence wellbeing and may precipitate distress;
- Developing skills to identify negative automatic thoughts, drawing on CBT techniques while intentionally cultivating wellbeing through planned activities;
- Recognising how negative automatic thoughts erode wellbeing, learning to challenge maladaptive cognitive patterns and moving towards more optimal functioning across the wellbeing domains.

A robust evidence base reviewed by Guidi and Fava (2021) indicates that WBT can enhance the facets of psychological wellbeing embedded in

Ryff's, (1989) model while reducing symptoms of anxiety and depression. More recent studies have shown several health benefits including reduction in fibromyalgia symptoms (Olivero et al., 2024), increased weight loss in obesity (Zhu et al., 2022), better diabetes management (Benasi et al., 2022), improved sleep quality (Benasi et al., 2023), and reduced alcohol use (Fantini et al., 2023).

Quality of Life Therapy

Quality of Life Therapy (QOLT; Frisch, 2006, 2016) is a manualised, wellbeing-focused therapeutic approach aimed at improving life satisfaction and positive functioning.

Quality of Life Therapy: a positive psychology wellbeing focused intervention that aims to enhance functioning and life satisfaction.

Frisch (2006) defined quality of life as the "subjective evaluation of the degree to which our most important needs, goals, and wishes have been fulfilled" (p. 22). On this basis, clients identify the domains that matter most to them and work systematically to increase satisfaction within those areas using structured, skills-based methods. QOLT has been applied both with clinical presentations and with non-clinical samples seeking greater happiness, meaning, and success (Frisch, 2013).

QOLT integrates CBT processes, particularly identifying and modifying maladaptive cognitions, but orients these tools towards building positive affect, meaning and engagement, rather than focusing on symptom reduction. Positive Psychology components include strengths work, gratitude, goal setting and meaning-focused exercises across 16 life areas, treating increases in positive emotion and life satisfaction as legitimate therapeutic outcomes (Frisch, 2013). Interventions are implemented within a CBT-style collaborative framework that links maintaining processes to real-world experiments and between-session practice.

Case formulation: A structured explanation of a person's difficulties, illnesses, strengths and processes that might maintain difficulties, used to guide intervention.

Assessment and **case formulation** typically begin with the quality of life inventory (QOLI), which rates satisfaction weighted by importance across 16 life domains (including health, self-esteem, work, love, friendships, learning, creativity, home and community). Frisch's (2006) manual provides step-by-step guidance for formulation, intervention planning and progress monitoring. Delivery is commonly individual or group-based, with structured sessions and homework to consolidate skills.

Content is organised around the CASIO framework – circumstances, attitudes, standards, importance and overall satisfaction – which provides a practical model for understanding and shifting how people evaluate and pursue goals across domains. This is complemented by core skills (such as problem-solving and life-management strategies) and domain-specific modules selected to fit the client's priorities. Session work is pragmatic and cumulative: Clients track links between mood and life satisfaction, practise cognitive and behavioural strategies to reduce obstacles to valued goals and implement incremental changes, with maintenance and relapse-prevention planning (Frisch, 2016).

Randomised trials (Frisch, 2016) reported on improvements in overall quality of life and life satisfaction relative to controls, with benefits across multiple life domains. However, Frisch emphasised the need for more independent, large-scale and longer-term evaluations across diverse clinical and non-clinical populations to strengthen conclusions about its effectiveness.

Positive Cognitive Behavioural Therapy

Positive Cognitive Behavioural Therapy (positive CBT; P-CBT) (Bannink & Geschwind, 2021) is a fourth-wave development of CBT that systematically integrates Positive Psychology with CBT and solution-focused brief therapy.

Positive CBT: A form of CBT that keeps core CBT methods but places greater emphasis on strengths, resources, solutions and positive emotion.

Bannink and Geschwind (2021) described P-CBT as a **transdiagnostic approach** for adults experiencing common mental health problems within routine outpatient and primary care contexts. The model is suited to individual or group delivery.

P-CBT maintains key CBT elements, such as structured sessions, **collaborative empiricism**, goal setting, behavioural experiments and **cognitive restructuring**, while shifting attentional emphasis towards solutions and positive resources. Rather than focusing on reducing what is wrong (symptoms and deficits), P-CBT emphasises building what is right (strengths, resources and positive emotions).

It retains the structured, collaborative principles of CBT, but reorients case formulation, therapeutic dialogue and homework towards clients' preferred future, the cultivation of well-being-enhancing skills (such as optimism, gratitude and self-compassion) and the exploration of exceptions to problems (times when things go well), rather than analysing problems.

The intervention is manualised, brief and structured. Sessions typically include agenda setting, review of between-session tasks, introduction and rehearsal of a specific P-CBT technique and homework planning, delivered within a standard CBT format (Bannink & Geschwind, 2021).

Across sessions, clients are invited to articulate their best hopes and preferred future. Problem talk is intentionally time-limited, followed by a shift towards goals, exceptions and successes.

Cognitive Behavioural Therapy (CBT): A therapeutic approach that addresses thoughts, behaviours, emotions and physical sensations, assuming that they are interconnected. It aims to modify unhelpful thoughts as a means to alter problematic emotions, physical sensations and behaviours.

Transdiagnostic approach: An approach designed to apply across a range of mental health problems rather than to only one diagnosis.

Collaborative empiricism: A CBT principle in which therapist and client work together to examine thoughts, behaviours and evidence in a systematic way.

Cognitive restructuring: A CBT technique that helps people identify and modify unhelpful or distorted patterns of thinking.

Core elements (Bannink, 2017) include:

- Specifying goals in concrete, future-oriented behavioural terms and tracking progress;
- Identifying exceptions to the problem (times when things went well) and coping behaviours, amplified through competence questions and empowerment;
- Attending to small positive changes, savouring them and linking them to the client's actions to strengthen agency and hope;
- Using CBT methods framed around what will be different when best hopes are realised and what supports movement in that direction;
- Assigning homework that combines positive practices with solution-focused tasks.

The therapeutic tone is encouraging and resource-focused, with deliberate use of strengths reflections to elicit positive emotions and broaden clients' repertoires of thought and action.

Given the model's relative newness, the evidence base remains limited. A **randomised controlled trial (RCT)** comparing P-CBT with traditional CBT for adults with depression reported that both conditions produced large symptom reductions, with P-CBT also showing significant reductions in negative affect and increases in happiness, positive affect, optimism and overall mental health. Participants also demonstrated lower dropout (Geschwind et al., 2019).

Positive Psychiatry

Psychiatry is a medical specialty concerned with the study, diagnosis, treatment and prevention of mental and behavioural disorders, with psychiatrists trained to assess both biological and psychosocial contributors to conditions such as mood, anxiety, psychotic and personality disorders and to provide interventions including medication and Psychotherapy (Black & Andreasen, 2011).

Psychiatry: the branch of medicine concerned with the diagnosis, treatment, and prevention of mental, emotional, and behavioural disorders.

Positive Psychiatry seeks to broaden the remit of Psychiatry by defining an additional aim – understanding and promoting psychological wellbeing. It does so through assessments and interventions that strengthen positive psychosocial characteristics and advance positive mental health outcomes in people with mental or physical illnesses (Jeste et al., 2015).

Positive Psychiatry: An approach within Psychiatry that adds the promotion of wellbeing and positive psychosocial characteristics to traditional aims such as diagnosis, treatment and relapse prevention.

Positive Psychiatry therefore formalises positive mental health outcomes and positive psychosocial characteristics as legitimate assessment and intervention targets alongside symptom management and relapse prevention, integrating diagnostic and pharmacological care with evidence-based positive interventions in a collaborative, person-centred manner. The approach draws on Positive Psychology concepts and interventions, **recovery-oriented care**, and **solution-focused principles** (Bannink & Peeters, 2021).

Bannink and Peeters (2021) illustrated how these principles can be operationalised across outpatient, inpatient, community mental health and primary care settings, delivered through individual, group and family or caregiver formats, and designed to complement established evidence-based treatments.

Recovery-oriented care: An approach that supports people in building a meaningful life and identity beyond illness.

Solution-focused principles: Practices that emphasise strengths, goals and possibilities rather than prolonged analysis of problems.

Person centred: an approach that places the individual's needs, values, preferences, experiences, and autonomy at the centre of care and decision-making.

Elements include:

- **Strengths- and values-informed assessment**, incorporating prior coping successes alongside symptoms and functional difficulties.
- **Collaborative formulation** that includes positive psychosocial characteristics as protective or promotive factors and explicit treatment targets.
- **Brief interventions** using solution-focused and positive psychology exercises within and between sessions.
- **Recovery-oriented dialogue** emphasising personal goals, identity beyond illness and pathways to participation and citizenship, rather than focusing solely on symptom metrics.

Direct evaluations of Positive Psychiatry remain limited. However, its rationale is supported by converging evidence that positive psychosocial characteristics are associated with better health and functioning outcomes, and that interventions targeting positive psychosocial characteristics can improve mental health outcomes across a range of populations (Jeste, 2018).

Applied Interdisciplinary Domains: An Overview

Across these domains, a clear set of common denominators emerges. First, all the approaches reposition applied work from an exclusive preoccupation with pathology, deficits or problem correction towards a more balanced model that also attends to resources and positive functioning. Whether in non-clinical growth-oriented contexts such as Positive Psychology Coaching or in clinical settings such as Positive Psychotherapy, Wellbeing Therapy, Positive CBT, Quality of Life Therapy and Positive Psychiatry, intervention targets include wellbeing-related outcomes alongside improvements in deficits or pathology.

Resource activation: The process of identifying and strengthening a client's existing strengths, supports and capacities.

Phase-based model: An intervention organised into sequential stages, each with a particular focus.

Second, while these approaches are new in terms of their integration, they embed positive psychological constructs and interventions within established applied frameworks with strong evidence of efficacy behind them. As a result, they preserve the foundations of their host disciplines while reorienting them towards **resource activation**, preferred futures and sustainable adaptation.

Third, across approaches, delivery is typically manualised or **phase-based**, but flexible enough to be tailored to individual priorities and context, whether in individual, group or broader care settings.

Fourth, these domains converge in treating change as both developmental and iterative, and the aim is not only immediate improvement but also the cultivation of enduring psychological resources.

However, the development of these interdisciplinary domains has introduced recurring conceptual, methodological and professional challenges.

The intervention literature across several domains remains vulnerable to common threats to validity, including small sample sizes, limited statistical power, inadequate comparators, selective reporting and inconsistent measurement. These limitations reduce confidence in effect estimates.

While manualised approaches improve fidelity and scalability, they may also reduce responsiveness when applied rigidly. The challenge is to maintain evidence-based structure while still tailoring interventions to client goals, readiness, comorbidity and context, particularly in complex clinical presentations.

Another challenge is how suffering and distress are treated. In both coaching and clinical contexts, an explicit focus on positive aspects can be experienced as invalidating if it minimises misery or implies that hardship reflects inadequate effort.

Additionally, as seen in the review, several approaches integrate Positive Psychology with CBT, yet the distinctiveness of these models is often under-specified.

Lastly, most of these practices remain under-researched, which restricts the field's capacity to draw balanced, comparative conclusions about their effectiveness.

These critiques do not negate the value of applied interdisciplinary domains; rather, they clarify what is required for responsible maturation.

Conclusion

Across the approaches reviewed in this chapter, a coherent pattern emerges: Positive Psychology is increasingly being embedded within established applied traditions as a way of broadening therapeutic and developmental aims beyond symptom reduction. Whether the primary context is non-clinical growth or clinical treatment and relapse prevention, these models share a commitment to identifying and cultivating psychological resources, strengthening meaning and relationships and supporting sustained functioning. This common thread suggests that promoting wellbeing is no longer positioned merely as an optional add-on, but as a legitimate and often central target of change.

At the same time, the chapter highlights that interdisciplinary integration is not a single uniform endeavour. Each domain varies in its assumptions about client populations, the role of diagnosis, the structure and duration of intervention, and the balance between strengths-building and problem-focused work. Manualised and assessment-driven approaches offer clear structure and transferability, but also depend on careful attention to fit, competence and context. Meanwhile, broader framings such as Positive Psychiatry indicate a shift at the level of service philosophy, redefining what counts as a meaningful outcome in mental healthcare, yet still require more direct evaluative research.

Looking ahead, the continued maturation of these applied domains will depend on three priorities. First, stronger and more independent evidence is needed, including longer-term follow-ups, comparative designs and clearer tests of mechanisms and boundary conditions. Second, professional standards must ensure appropriate training, ethical safeguards and clarity about who is qualified to deliver which interventions. Third, cultural responsiveness and equity considerations need to be treated as foundational rather than peripheral, so that wellbeing-oriented practice does not default to narrow ideals or inadvertently shift responsibility from systems to individuals. With these developments, applied interdisciplinary domains can become a robust bridge between the science of wellbeing and the diverse realities of practice.

References

Bannink, F.P. (2017). Positive CBT in practice. In C. Proctor (Ed.), Positive psychology interventions in practice (pp. 15–28). Springer.

Bannink, F.P., & Geschwind, N. (2021). Positive CBT. Hogrefe.

Bannink, F.P., & Peeters, F. (2021). Practicing positive psychiatry. Hogrefe Publishing GmbH.

Beck, J. (2011). Cognitive behavior therapy. Guildford.

Benasi, G., Gostoli, S., Zhu, B., Offidani, E., Artin, M.G., Gagliardi, L., Rignanese, G., Sassi, G., Fava, G.A., & Rafanelli, C. (2022). Well-Being therapy and lifestyle intervention in type 2 diabetes: A pilot randomized controlled trial. Biopsychosocial Science and Medicine, 84(9), 1041–1049.

Biswas-Diener, R. (2020). The practice of positive psychology coaching. The Journal of Positive Psychology, 15(5), 701–704.

Black, D.W., & Andreasen, N.C. (2011). Introductory textbook of psychiatry. American Psychiatric Pub.

Boniwell, I., Kauffman, C., & Silberman, J. (2014). The positive psychology approach to coaching. In E. Cox, T. Bachkirova, & D. Clutterbuck (Eds.), The complete handbook of coaching (pp. 157–169). Sage.

Fantini, L., Gostoli, S., Artin, M.G., & Rafanelli, C. (2023). An intervention based on well-being therapy to prevent alcohol use and other unhealthy lifestyle behaviors among students: A three-arm cluster randomized controlled trial. Psychology, Health & Medicine, 29(5), 930–950.

Fava, G.A. (2016). Well-being therapy: Current indications and emerging perspectives. Psychotherapy and Psychosomatics, 85(3), 136–145.

Frisch, M.B. (2006). Quality of life therapy. Wiley.

Frisch, M.B. (2013). Evidence-based well-being/positive psychology assessment and intervention with quality of life therapy and coaching and the Quality of Life Inventory (QOLI). Social Indicators Research, 114(2), 193–227.

Frisch, M.B. (2016). Quality of life Therapy. In S. Joseph (Ed.), The Wiley handbook of positive psychology (pp. 409–424). Wiley.

Geschwind, N., Arntz, A., Bannink, F., & Peeters, F. (2019). Positive cognitive behavior therapy in the treatment of depression: A randomized order within-subject comparison with traditional cognitive behavior therapy. Behaviour Research and Therapy, 116, 119–130.

Grant, A.M., & Atad, O.I. (2022). Coaching psychology interventions vs. positive psychology interventions: The measurable benefits of a coaching relationship. The Journal of Positive Psychology, 17(4), 532 544.

Guidi, J., & Fava, G.A. (2021). Conceptual and clinical innovations of well-being therapy. International Journal of Cognitive Therapy, 14(1), 196–208.

Jeste, D.V. (2018). Positive psychiatry comes of age. International Psychogeriatrics, 30(12), 1735–1738.

Jeste, D.V., Palmer, B.W., Rettew, D.C., & Boardman, S. (2015). Positive psychiatry: Its time has come. Journal of Clinical Psychiatry, 76(6), 675–683.

McLeod, J. (2025). An introduction to counselling and psychotherapy. Open University Press.

Olivero, A., Cuniberti, F., & Leombruni, P. (2024). Well-being therapy for fibromyalgia: A case report. The Journal of Nervous and Mental Disease, 212(6), 352–357.

Palmer, S., & Whybrow, A. (2006). The coaching psychology movement and its development within the British Psychological Society. International Coaching Psychology Review, 1(1), 5–11.

Pelaez Zuberbuhler, J., Corbu, A., Christensen, M., & Salanova, M. (2024). The effectiveness of positive psychological coaching at work: A systematic review. Coaching: An International Journal of Theory, Research and Practice, 17(2), 163–188.

Rashid, T. (2015). Positive psychotherapy: A strength-based approach. The Journal of Positive Psychology, 10(1), 25–40.
Rashid, T., & Seligman, M.E.P. (2018). Positive psychotherapy. Oxford University Press.
Richter, S., van Zyl, L.E., Roll, L.C., & Stander, M.W. (2021). Positive psychological coaching tools and techniques: A systematic review and classification. Frontiers in Psychiatry, 12, 667200.
Ryff, C.D. (1989). Happiness is everything, or is it? Explorations on the meaning of psychological well-being. Journal of Personality and Social Psychology, (57), 1069–1081.
Seligman, M.E.P. (2012). Flourish. Free Press.
Van Nieuwerburgh, C., & Biswas-Diener, R. (2020). Positive psychology approaches to coaching. In J. Passmore (Ed.), The coaches' handbook (pp. 314–321). Routledge.
Van Zyl, L.E., Roll, L.C., Stander, M.W., & Richter, S. (2020). Positive psychological coaching definitions and models: A systematic literature review. Frontiers in Psychology, 11, 793.
Zhu, B., Gostoli, S., Benasi, G., Patierno, C., Petroni, M.L., Nuccitelli, C., Marchesini, G., Fava, G.A., & Rafanelli, C. (2023). Promoting weight loss and psychological well-being in patients with obesity: A sequential combination of behavioural lifestyle intervention and well-being therapy. Clinical Psychology & Psychotherapy, 30(2), 422–435.

Section 4

Key Sub-Disciplines

This Section in Summary

Chapter 7: Positive Education

- Positive Education emerged as a response to attainment-focused schooling, arguing that schools should support wellbeing alongside academic achievement.
- It is best understood as a whole-school orientation, integrating Positive Psychology concepts and interventions with curriculum, pedagogy, relationships, culture, and systems.
- The field developed in waves, moving from student-focused interventions to broader whole-school models, and, more recently, to context-sensitive approaches attentive to culture, equity, and pedagogy.
- Evidence suggests modest but generally positive effects on student wellbeing, engagement, school climate, some academic outcomes, and staff wellbeing.
- Key limitations include weak and uneven evidence, limited **generalisability**, and the need for greater conceptual clarity, rigour, and integration with educational practice.

Chapter 8: Positive Work and Organisations

- Positive Work and Organisations emerged to address the gap between what work currently offers and what people need to flourish, reframing occupational wellbeing as central to sustainable organisational success.
- The field integrates Positive Psychology and Management scholarship, focusing on how employees and organisations can flourish.
- Its remit is broad, covering themes such as employee wellbeing, engagement, meaning, strengths, psychological capital, leadership, relationships, work–life balance, and **organisational culture**.
- The field has grown rapidly but faces important critiques, including weak meta-theoretical grounding, methodological limitations, excessive

DOI: 10.4324/9781032663111-10

focus on individuals, and the risk of instrumentalising wellbeing for productivity.
- Workplace interventions show generally small-to-moderate benefits for psychological and relational outcomes, but less consistent effects on performance.

Chapter 9: Positive Health

- Positive Health is an interdisciplinary approach that integrates Positive Psychology, **Lifestyle Medicine**, and allied health sciences to promote flourishing.
- It aims to broadens traditional healthcare frameworks by moving beyond a disease-centred model to emphasise prevention, adaptation and self-management.
- Positive Health arose in response to system pressures alongside advances in theory and empirical work that links between Positive Psychology concepts and interventions and physical health outcomes.
- Research on the efficacy of Positive Health interventions suggests modest psychological and behavioural benefits, but limited physical health outcomes.
- Challenges include uneven implementation and methodological weaknesses.

Chapter 10: Positive Economic Psychology

- Positive Economic Psychology is a new interdisciplinary field that integrates Positive Psychology and Economic Psychology to understand and promote financial and economic wellbeing.
- It emerged as a corrective to deficit-focused Economic Psychology, shifting attention from bias, error, and dysfunction towards strengths, adaptive behaviour, and prosperity.
- Its mission is both scientific and applied, aiming to develop research, interventions, and policies that foster financial wellbeing, economic resilience, and fairer economic outcomes.
- The field is guided by a humanistic, non-paternalistic approach, emphasising agency, constructive language, capability-building, and support for ethical and effective economic decision-making.
- Its future promise lies in combining the strengths of both parent disciplines to offer a more balanced, multi-level, and intervention-oriented framework for improving economic life.

Chapter 7

Positive Education

Positive Education has emerged in response to a growing recognition that many contemporary approaches to schooling have been guided by an overly narrow definition of success, one that privileges academic attainment while insufficiently attending to the lived experience of students and staff. In many systems, educational quality is treated as synonymous with grades, standardised test scores and credentials, reinforcing a performative culture in which measurable outcomes become the dominant proxy for learning and development. Yet this emphasis has increasingly sat alongside evidence of persistent disengagement, heightened stress and rising mental health difficulties among young people, as well as significant strain among teachers. Against this backdrop, the emergence of Positive Education reflects a widening consensus that the purposes of education require re-examination: Schooling should not only prepare students to achieve but also support them to flourish (Kern & Wehmeyer, 2021).

Positive Education: An interdisciplinary area applying Positive Psychology to schools, learning and student development.

Positive Psychology offered a compelling counterbalance by foregrounding strengths, optimal functioning and flourishing, constructs that resonate with education's enduring (if sometimes eclipsed) aims of developing whole persons. The logic is straightforward: Schools are not merely sites for knowledge transmission; they are formative developmental ecologies. They shape identities, relationships, emotional repertoires and beliefs about agency and possibility. If education is one of society's most universal and sustained interventions, then it is also one of the most powerful contexts in which to cultivate the capabilities and conditions that enable both doing well and feeling good. Positive Education thus reframes wellbeing not as an add-on or a remedial concern, but as a core educational outcome that can be intentionally taught, modelled and embedded in the structures and cultures of schools.

DOI: 10.4324/9781032663111-11

This chapter introduces Positive Education as a conceptual shift and a set of practical approaches aimed at aligning educational excellence with wellbeing. It first defines Positive Education and examines why integrating Positive Psychology with Education became necessary. The following sections offer a brief historical account of the field's development and explore how Positive Education is implemented in practice.

Conceptualising Positive Education

> **Positive Education** is defined as an approach to schooling that integrates academic learning with the cultivation of wellbeing (Seligman et al., 2009), through the application of Positive Psychology within educational settings, bringing the science of wellbeing together with effective teaching practices to support flourishing among individuals and school communities (Green et al., 2021).

Across these perspectives, Positive Education is positioned as an applied, empirical endeavour, aiming to incorporate evidence-based insights on topics that are central to Positive Psychology into curriculum design, pedagogy and school culture.

Recent conceptions have underscored that Positive Education is not simply a set of discrete interventions or stand-alone programmes. Kern and Wehmeyer (2021) described it as a broader orientation, understood as a multidimensional, whole-school endeavour. It includes explicit teaching of wellbeing-related skills, the cultivation of environments where these capacities are acquired through everyday experiences and the alignment of policies, practices and relationships so that wellbeing and academic learning are treated as mutually reinforcing aims of schooling (White & Kern, 2018).

Beyond Attainment: A Wellbeing Imperative

The impetus to integrate Positive Psychology with Education arose amid growing concern about the limitations of an achievement-oriented model of schooling. For much of the late 20th century, educational success was primarily assessed through grades, standardised test scores and credentials, even as evidence accumulated of widespread student disengagement, a weaker sense of school belonging and increasing rates of mental health difficulties among young people (Kern & Wehmeyer, 2021). Recent global estimates indicate that around 10–20% of children and adolescents live with a diagnosable mental health condition, and that a substantial proportion of lifetime mental disorders first emerge before age 25 (Kieling et al., 2024). Educators have also reported high levels of stress and burnout, prompting questions about the sustainability of prevailing systems and the kinds of learning environments they generate (Green et al., 2021).

Against this background, Positive Psychology's call for a science that focuses on positive subjective experience, positive individual traits and positive institutions (Seligman & Csikszentmihalyi, 2000) provided education with both a vocabulary and an evidence base for focusing on cultivating strengths, optimal functioning and flourishing within schools.

In parallel, developments in youth mental health and public policy strengthened the case for a more proactive, school-based approach to wellbeing. International bodies and governments, including the OECD and the WHO, have urged educational systems to attend to students' social and emotional development and wellbeing alongside core academic aims (Kern & Wehmeyer, 2021).

Positive Education responded by making schools a primary context for building the knowledge, skills and conditions that support young people (and the adults who teach them) to feel good and function well, rather than treating wellbeing as an optional add-on or an individual responsibility (Waters & Loton, 2019). In doing so, Positive Education reframed schooling's purpose: Not only to transmit knowledge and prepare students for economic and civic participation but also to foster the capacities needed to navigate adversity, contribute to others, and build lives that are worth living (Kern & Wehmeyer, 2021).

A further driver was the recognition that earlier school-based mental health efforts, while valuable, were conceptually and practically incomplete. Historically, interventions were remedial and focused on psychological treatment. Bringing Positive Psychology into Education therefore enabled a shift from predominantly deficit-focused framings of students' and staff wellbeing towards a more balanced model that treats mental, physical and social wellbeing as educational outcomes in their own right (Kern & Wehmeyer, 2021).

The Development of Positive Education

Although the term Positive Education only gained currency from 2009, the ideas it captures have deeper roots in Education. Traditions such as **character education**, civic and moral education and positive youth development have long sought to cultivate virtues, purpose and human potential in young people (Romer & Hansen, 2021; Kristjansson, 2012). Positive Psychology added a stronger emphasis on child wellbeing and on the development of positive communities and institutions, helping to establish the foundations for a more coherent field (Waters, 2011).

Character education: An educational tradition focused on cultivating virtues, moral development and responsible citizenship.

Civic and moral education: the teaching of knowledge, values, responsibilities, and ethical principles that support responsible citizenship and respectful participation in society.

Positive youth development: an approach that promotes young people's strengths, skills, relationships, and opportunities to support healthy development and successful participation in society.

A pivotal moment came when Seligman and colleagues' (2009) partnered with Geelong Grammar School in Australia to introduce a whole-school effort to embed Positive Psychology constructs into the school's curriculum, pedagogy and culture. This and comparable early initiatives aligned with what Kern and Wehmeyer (2021) described as the first wave of Positive Education. During this period, the application of Positive Psychology within schools typically centred on student programmes delivered by teachers.

As the field developed, its focus extended beyond student-facing programmes to include teachers, leaders and whole-school systems. Second-wave perspectives stressed that wellbeing is both "taught" and "caught": It depends not only on explicit instruction but also on the implicit norms, relationships and everyday practices that constitute the school's culture, with lasting impact requiring alignment across policy, leadership and staff development (Norrish, 2015; White & Kern, 2018).

More recently, both advocates and critics have increasingly foregrounded context, culture, equity and pedagogy. These concerns underpin what Kern and Wehmeyer (2021) described as a third wave: Positive Education as a broad perspective rather than a bounded sub-discipline, one that seeks to integrate Positive Psychology with established educational traditions, systems thinking and locally grounded practices in the service of flourishing educational communities.

Positive Education in Practice

In practice, Positive Education operates across several interconnected layers. One useful distinction is between approaches, themes, interventions and implementation models. At the broadest level are core approaches, established traditions and frameworks such as **social and emotional learning**, character strengths, growth mindset, resilience, positive youth development and coaching, which provide guiding theories and practical toolkits for strengthening wellbeing and capability in schools (Green et al., 2021).

Across and within these approaches, a set of recurring themes commonly appears, including emotion regulation, relationships, purpose, intrinsic motivation and agency. These themes are then operationalised through concrete interventions, delivered through classroom lessons, group-based programmes, feedback and assessment cycles or coaching conversations.

Finally, schools adopt implementation models to organise and sustain this work, often through whole-school change processes designed to embed wellbeing within culture, systems, and everyday practices (White & Kern, 2018). The sections that follow illustrate a few examples of how Positive Education is applied.

- **Social and emotional learning (SEL):** This approach builds the capacities needed to understand and manage emotions, sustain relationships and make responsible decisions. It is commonly organised around a small set of competencies (such as self-awareness, self-management and relationship skills) that are translated into sequenced, developmentally appropriate lessons and reinforced through school-wide practices (Green et al., 2021). Since SEL programmes have been shown to improve social–emotional skills, behaviour and academic outcomes, they often function as a practical bridge between wellbeing and learning within Positive Education. In schools, they may be visible as a dedicated curriculum strand, integrated routines and pedagogies within existing subjects and policies designed to create safe, supportive and inclusive climates.
- **Strengths-based character education:** This strand focuses on identifying and cultivating character strengths (such as curiosity, kindness, perseverance and gratitude) as resources for learning, relationships and contribution (Green et al., 2021). Schools draw on the VIA Classification (Niemiec, 2017) (see Chapter 2) to help students and staff recognise strengths and apply them in everyday contexts. When integrated strategically, **strengths-based approaches** have been linked to higher wellbeing, engagement and academic motivation, alongside reductions in distress, while providing a shared aspirational vocabulary for school culture (Waters & Loton, 2019).
- **Growth mindset:** This perspective emphasises the belief that abilities can be developed through effort, effective strategies and support, rather than being fixed traits (Dweck & Yeager, 2019). Within Positive Education, this approach links academic learning and wellbeing: It encourages students to interpret difficulty as part of learning, persist through setbacks, seek feedback and remain engaged, which can buffer against withdrawal. In practice, schools embed this orientation through classroom norms that treat mistakes as learning opportunities, feedback that highlights process and strategy, explicit teaching about brain plasticity and reflective activities that support constructive interpretations

of failure. At the same time, evidence-informed guidance cautions against false growth mindset, where slogans replace substantive change, and highlights the need for teacher learning and alignment with assessment, grouping and disciplinary practices (Green et al., 2021).

- **Resilience-oriented approaches:** This work aims to strengthen students' capacity to cope with stress, recover from setbacks and adapt to changes following adversity. Programmes such as the Penn Resilience Program (see Chapter 5) focus on preventing depression and developing optimistic explanatory styles, alongside the development of a broader set of capacities (Green et al., 2021). These are delivered through small-group provision, classroom programmes or trauma-informed pedagogies. Resilience work also attends to contextual factors such as pedagogy, relationships and structural disadvantage, rather than locating adversity within the individual (Arguis-Rey, 2021).
- **Positive youth development (PYD):** This perspective foregrounds developmental processes and virtue-oriented aims, focusing on the conditions that enable young people to realise their potential and contribute to their communities. PYD frameworks emphasise assets such as competence, confidence, connection, character and caring, developed through meaningful opportunities for participation, leadership and service (Romer & Hansen, 2021). Within Positive Education, it is reflected in initiatives that strengthen student voice and agency, connect learning to community challenges and cultivate long-term goals and purpose. This commonly involves project- and service-based learning, student-led action projects and partnerships with families and community organisations, positioning students as active co-creators of learning and school culture.

Several critiques have been highlighted in these applications, with researchers identifying design weaknesses in evaluating their impact, such as heavy reliance on **self-report measures**, use of small convenience samples, limited use of randomised controlled trials and a scarcity of longitudinal and replication studies. As a result, only a subset of programmes has been examined using robust methods (Cabanas & González-Lamas, 2022).

Generalisability: The extent to which findings from a study can be applied to wider populations or other settings.

A further concern is that these programmes have been implemented in relatively privileged contexts. With limited evidence from diverse, under-resourced, non-Western contexts, claims of broad generalisability remain unsubstantiated (Cabanas & González-Lamas, 2022).

Many interventions remain predominantly focused on intra-individual factors, which risks individualising problems that are partly produced by school structures, classroom climates, and broader disadvantage (Ciarrochi et al., 2016).

Finally, the proliferation of loosely connected programmes and constructs, combined with uneven engagement with educational theory, pedagogy and curriculum scholarship, can produce an implementation landscape that is difficult for teachers to navigate. Calls for integrative frameworks emphasise unifying Positive Psychology with educational knowledge, strengthening pedagogical guidance, and clarifying how wellbeing work fits within teaching and learning (Thomas et al., 2016; White, 2016).

Taken together, the future of Positive Education depends not only on demonstrating effectiveness but also on ensuring stronger conceptual coherence, methodological rigour and contextual sensitivity, integrating more fully with pedagogy, curriculum and whole-school structures rather than being delivered as a fragmented set of add-on initiatives.

Evidence on Outcomes and Impacts

Across the literature, Positive Education is linked to four clusters of outcomes:

- **Student wellbeing and functioning:** Intervention studies commonly report improvements in outcomes such as students' life satisfaction, positive affect, optimism, hope, self-esteem, engagement, social–emotional competence and school belonging following Positive Education initiatives (Waters, 2011; Shoshani et al., 2016; Norrish, 2015; White & Kern, 2018). There is also evidence for reductions in ill-being, including depressive symptoms, anxiety, stress and behavioural problems (Kallapiran et al., 2015; Waters & Loton, 2019). However, effects are typically small to moderate and, at times, concentrated in particular subgroups (students with low baseline wellbeing), and are more consistent post-intervention than at longer-term follow-up (Waters, 2011; Cabanas & González-Lamas, 2022).
- **Academic outcomes:** Research evidence suggests that these interventions can yield modest improvements in students' academic achievement, alongside more reliable gains in academic attitudes and learning behaviours such as motivation, perseverance, self-efficacy and school engagement (Shoshani et al., 2016; Waters & Loton, 2019). Growth mindset and related work on agency and self-regulation have been associated with persistence, task orientation and adaptive learning behaviours, although recent syntheses cautioned that average effects on grades and test scores are small and contingent on context and implementation quality (Dweck & Yeager, 2019). Longitudinal work also

indicated that positive emotions predict slightly improved achievement over time, while negative emotions often show associations with declines in performance, highlighting the importance of addressing both (Cabanas & González-Lamas, 2022).

- **Social, relational, and school climate outcomes:** Several initiatives reported improvements in classroom climate, peer relations, perceived social support and school connectedness (Allen et al., 2017; Waters & Loton, 2021; Green et al., 2021). Case studies also described gains in staff morale, a shared language for wellbeing, and stronger alignment between values, policies, and everyday practice (Norrish, 2015; Hoare et al., 2017; White & Kern, 2018).
- **Staff outcomes:** Where staff are included, Positive Education initiatives have been associated with improvements in teacher wellbeing, work engagement, and in some cases improved classroom practice (Kern et al., 2014; Allison et al., 2020; Hoare et al., 2017). Nonetheless, the evidence base on teachers and leaders remains small (Waters & Loton, 2019; Kern & Wehmeyer, 2021).

Taken together, the evidence supports a cautious but broadly favourable conclusion: Well-designed, context-sensitive Positive Education initiatives can enhance aspects of student wellbeing and learning while contributing to more relationally supportive and values-aligned school cultures. However, effects are typically modest, uneven across programmes and dependent on implementation quality, system context and whether efforts move beyond the individual level to address pedagogy, culture and structural conditions.

Conclusion

Positive Education has emerged as a response to the limits of attainment-focused schooling, reframing educational success so that flourishing is treated as a core outcome alongside learning. Located at the intersection of Education and Positive Psychology, it reframes some long-standing questions about what is worth learning and what kinds of lives and communities schools should help cultivate. It also reconnects contemporary schooling with earlier educational traditions concerned with character, citizenship and human potential, while adding a distinctively positive-psychological emphasis on wellbeing, strengths and supportive institutions.

The chapter has shown that Positive Education is best implemented not as a set of discrete programmes, but as a whole-school orientation that integrates explicit wellbeing learning with experiential learning derived from the school environment. Well-designed, context-sensitive initiatives can produce modest improvements in student wellbeing, engagement and some learning-related outcomes, and school climate and educator wellbeing may also benefit. However, effects are uneven and contingent on implementation quality and context.

The critiques reviewed here highlight the conditions needed for the field's maturation: Clearer concepts, stronger research designs and greater attention to pedagogy, culture and structural inequality to avoid decontextualised framings of wellbeing. If Positive Education evolves with greater rigour and deeper sensitivity to context, it can help create learning communities where students and staff can achieve and thrive.

References

Allen, K.A., Kern, M.L., Vella-Brodrick, D., & Waters, L. (2017). School values: A comparison of academic motivation, mental health promotion, and school belonging with student achievement. The Educational and Developmental Psychologist, 34(1), 31–47.

Allison, L., Waters, L., & Kern, M.L. (2020). Flourishing classrooms: Applying a systems-informed approach to positive education. Contemporary School Psychology, 2, 395–405.

Arguis-Rey, R. (2021). Positive education in practice. In M.L. Kern, & M.L. Wehmeyer (Eds.), The Palgrave handbook of positive education (pp. 49–74). Palgrave.

Cabanas, E., & González-Lamas, J. (2022). A critical review of positive education: Challenges and limitations. Social Psychology of Education, 25(5), 1249–1272.

Ciarrochi, J., Atkins, P.W., Hayes, L.L., Sahdra, B.K., & Parker, P. (2016). Contextual positive psychology: Policy recommendations for implementing positive psychology into schools. Frontiers in Psychology, 7, 1561.

Dweck, C.S., & Yeager, D.S. (2019). Mindsets: A view from two eras. Perspectives on Psychological Science, 14(3), 481–496.

Green, S., Leach, C., & Falecki, D. (2021). Approaches to positive education. In M.L. Kern, & M.L. Wehmeyer (Eds.), The Palgrave handbook of positive education (pp. 21–48). Palgrave.

Hoare, E., Bott, D., & Robinson, J. (2017). Learn it, live it, teach it, embed it: Implementing a whole school approach to foster positive mental health and wellbeing through positive education. International Journal of Wellbeing, 7(3), 56–71.

Kallapiran, K., Koo, S., Kirubakaran, R., & Hancock, K. (2015). Effectiveness of mindfulness in improving mental health symptoms of children and adolescents: A meta-analysis. Child and Adolescent Mental Health, 20(4), 182–194.

Kern, M.L., Waters, L., Adler, A., & White, M. (2014). Assessing employee wellbeing in schools using a multifaceted approach: Associations with physical health, life satisfaction, and professional thriving. Psychology, 5(6), 500–513.

Kern, M.L., & Wehmeyer, M.L. (2021). Introduction and overview. In M.L. Kern, & M.L. Wehmeyer (Eds.), The Palgrave handbook of positive education (pp. 1–20). Palgrave.

Kieling, C., Buchweitz, C., Caye, A., Silvani, J., Ameis, S.H., Brunoni, A.R., Cost, K.T., Courtney, D.B., Georgiades, K., Ries Merikangas, K., Henderson, J.L., Polanczyk, G.V., Rohde, L.A., Salum, G.A., & Szatmari, P. (2024). Worldwide prevalence and disability from mental disorders across childhood and adolescence: Evidence from the global burden of disease study. JAMA Psychiatry, 81(4), 347–356.

Kristjansson, K. (2012). Positive psychology and positive education: Old wine in new bottles? Educational Psychologist, 47(2), 86–105.

Niemiec, R.M. (2017). Character strenghts interventions. Hogrefe.

Norrish, J.M. (2015). Positive education: The Geelong Grammar School Journey. Oxford University Press.

Romer, D., & Hansen, W. (2021). Positive youth development and positive education. In M.L. Kern, & M.L. Wehmeyer (Eds.), The Palgrave handbook of positive education (pp. 93–111). Palgrave.

Seligman, M.E.P., & Csikszentmihalyi, M. (2000). Positive psychology: An Introduction. American Psychologist, (55), 5–14.

Seligman, M.E.P., Ernst, R.M., Gillham, J., Reivich, K., & Linkins, M. (2009). Positive education: Positive psychology and classroom interventions. Oxford Review of Education, 35(3), 293–311.

Shoshani, A., Steinmetz, S., & Kanat-Maymon, Y. (2016). Effects of the Maytiv positive psychology school program on early adolescents' well-being, engagement, and achievement. Journal of School Psychology, 57, 73–92.

Thomas, N., Graham, A., Powell, M.A., & Fitzgerald, R. (2016). Conceptualisations of children's wellbeing at school: The contribution of recognition theory. Childhood, 23(4), 506–520.

Waters, L. (2011). A review of school-based positive psychology interventions. The Australian Educational and Developmental Psychologist, 28(2), 75–90.

Waters, L., & Loton, D. (2019). SEARCH: A meta framework and review of the field of positive education. International Journal of Applied Positive Psychology, 4(1–2), 1–46.

Waters, L., & Loton, D. (2021). Tracing the growth, gaps, and characteristics in positive education science: A long term, large scale review of the field. Frontiers in Psychology, 12, 774967.

White, M.A. (2016). Why won't it stick? Positive psychology and positive education. Psychology of Well-Being, 6(1), 2.

White, M.A., & Kern, M.L. (2018). Positive education: Learning and teaching for wellbeing and academic mastery. International Journal of Wellbeing, 8(1), 1–17.

Chapter 8

Positive Work and Organisations

In the complex fabric of our lives, work holds a pivotal position. For many, it is not just a way to meet material necessities but also a foundation for identity, purpose, personal development, and social interaction. Our jobs mould our daily activities, colour how we view ourselves, and play a crucial role in determining our happiness and fulfilment. However, the professional sphere can also be a source of tension, conflict and distress. As we journey through the 21st century, focusing on and elevating occupational wellbeing is no longer a luxury but a strategic imperative essential for organisational sustainability.

Positive Work and Organisations has emerged as a vibrant and increasingly influential area of scholarship and practice concerned with how work can be designed, led and experienced in ways that promote human flourishing while also supporting sustainable organisational performance and productivity.

> **Positive Work and Organisations:** An interdisciplinary area applying Positive Psychology to workplaces, leadership, teamwork and organisational life.

Its rise reflects a growing recognition that, for many people, work is falling short of being engaging, healthy or even tolerable. Gallup's (2022) global report on the state of work encapsulates this starkly, concluding that, for most people, "work sucks" (p. 2). Gallup estimated that 23% of employees are engaged, 59% are not engaged (often framed as **quiet quitting**) and 18% are actively disengaged. Wellbeing indicators are similarly sobering: Across 160 countries, 33% of employees are classified as "thriving," with the remainder "struggling" or "suffering" (Gallup, 2022). Occupational stress remains widespread: 44% report persistent stress, with 51% planning to leave their jobs (Gallup, 2023). Despite modest improvements over earlier decades, these

> **Quiet quitting:** A term used to describe employees who are not engaged.

DOI: 10.4324/9781032663111-12

figures underscore a persistent gap between what work currently offers and what it could enable under more supportive organisational conditions.

Set against this bleak context, Positive Work and Organisations offers a timely counterpoint by examining the conditions under which employees and organisations can function well and flourish. It considers workplaces as far more than sites of income generation; they are social and developmental contexts that shape identities, cultivate skills, influence life trajectories, and inform beliefs about the self and society. At its best, work offers structure, opportunities for learning, achievement, autonomy, growth, social connection, recognition and respect. For many people, it is also a vital source of meaning, purpose and contribution beyond the self. Because work is so closely tied to fundamental human needs and values, its quality carries profound implications for wellbeing.

This chapter positions Positive Work and Organisations as a conceptual reorientation and a set of practical approaches that align organisational practices and outcomes more closely with employee wellbeing. It begins by defining the field as an interdisciplinary science and domain of practice, and then reviews its core concerns, interventions and their impact.

Conceptualising Positive Work and Organisations

> **Positive Work and Organisations** (also referred to as Positive Work and Organisational Psychology) is a field that brings together Positive Psychology and Management scholarship. It is defined as the study and application of psychological mechanisms that promote employee and organisational flourishing (Warren et al., 2017).
>
> As an applied science, it is oriented towards "developing strategies to enhance positive functioning and creating evidence-based intervention strategies to help facilitate individual wellbeing and organisational flourishing" (Van Zyl et al., 2024, p. 700).

The term Positive Work and Organisations is an umbrella term that encompasses three sub-domains:

- **Positive Organisational Psychology (POP)**: This sub-domain is described as the scientific study of positive subjective experiences in the workplace. It centres on employees and the interface between them and their organisations, with a strong applied aim: Developing interventions that enhance quality of life within work settings (Donaldson & Ko, 2010). It therefore focuses on topics such as occupational wellbeing, positive leadership, job satisfaction, engagement, motivation, positive relationships and meaningful work.

- **Positive Organisational Behaviour (POB)**: This strand is defined as "the study and application of positively oriented human resource strengths and psychological capacities that can be measured, developed, and effectively managed for performance improvement in today's workplace" (Luthans, 2002, p. 59). It concentrates on individual positive psychological resources that are related to employee wellbeing or performance, such as strengths, hope, optimism, resilience and prosocial behaviours (Luthans, 2002).
- **Positive Organisational Scholarship (POS)**: This sub-field is framed as "the study of that which is positive, flourishing, and life-giving in organisations" (Cameron & Caza, 2004, p. 731). If focuses on organisational features and on processes that occur in organisations and their outcomes for employees and for organisations. It explores the interpersonal or structural dynamics activated in and through organisations (Cameron & Caza, 2004), covering topics such as organisational virtuousness, positive deviance, and appreciative cultures (Cameron et al., 2003). Its primary emphasis is on the accomplishment of work-related outcomes through positive means.

As is evident from these descriptions, the three sub-domains overlap to some degree, which resulted in conceptual ambiguity. To provide greater coherence, Warren et al. (2017) proposed the umbrella term Positive Work and Organisations (PWO) to integrate these strands. The purpose of PWO is "to encourage dialogue across subfields and serve as a clearinghouse for best practices in Positive Psychology theory building and practice" (Donaldson et al., 2019, p. 114).

Two concepts are central to the field and warrant closer clarification:

- **Flourishing employees:** Within the work domain, flourishing is considered a state of optimal occupational wellbeing, where the person is satisfied with their work, doing what is morally worth doing, and functioning optimally both at work and at the interface between work and other life domains. Flourishing employees possess a positive mental state and engage in behaviours that contribute to their organisations (Seligman, 2012).
- **Flourishing organisation:** A flourishing organisation is one that embeds positive organisational values and practices in its day-to-day interactions. Positive organisations achieve high performance and profitability by bringing out the best in employees to help them engage, flourish and grow. They also leverage employees' strengths and talents by designing work that is meaningful and empowering (Cameron, 2012).

The Remit of Positive Work and Organisations

There are numerous topics that fall within the remit of PWO (Martin-Del-Rio et al., 2021; Warren et al., 2017; Donaldson & Ko, 2010; Luthans & Youssef, 2020) and these can be classified into the following themes:

> **The happy-productive employee model:** proposes that employees with higher levels of happiness tend to be more productive and perform better at work.

- **Employee wellbeing:** This area examines workers' wellbeing across multiple interlinked domains – physical, mental, social, occupational and financial. Within occupational wellbeing, it considers how employment conditions, career trajectories and everyday work experiences shape functioning and quality of life. Applied work in this space focuses on identifying risks and protective factors, strengthening resources, and developing interventions such as stress management and recovery practices, burnout prevention and evidence-informed workplace wellness initiatives.
- **Happiness at work:** This theme examines the conditions that shape individuals' satisfaction and positive affect at work, and considers how job satisfaction influences outcomes such as performance and organisational commitment. It is often discussed in relation to the happy–productive employee model (Cropanzano & Wright, 2001) which proposes that employees who feel happier at work tend to perform better, since positive affect supports motivation, persistence and more constructive work behaviours.

> **Organisational citizenship behaviours:** Voluntary, helpful behaviours that support colleagues or the organisation but are not formally required by the job.

- **Positive organisational behaviours:** This theme encompasses research on individual and collective behaviours that help cultivate constructive, supportive work environments, such as optimism, resilience, self-efficacy and self-regulation. It also includes relational and prosocial behaviours that strengthen teams and organisations, for example cooperation, organisational citizenship behaviours, kindness and peer support.
- **Engagement and performance:** This topic examines what energises and sustains employees' engagement and effectiveness at work, and how these translate into performance. It considers individual factors such as motivation, strengths and work-related meaning, alongside organisational factors such as job design, the availability of resources,

autonomy, supportive leadership, learning opportunities and recognition. It also explores how these influences interact.

- **Strengths-based approaches:** These approaches emphasise identifying, developing and using individual and team strengths. In practice, this may involve strengths assessment and feedback, role crafting to align tasks with what people do best, building complementary strengths in teams, and shaping learning, coaching and performance conversations around amplifying capabilities. Closely related is **Appreciative Inquiry**, an organisational development approach that builds on existing organisational strengths by systematically exploring successes, resources and possibilities and using these to envision and co-create desired futures. Their core premise is that these practices can enhance energy, confidence, engagement, collaboration and effectiveness, while still addressing weaknesses when they limit performance or wellbeing.

> **Appreciative Inquiry:** An organisational development approach that builds change by identifying existing strengths, successes and possibilities rather than focusing mainly on problems.

- **Meaning and purpose at work:** This area examines how people experience their work as significant and worthwhile, and how this sense of meaning shapes motivation, engagement and performance. It explores where meaning comes from and how organisations can support it through job design, leadership and organisational narratives. Common topics include **work orientations** (viewing work as a job, a career or a calling) and career calling, which help employees connect everyday tasks to a larger purpose.

> **Work orientation:** The way a person understands their work as a job, a career or a calling.

- **Psychological Capital (PsyCap):** PsyCap refers to a set of psychological resources that support effective functioning at work. Research in this area examines how these capacities shape how employees interpret challenges, set goals, persist through setbacks and recover after adversity, and how they relate to outcomes such as engagement, performance, adaptability and wellbeing.

> **Psychological Capital:** A set of positive psychological resources at work consisting of hope, efficacy, resilience and optimism.

- **High-quality work relationships:** This domain examines how supportive, trusting, growth-oriented work relationships are formed, sustained and linked to positive outcomes. It focuses on the quality of everyday interactions among colleagues, leaders and followers. Key topics include high-quality connections and relational energy, leader–member exchange, psychological safety, trust and fairness, inclusion and belonging, compassion and civility, social support, constructive conflict and repair. Research also considers how high-quality relationships shape wellbeing, engagement, performance, creativity, adaptability and retention, while recognising that poor relationships can undermine health and organisational effectiveness.

- **Positive change management:** This theme focuses on how organisational change can be designed and led in ways that strengthen, rather than deplete, employee and organisational functioning. It examines approaches that build psychological safety, participation and trust, communicate a compelling purpose and clear rationale for change, and support adaptation through learning, capability-building and adequate resources. It also considers how leaders can harness positive emotions, strengths and collective efficacy during transitions, reduce uncertainty and change fatigue, and create processes that leave the organisation healthier and more resilient after change than before.
- **Work-life balance:** This topic examines how work intersects with other life domains and how people manage the boundaries, demands and spillover between them. It explores individual strategies, such as boundary-setting, time and energy management, and negotiation of roles, alongside organisational conditions that shape balance, such as workload and scheduling, flexibility and remote arrangements, supportive leadership, leave policies, and cultures that respect non-work time. A further focus is on outcomes such as stress, wellbeing, engagement, retention and the extent to which work can either enrich life outside work or create conflict and depletion.
- **Positive leadership:** This topic examines leadership

Transformational leadership: a leadership approach in which leaders inspire and motivate followers to exceed expectations by providing a compelling vision, intellectual stimulation, and individualised support.

Authentic leadership: a leadership approach characterised by self-awareness, transparency, ethical behaviour, and consistency between a leader's values and actions.

Servant leadership: a leadership approach that prioritises serving and developing followers, emphasising their wellbeing, growth, and empowerment.

approaches that cultivate healthy, high-functioning teams and constructive workplace climates, such as transformational, authentic and servant leadership. It focuses on how leaders can inspire and motivate by articulating a compelling vision, modelling integrity and optimism, and fostering trust, psychological safety and inclusion. It also considers everyday leadership practices that bring out the best in others, including recognition and appreciation, supporting development and building high-quality relationships.

- **Organisational culture and climate:** This area examines the shared values, norms and assumptions that shape how things are done in organisations (culture), alongside employees' perceptions of what is expected, supported and rewarded in everyday working life (climate). It also incorporates the **psychological contract** – the implicit, subjective beliefs employees and employers hold about mutual obligations. Research in this cluster explores how culture, climate and psychological contracts interact to influence morale, wellbeing, trust, collaboration, learning, productivity, ethical behaviour and retention, and how perceived contract fulfilment or breach can strengthen commitment or trigger disengagement and turnover intentions.

> **Organisational culture:** The shared values, norms and assumptions that shape how things are done within an organisation.
>
> **Organisational climate:** Employees' shared perceptions of what is expected, supported and rewarded in everyday working life.
>
> **Psychological contract:** Employees' and employers' subjective beliefs about their mutual obligations and expectations in the workplace.

These themes highlight PWO's dual emphasis on how people thrive at work and how organisations create the conditions for thriving. Its remit spans individual experiences, the development of psychological resources, and the relational and structural features of work. This breadth reflects the field's integrative ambition: To connect rigorous psychological theory with organisational practice and to translate insights into strategies that simultaneously enhance employee functioning and organisational effectiveness.

The Development of Positive Work and Organisations

In a bibliometric review and mapping analysis, Martin-Del-Rio et al. (2021) suggested that PWO is among the fastest-growing interdisciplinary sub-domains within Positive Psychology. Their analysis highlighted its multidisciplinary reach and the extent to which its theories and methods travel beyond conventional boundaries. This diffusion has supported collaboration and knowledge exchange, strengthening the field's impact, visibility and credibility.

Despite rising publication volume, however, there are signs that PWO's influence may be weakening. Martin-Del-Rio et al. (2021) found that the publications attracting the greatest scientific attention clustered between 2001 and 2011, with critics arguing that PWO has produced relatively few revolutionary ideas since then, and that some newer work has generated mainly "ephemeral frontier knowledge" that does not cumulate to advance theory or enable sustained knowledge-building (Van Zyl et al., 2024, p. 701).

Van Zyl et al. (2024) attributed PWO's rapid rise to strategic visibility and contextual fit. They emphasised the role of influential scholars in promoting PWO, early large-scale funding that enabled high-profile programmes and international collaboration, and social and political shifts that foregrounded wellbeing and agency, making organisations more receptive to positive approaches to work. They also highlighted PWO's applied, results-oriented promise: Developable strengths, positive psychological states and healthier work environments are often framed as routes to performance. Its traction was further amplified by the **mainstreaming** of constructs such as work engagement and strengths at work, by endorsements and implementation through large consultancy and analytics firms, and by institutional recognition that strengthened its credibility, funding prospects and reach.

> **Mainstreaming:** The process through which ideas that were once specialised become widely accepted within a discipline or society.

However, several factors seem to undermine the field's progression leading to the observed stagnation (Van Zyl et al., 2024). These include a lack of meta-theoretical grounding, heavy borrowing across traditions, methodological problems, the instrumentalisation of concepts such as wellbeing and meaning as routes to productivity, the individualisation of responsibility while deflecting attention from detrimental working conditions, lagging behind changes in work structures and technology, the use of simplified proxies to measure complex concepts, ethical risks, as well as a declining pipeline of future professionals and variable practitioner competence. These factors limit theoretical and empirical developments, reduce confidence in research claims, damage the field's credibility and reputation, and lead to the slow uptake of ideas and interventions by stakeholders.

Van Zyl et al. (2024) proposed that PWO is currently entering its second wave in response to stagnation in its scholarship and the rapidly changing nature of work, by explicitly embracing technological transformations. They defined this wave as an evidence-based, data-driven approach using technological advances and human-centred designs to enhance positive characteristics of individuals and organisations, in service of functioning, wellbeing and performance. PWO 2.0 expands the field's remit beyond conventional organisational settings to digital or decentralised workforces, with artificial human companions, and calls for stronger designs and purposeful use of machine learning, big data analytics, natural language processing and passive assessment to capture work experiences in real time.

The second wave also implies a shift in practice and professional identity: Practitioners are positioned less as facilitators and more as developers, analysts and data-driven technologists who help design and govern environments that support wellbeing. It also encourages multi-level thinking, expanded interdisciplinarity, culturally sensitive and inclusive perspectives, and deeper stakeholder collaboration to keep the science usable in real organisational contexts.

Overall, these developments suggest that PWO's first wave achieved rapid expansion through strategic promotion, strong socio-economic resonance and an applied promise. However, the past decade revealed some vulnerabilities in theoretical novelty and cumulative progress. The second wave agenda can be read as both a corrective and an opportunity: A bid to renew the field's intellectual traction by aligning its concepts, methods and professional competencies with digitally mediated work realities. If PWO 2.0 succeeds, it may restore the discipline's capacity to generate distinctive, robust knowledge and ethically grounded interventions at scale. If it fails, the field risks further fragmentation, credibility loss and being outpaced by adjacent domains that are moving faster in technological capability and organisational influence.

Applied Interventions and Their Impact

In their systematic review of Positive Psychology interventions in organisational contexts, Donaldson et al. (2019) found that five categories of interventions are commonly implemented in workplaces:

- **Wellbeing interventions:** These can range from environmental or ergonomic provisions to physical activity programmes and mindfulness sessions, as well as health and safety training, resilience building, stress management and self-care. Most are delivered in group formats and are intended to encourage employees to adopt and sustain wellbeing-promoting practices. Such interventions typically target changes in individuals' attitudes or behaviours rather than factors related to work conditions. Hence, broader environmental change is more likely to be indirect and gradual through the development of a workplace culture that normalises self-care. Research indicates that wellbeing interventions can reduce absenteeism and turnover intentions while improving job satisfaction (Boehm & Lyubomirsky, 2008; Layous et al., 2013). This aligns with the happy–productive employee thesis, which proposes that happier employees tend to perform better than those who are less happy (Cropanzano & Wright, 2001).

- **Psychological Capital (PsyCap) Interventions:** These interventions develop a set of four psychological resources (Luthans & Youssef-Morgan, 2017):

    - **Self-efficacy:** Confidence in one's ability to succeed in challenging work tasks;
    - **Optimism:** Positive expectations regarding one's work and the organisation's prospects;
    - **Hope:** The capacity to generate goals and pathways, and to reroute pathways when obstacles arise;
    - **Resilience:** The ability to recover, adapt, and continue functioning effectively following adversity.

  Avey et al. (2010) reported that PsyCap interventions are linked to a range of desirable outcomes, including stronger job performance, higher engagement and more citizenship behaviours. However, echoing the earlier critique, PsyCap interventions typically focus on developing individuals rather than altering organisational systems or working conditions. That said, they have also been implemented with leaders (Luthans et al., 2014; Pitichat et al., 2018), and the findings suggest that strengthening leaders' PsyCap may have wider ripple effects, shaping culture and everyday practices.
- **Strengths interventions:** Peterson and Seligman's (2004) Values in Action (VIA) framework and its inventory of character strengths and virtues (see Chapter 2) have become one of the most widely used strengths-based tools in workplace settings. In organisational applications, strengths interventions are geared towards helping employees identify their signature strengths, develop them further and apply them intentionally in their work. Evidence indicates that strengths interventions can enhance employee wellbeing, performance, engagement and the experience of work as meaningful. They are also commonly incorporated into leadership development initiatives and used within coaching contexts (MacKie, 2014).
- **Gratitude interventions:** Wood et al. (2010) conceptualised workplace gratitude as "noticing and appreciating the positive in one's work life" (p. 891). Gratitude interventions involve structured, intentional

activities designed to strengthen gratitude as a habitual orientation at work. Research findings suggest that gratitude-based interventions can be a robust means of enhancing employee wellbeing, happiness and health, while also strengthening workplace relationships and encouraging prosocial behaviours (Wood et al., 2010; Boggiss et al., 2020).

- **Job crafting interventions:** Job crafting refers to a self-directed process through which employees modify aspects of their work to improve the fit between job demands and their personal needs, abilities, interests, and strengths (Wrzesniewski & Dutton, 2001). Evidence from job crafting interventions suggest that when employees can exert greater control over key features of their roles, they are able to align work demands with personal strengths, often with benefits for performance, wellbeing and work engagement (Tims et al., 2022). Unlike many interventions that primarily target individuals' internal states, job crafting alters what people do at work, creating the potential for incremental, bottom-up organisational change.

Job crafting: A self-directed process in which employees modify aspects of their work to improve fit with their strengths, needs and interests.

Donaldson et al. (2019) reported several notable patterns in the overall effects of these interventions. Effect sizes differed substantially across studies, though most were in the small-to-moderate range. Workplace interventions are associated with significant improvements in outcomes such as wellbeing, engagement, leader–member exchange, self-esteem, workplace trust, forgiveness, prosocial behaviour, leadership and calling. Notably, however, they did not produce significant improvements in performance.

Overall, this body of work suggests that PWO interventions are effective for strengthening psychological and relational outcomes, rather than producing direct gains in performance. One implication is that many interventions operate through gradual, indirect pathways that may take time to translate into measurable productivity outcomes, or may be constrained by job design, workload and wider organisational systems. This highlights a key message: Resource-building interventions are valuable, but their impact is likely to be maximised when paired with changes to the work environment, so that individual gains are not undermined by structural barriers and can accumulate into sustained, organisation-level benefit.

Conclusion

This chapter positioned Positive Work and Organisations as an intellectual reorientation and an applied agenda for bringing the realities of work into closer alignment with human flourishing and sustainable organisational functioning. It has shown how PWO integrates insights from Positive Psychology and Management scholarship to illuminate the individual, relational and systemic conditions under which people can thrive at work. At the same time, the review underscores a key tension: Many PWO approaches strengthen psychological and relational outcomes, yet effects on performance are less consistent and may depend on whether interventions are matched with changes to working conditions and organisational systems.

Additionally, the chapter has highlighted that the discipline's growth has been accompanied by substantive critiques. These critiques matter not only academically but strategically: They shape whether PWO is perceived as a rigorous, cumulative science capable of guiding high-stakes organisational decisions, or as a set of attractive ideas vulnerable to simplification and short-lived trend adoption. Addressing these challenges requires tighter theory, stronger and more pluralistic methods, better replication and evaluation, and more credible science–practice partnerships.

Looking ahead, the chapter suggests that PWO's future relevance will be determined by its ability to evolve with the changing nature of work. The PWO 2.0 agenda signals a shift towards engaging technology, datafication and AI-mediated working life, while insisting on human-centred design and ethical governance. If pursued well, this direction offers a route to renewed theoretical traction and practical impact. The field's next phase is therefore less about adding new constructs, and more about deepening its capacity to shape work as a developmental, relational and ethical environment fit for the complexities of the 21st century.

References

Avey, J., Luthans, F., & Youssef, C. (2010). The additive value of positive psychological capital in predicting work attitudes and behaviors. Journal of Management, 36(2), 430–452.

Boehm, J.K., & Lyubomirsky, S. (2008). Does happiness promote career success? Journal of Career Assessment, 16(1), 101–116.

Boggiss, A.L., Consedine, N.S., Brenton-Peters, J.M., Hofman, P.L., & Serlachius, A.S. (2020). A systematic review of gratitude interventions: Effects on physical health and health behaviors. Journal of Psychosomatic Research, 135, 110165.

Cameron, K.S. (2012). Positive leadership. Berrett-Koehler Publishers.

Cameron, K.S., & Caza, A. (2004). Introduction: Contributions to the discipline of positive organizational scholarship. American Behavioral Scientist, 47(6), 731–739.

Cameron, K.S., Dutton, J.E., & Quinn, R.E. (2003). Introduction. In K.S. Cameron, & J.E. Dutton (Eds.), Positive organizational scholarship (pp. 48–65). Berrett-Koehler.

Cropanzano, R., & Wright, T.A. (2001). When a "happy" worker is really a "productive" worker: A review and further refinement of the happy-productive worker thesis. Consulting Psychology Journal, 53(3), 182.
Donaldson, S.I., & Ko, I. (2010). Positive organizational psychology, behavior, and scholarship: A review of the emerging literature and evidence base. The Journal of Positive Psychology, 5(3), 177–191.
Donaldson, S.I., Lee, J.Y., & Donaldson, S.I. (2019). Evaluating positive psychology interventions at work: A systematic review and meta-analysis. International Journal of Applied Positive Psychology, 4(3), 113–134.
Gallup. (2022). State of the global workplace 2022 report. Gallup.
Gallup. (2023). State of the global workplace 2023 report. Gallup.
Layous, K., Sheldon, K., & Lyubomirsky, S. (2013). What is the optimal way to deliver a positive activity intervention? The case of writing about one's best possible selves. Journal of Happiness Studies, 14(2), 635–654.
Luthans, B.C., Luthans, K.W., & Avey, J.B. (2014). Building the leaders of tomorrow: The development of academic psychological capital. Journal of Leadership & Organizational Studies, 21(2), 191–199.
Luthans, F. (2002). Positive organisational behaviour: Implications for the workplace. Academy of Management Executive, 16, 57–76.
Luthans, F., & Youssef-Morgan, C.M. (2017). Psychological capital: An evidence-based positive approach. Annual Review of Organizational Psychology and Organizational Behavior, 4, 339–366.
Luthans, F., & Youssef-Morgan, C.M. (2020). Positive workplaces. In C.R. Snyder, S.J. Lopez, L.M. Edwards, & S.C. Marques (Eds.), The Oxford Handbook of Positive Psychology (3rd ed., pp. 211–240). Oxford University Press.
MacKie, D. (2014). The effectiveness of strength-based executive coaching in enhancing full range leadership development: A controlled study. Consulting Psychology Journal, 66(2), 118 137.
Martin-Del-Rio, B., Neipp, M.C., García-Selva, A., & SolanesPuchol, A. (2021). Positive organizational psychology: A bibliometric review and science mapping analysis. International Journal of Environmental Research and Public Health, 18(10), 5222.
Peterson, C., & Seligman, M.E.P. (2004). Character strengths and virtues. APA.
Pitichat, T., Reichard, R.J., Kea-Edwards, A., Middleton, E., & Norman, S.M. (2018). Psychological capital for leader development. Journal of Leadership & Organizational Studies, 25(1), 47–62.
Seligman, M.E.P. (2012). Flourish. Free Press.
Tims, M., Twemlow, M., & Fong, C.Y.M. (2022). A state-of-the-art overview of job-crafting research: Current trends and future research directions. Career Development International, 27(1), 54–78.
Van Zyl, L.E., Dik, B.J., Donaldson, S.I., Klibert, J.J., Di Blasi, Z., Van Wingerden, J., & Salanova, M. (2024). Positive organisational psychology 2.0: Embracing the technological revolution. The Journal of Positive Psychology, 19(4), 699–711.

Warren, M.A., Donaldson, S.I., & Luthans, F. (2017). Taking positive psychology to the workplace: Positive organizational psychology, positive organizational behavior, and positive organizational scholarship. In M.A. Warren & S.I. Donaldson (Eds.), Scientific advances in positive psychology (pp. 195–227). Praeger.

Wood, A., Froh, J., & Geraghty, A. (2010). Gratitude and well-being: A review and theoretical integration. Clinical Psychology Review, 30(7), 890–905.

Wrzesniewski, A., & Dutton, J. (2001). Crafting a job: Revisioning employees as active crafters of their work. The Academy of Management Review, 26(2), 179–179.

Chapter 9

Positive Health

Positive Health emerged in response to increasing critiques that contemporary approaches to health and healthcare have been underpinned by narrow interpretations of health and illness, and of what healthcare is for. Within this framing, "good health" is commonly defined as the absence of disease, the identification and treatment of illness are prioritised over prevention, and progress is monitored primarily through **biomedical indicators** and the tracking of service activity.

However, this disease-centred approach is increasingly at odds with the realities of persistent **multimorbidity**, the rising burden of long-term conditions, enduring health inequalities and escalating stress and burnout among health professionals. Against this background, the turn towards Positive Health reflects an understanding that supporting people to thrive involves more than treating illness or managing symptoms; it also involves prevention and cultivating the resources that enable individuals and communities to live well (Lianov et al., 2019).

Positive Health: An interdisciplinary area linking Positive Psychology with health and physical functioning.

Lifestyle Medicine: An evidence-based clinical discipline using lifestyle change as a primary way to prevent, manage and reverse chronic disease.

Biomedical indicators: Medical measures used to track health or disease, such as blood pressure, biomarkers or physiological functioning.

Multimorbidity: The presence of two or more long-term health conditions in a person.

Grounded in Positive Psychology, Lifestyle Medicine, Health Psychology and related disciplines, Positive Health conceptualises good health not as perfection or the absence of disease, but as a multidimensional,

DOI: 10.4324/9781032663111-13

dynamic state in which individuals can function, adapt and experience wellbeing across physical, mental and social domains.

This chapter presents Positive Health as a conceptual shift and a set of practical approaches designed to connect health improvement with broader understandings of wellbeing across the life course. It begins by defining Positive Health, and the chapter then examines how the field is enacted in healthcare delivery. It concludes with a review of evidence on the effectiveness of its interventions.

Conceptualising Positive Health

Positive Health is an emerging scientific and applied discipline that integrates Positive Psychology with Lifestyle Medicine and other allied health sciences to promote flourishing across life domains and across the life span (Lianov et al., 2019).

Lifestyle Medicine is an evidence-based clinical discipline using therapeutic lifestyle interventions as a primary modality to prevent, manage and reverse lifestyle-related chronic conditions, addressing behavioural and social drivers of health rather than relying primarily on medical and pharmacological interventions (Lippman et al., 2024). It is commonly structured around six domains: Nutrition, physical activity, sleep, stress management, avoidance of harmful substances and positive social connection. Delivery typically follows a person-centred, whole-person approach that integrates behavioural science to support sustained behaviour change (Giurca et al., 2025).

As a science, Positive Health investigates how positive psychological resources interact with lifestyle-related factors to shape biological pathways. In doing so, Positive Health extends the scope of **Behavioural Medicine** by centring on **vantage resources** and positive outcomes, rather than focusing predominantly on reducing pathology and risk (O'Boyle et al., 2023).

Behavioural Medicine: An interdisciplinary field examining how behaviour, psychology and biology interact in health and illness.

Vantage resources: Positive resources that enhance functioning, wellbeing and resilience, rather than merely reduce risk.

As a practice, Positive Health is operationalised through approaches that embed evidence-based Positive Psychology principles and interventions within healthcare (Lianov et al., 2020).

While acknowledging determinants of illness and disease, Positive Health foregrounds the processes that enable optimal wellbeing, adopting an integrated systems view in which mind and body are inseparable and health is understood within the wider social, cultural and environmental context. The approach is relevant not only for those living with illness or disability, but for everyone seeking to live well (O'Boyle et al., 2023).

It is worth highlighting that the term "health" is used in the Positive Health literature in its everyday sense, referring primarily to the physical aspects of a person's functioning, which aligns more closely with medical terminology and does not reflect contemporary Positive Psychology conceptions of the difference between *health* and *wellbeing* (see Chapter 3). This creates conceptual slippage and merits further discussion. Lianov (2024) argued that stronger cross-disciplinary work is needed to harmonise terminology.

Positive Health: The Case for Integration

The emergence of Positive Health as an interdisciplinary enterprise has been driven by pragmatic system pressures alongside advances in theory and empirical research:

- **Dissatisfaction with deficit models of health:** A key driver for the emergence of Positive Health has been the recognition that biomedical, pathology-focused approaches are poorly suited to address contemporary burdens such as long-term conditions, multimorbidity and illness management. In these contexts, a focus on symptoms leaves core questions unanswered about living well with illness and sustaining functional adaptation. Related critiques of defining health as the absence of disease underscore its limited utility for health promotion, rehabilitation and chronic care, where progress often depends on behavioural change, engagement, adherence, self-care, resilience and the support available to the patient (O'Boyle et al., 2023).
- **A conceptual broadening of health:** Much like Positive Psychology's agenda with regard to Applied Psychology (see Chapter 1), Positive Health seeks to rebalance and extend contemporary health models by incorporating and fostering the positive dimensions of health. Grounded in the WHO's (1948) definition of health as "complete physical, mental and social wellbeing," and informed by later work conceptualising health as the capacity to adapt and self-manage in the face of challenges (Huber et al., 2011), Positive Health adopts a salutogenetic orientation (Antonovsky, 1979) that centres on the origins of health rather than the origins of illness, emphasising the resources that sustain optimal functioning. Building on these foundations, Dunne et al. (2025) introduced

meliotropism: An action-oriented tendency towards health-promoting behaviours that benefit both self and others, offering a language for movement towards flourishing.

Meliotropism: An action-oriented tendency towards behaviours that promote health and flourishing for oneself and others.

- **Chronic disease burden:** With ageing populations and rising lifestyle-related conditions, chronic illnesses now account for a substantial share of service demand, placing sustained strain on conventional models of care. Since lifestyle-related diseases contribute considerably to global morbidity and mortality, effective prevention and long-term management rely on behaviour change and on addressing risks that can derail these efforts (Bohlmeijer & Westerhof, 2021). Against this backdrop, Positive Health has gained traction by aligning with a preventive and early-intervention agenda, and by emphasising adaptive capacities and health-promoting behaviours as pathways to reducing morbidity (Huber et al., 2011).
- **Increasing costs of healthcare:** Escalating expenditure on medical and surgical interventions, particularly in the context of chronic disease, has also prompted interest in Positive Health. Long-term conditions typically require ongoing monitoring, recurrent treatment, polypharmacy and costly procedures, meaning that costs accrue over years. This has highlighted the limitations of reactive, treatment-centred approaches, which can yield diminishing returns while overlooking the upstream determinants and the capabilities required to live well with chronic illness. Rather than seeking to do more with less, Positive Health argues for rebalancing investment towards scalable strategies that prevent illness, preserve functioning, reduce complications and slow deterioration (O'Boyle et al., 2023).
- **Increase in mental illness:** Rising rates of mental health problems have been another catalyst for Positive Health, since they expose the limits of contemporary psychological treatment models when demand outstrips service capacity. As needs increase, the case strengthens for scalable approaches that build protective resources, support adaptive functioning and enable recovery-oriented living (O'Boyle et al., 2023).
- **New scientific findings:** Novel scientific advances have accelerated Positive Health by making the **mind–body** links more visible. As research clarified mechanisms such as the **microbiome–gut–brain axis** (a system through which gut microbes influence mood and behaviour and vice versa), epigenetic regulation (the ways in which stress can switch genes on or off without changing the DNA), neuroplasticity (the brain's capacity to reorganise its structure and functioning in response to thoughts and emotions) and **psycho-neuro-immunological pathways** (the ways in which psychological processes influence the nervous

and immune systems), it has become increasingly difficult to maintain a strict divide between psychological and physical health (O'Boyle et al., 2023). These developments indicate that lived experience can influence physiology, shaping vulnerability, disease progression and recovery. This supports Positive Health's view of health as a dynamic capacity emerging from interacting biological, psychological and social systems.

Mind–body integration: The view that psychological and physical health are deeply interconnected rather than separate.

Microbiome–gut–brain axis: The two-way system through which gut microbes and the brain influence each other, affecting mood, behaviour and health.

Psycho-neuro-immunological pathways: The ways psychological processes affect the nervous and immune systems, influencing health and disease.

- **Accumulating evidence linking Positive Psychology concepts to health outcomes**: A key impetus has been the growing empirical literature indicating that a range of Positive Psychology constructs are associated with meaningful physical health outcomes. For instance, research on psychological wellbeing has linked it to improved neuroendocrine, immune, cardiovascular and sleep-related markers (Ryff et al., 2004; Boehm & Kubzansky, 2012). Happiness has been associated with better health, ageing, and longevity (Steptoe et al., 2015), optimism has been linked to fewer health complaints, constructive health behaviours and improved management of long-term conditions (Scheier & Carver, 2018), and positive relationships has been shown to influence morbidity and mortality (Holt-Lunstad & Uchino, 2015). This evidence base has supported a more integrated Positive Psychology–Health agenda by identifying pathways and measurable outcomes (Lianov et al., 2020).
- **Growth of intervention science:** Integration has also been propelled by the rise of experimental evidence showing that physical health can be cultivated through the use of Positive Psychology interventions. Meta-analytic findings indicated that these interventions can enhance physical wellbeing and reduce illness symptoms (see below). In addition, many positive interventions are comparatively low-cost, scalable and compatible with stepped-care or self-management models, and these features make them attractive to health systems under strain.
- **Expansion of the wellness industry:** The rapid expansion of the **wellness industry** has also been a catalyst for the emergence of Positive Health, largely because it exposed a widening gap between

Wellness industry: A commercial sector offering products and services aimed at improving wellbeing, health or lifestyle.

public demand for well-being-oriented support and the standards typically applied within healthcare systems. As commercial wellness offerings proliferated, often making broad claims about improving health, concerns increased about variable quality, unclear mechanisms, exaggerated promises and the potential for harm. This created a rationale for frameworks that could distinguish credible, empirically supported approaches from those driven primarily by profit (Allem, 2024).

- **Lifestyle Medicine and Positive Psychology:** Lifestyle Medicine provides a natural bridge to Positive Psychology since both treat everyday patterns of living as primary levers for health. It focuses on modifiable behaviours as routes to preventing, managing, and reversing chronic disease (Burke & Dunne, 2022). Positive Psychology offers practices that can be embedded as healthy habits, alongside models of behaviour change (Lianov et al., 2019). This fit is pragmatic as well as conceptual: Lifestyle changes often falter not because people lack knowledge, but because sustaining them is psychologically demanding. Positive Psychology contributes mechanisms that make constructive lifestyle behaviours more durable (Lianov et al., 2019).

Taken together, these drivers suggest that contemporary health challenges require models that move beyond treating illness to supporting adaptation, self-management and sustainable functioning. Rising chronic disease and mental ill-health, alongside service capacity constraints, have increased the demand for scalable approaches that strengthen protective resources alongside clinical care. Meanwhile, dissatisfaction with deficit-focused paradigms has positioned Positive Health as a coherent framework for integrating what matters to patients with what health systems can deliver and measure. This convergence is evidence-informed: Research has clarified mechanisms that link lived experience and psychosocial resources to physiology, morbidity and longevity, while scalable wellbeing interventions, Lifestyle Medicine and the need to protect the public amid an expanding wellness market reinforce the practical case for integration.

Implementing Positive Health Interventions

The applied side of Positive Health entails embedding Positive Psychology evidence-based interventions within routine medical care so that, alongside treating disease, services build patients' psychological resources.

The literature on Positive Health interventions indicates that participants are predominantly adult populations from Western countries. Interventions have been delivered to people living with a broad range of conditions, including chronic pain, diabetes, hypertension, asthma, HIV, cancer, neuromuscular disorders, spinal cord injury, multiple sclerosis, metabolic syndrome, brain injury, lung illness, kidney disorders, skin disorder and other chronic health problems (Feig et al., 2022; Ghosh & Deb, 2017; DuBois et al., 2012). Cardiac conditions received particularly strong attention within this evidence base (DuBois et al., 2012). Some programmes also target health professionals (Townsley et al., 2023).

Some interventions aim to support behavioural change, for example increasing physical activity, improving treatment or medication adherence, maintaining diet and supporting smoking cessation. In addition, some trials focus on reducing illness burden and symptoms, lowering hospitalisation or relapse risk, or mitigating common psychological sequelae of chronic illness, particularly stress, depression and anxiety (Casellas-Grau et al., 2013; Chakhssi et al., 2018; Feig et al., 2022).

Intervention duration varies considerably, ranging from single sessions to intensive protocols delivered over a year (Feig et al., 2022). Programmes range from single-component exercises to multi-component interventions. Delivery is often remote, including videoconferencing, self-administered materials, email-based exercises or through smartphone or web apps. Fewer interventions are delivered in person, either individually or in groups (Feig et al., 2022; Ghosh & Deb, 2017). Most interventions are facilitated by trained practitioners who lead sessions or meetings and monitor progress, though some protocols are self-guided (Feig et al., 2022).

The contents of these interventions vary. Some programmes are structured around psychological wellbeing frameworks (such as PERMA), with sessions targeting each component of the model (see Chapter 3) (Feig et al., 2022). Other interventions include themes such as strengths-work, goal-setting, gratitude, savouring, positive reappraisal, acts of kindness, hope, optimism, self-efficacy, expressive writing, meaning and purpose, resilience building, post-traumatic growth, stress management and mindfulness training (Feig et al., 2022; Ghosh & Deb, 2017). Alongside the interventions, most programmes include psychoeducational contents and homework (Feig et al., 2022).

Lianov (2024) noted that weaving Positive Health interventions into everyday health practice has been challenging, since it requires deliberate planning for how they fit within existing clinical pathways, including the choice of settings, delivery modality and mechanisms to sustain fidelity and engagement. System-level constraints further impede uptake, including time pressures in consultations, limited clinician training in Positive Psychology and high levels of staff stress.

Overall, the literature shows a field that is currently conceptually mature but operationally uneven. Interventions are well-specified, theoretically and empirically anchored, and adaptable, with an emphasis on strengthening psychological resources and supporting health-related behaviours. However, although there have been efforts to integrate interventions more systematically within healthcare systems, research suggests that they are still commonly positioned as optional add-ons rather than core components of standard treatment (Lianov et al., 2020). This indicates that the evidence base has not yet translated into routine, system-level delivery. Addressing this implementation gap will require greater attention to integration within clinical pathways, workforce training, and attention to equity in design and reach (Lianov, 2024). As the field moves forwards, the central challenge is not only whether positive interventions can benefit medical populations, but how they can be sustainably embedded, scaled and normalised as part of routine healthcare.

Interventions Outcomes and Effects

Across the literature, Positive Health interventions map onto four outcome clusters:

- **Patients' health behaviours:** Evidence drawn from experimental studies introducing Positive Health interventions indicates low-to-mid-range improvements in physical activity, treatment or medication adherence, self-care behaviours and reduced smoking, while diet-related outcomes are reported as inconsistent across reviews (Schiavon et al., 2017; Feig et al., 2022).
- **Psychological wellbeing:** Across diverse patient groups who were offered Positive Health interventions, improvements were observed in psychological wellbeing, happiness, optimism, hope, self-esteem, engagement and post-traumatic growth alongside reductions in stress, depression, anxiety, catastrophising and negative affect. Effects are typically small-to-moderate and short term (Casellas-Grau et al., 2013; Chakhssi et al., 2018; Ghosh & Deb, 2017; Schiavon et al., 2017; Labarthe et al., 2016). Mindfulness interventions show slightly stronger effects, including reductions in stress, anxiety, depression, suicidal ideation, self-harm, rumination, substance misuse and symptom relief across several mental conditions. They also show gains in psychological wellbeing, life satisfaction, emotion regulation, positive emotions, hope, sense of coherence, sense of control, autonomy and independence, coping, resilience, spirituality, self-compassion, self-esteem, self-acceptance, benevolence, trust, empathy, forgiveness, improved social relationships, social adjustment and humour. There is

also some evidence of longer-term maintenance with continued practice (Creswell, 2017; Keng et al., 2011; Marchand, 2012).

- **Physical health:** Evidence points to interventions leading to reductions in chronic pain (Muller et al., 2016), as well as improved cardiac outcomes (DuBois et al., 2012; Huffman et al., 2017), including lower post-surgical readmission rates, reduced mortality in older adults, better recovery and survival following cardiac procedures, and fewer adverse cardiac events among those with established disease. However, these effects are small-to-medium, short-lived and some studies show no significant effects. In cancer populations, there is similarly little evidence for effects on survival or biomarkers (DuBois et al., 2012). Mindfulness interventions in clinical samples have reported slightly stronger and more consistent effects across several physiological and functional indicators, including improvements in blood pressure, pain, immune function, sleep, skin conditions and memory (Witek-Janusek et al., 2008; Kabat-Zinn et al., 1998; Creswell, 2017; Shapiro et al., 2003).
- **Staff outcomes:** Interventions delivered to healthcare staff showed measurable reductions in stress, burnout, anxiety and depressive symptoms, alongside increases in psychological wellbeing, job and life satisfaction, self-compassion, relaxation and resilience. However, long-term outcomes are variable (Townsley et al., 2023; Ong et al., 2024).

A key critique of this body of evidence refers to methodological weaknesses in Positive Health experimental research, including a paucity of **longitudinal designs**, absence of control groups, risks of bias and underpowered studies, inconsistent measurement approaches and significant heterogeneity in both intervention content and delivery modalities (Feig et al., 2022). Many trials also fail to articulate the mechanisms of change that can explain how or why the interventions influence health outcomes (Feig et al., 2022).

Another critique is that the evidence base is dominated by studies conducted in Western settings with largely White and highly educated samples, with comparatively scarce inclusion of racial or ethnic minority groups or other cultural contexts, hence raising concerns about transferability across cultures (Huffman et al., 2023).

Additionally, as noted, intervention effects are variable and frequently short-lived, with a subset of studies reporting null findings (Huffman et al., 2023). This may indicate differential responsiveness, suggesting that Positive Psychology approaches are not universally effective, thereby strengthening the case for identifying moderators of impact and tailoring intervention selection and dose accordingly (Casellas-Grau et al., 2013).

Overall, the available body of research indicates that Positive Health interventions function as moderately effective, low-intensity approaches for improving psychosocial outcomes and inducing behavioural changes.

There is, however, limited evidence that these approaches may contribute to improved health prognosis, reinforcing the case for stronger integration in routine healthcare provision, alongside greater methodological rigour in evaluating these interventions.

Conclusion

This chapter positioned Positive Health as both a conceptual reorientation and an emerging applied discipline that responds to the misfit between the disease-centred healthcare system and contemporary realities of multimorbidity, rising mental illness, widening inequalities and constrained service capacity. By integrating insights from Positive Psychology, Lifestyle Medicine and allied health sciences, Positive Health reframes "good health" as a dynamic capacity for functioning, adaptation and self-management across physical, mental and social domains.

The review of its implementation and outcomes displays a field with considerable promise: Interventions are often low-intensity and scalable, show consistent benefits for psychosocial wellbeing and some health behaviours, and display particularly encouraging patterns in mindfulness approaches and in selected clinical contexts such as cardiac care.

At the same time, the chapter has highlighted a set of limiting conditions that require addressing if Positive Health is to become more than an add-on to usual care. Future progress therefore depends on advancing the field as a translational enterprise: Sharpening constructs and mechanisms, strengthening study designs and long-term evaluation, identifying moderators to enable targeted delivery, and embedding interventions within routine care pathways in ways that are feasible under constraints and equitable in reach. If these foundations are established, Positive Health can fulfil its broader promise: Helping health systems do more than treat illness by empowering people and communities to thrive, equitably and sustainably.

References

Allem, J.P. (2024). The need for research on the wellness industry's impact on health decisions. American Journal of Preventive Medicine, 67(4), 627–630.

Antonovsky, A. (1979). Health, stress, and coping. Jossey-Bass.

Boehm, J.K., & Kubzansky, L.D. (2012). The heart's content: The association between positive psychological well-being and cardiovascular health. Psychological Bulletin, 138(4), 655.

Bohlmeijer, E., & Westerhof, G. (2021). The model for sustainable mental health: Future directions for integrating positive psychology into mental health care. Frontiers in Psychology, 12, 747999.

Burke, J., & Dunne, P.J. (2022). Lifestyle medicine pillars as predictors of psychological flourishing. Frontiers in Psychology, 13, 963806.

Casellas-Grau, A., Font, A., & Vives, J. (2013). Positive psychology interventions in breast cancer. A systematic review. Psycho-Oncology, 23(1), 9–19.

Chakhssi, F., Kraiss, J.T., Sommers-Spijkerman, M., & Bohlmeijer, E.T. (2018). The effect of positive psychology interventions on well-being and distress in clinical samples with psychiatric or somatic disorders: A systematic review and meta-analysis. BMC Psychiatry, 18(1), 211.

Creswell, J.D. (2017). Mindfulness interventions. Annual Review of Psychology, 68, 491–516.

DuBois, C.M., Beach, S.R., Kashdan, T.B., Nyer, M.B., Park, E.R., Celano, C.M., & Huffman, J.C. (2012). Positive psychological attributes and cardiac outcomes: Associations, mechanisms, and interventions. Psychosomatics, 53(4), 303–318.

Dunne, P.J., Byrne, E., Burke, J., & Duggan, A. (2025). Meliotropism: A new concept in positive health sciences and human flourishing. Health Promot. Int., 11, 11–18.

Feig, E.H., Madva, E.N., Millstein, R.A., Zambrano, J., Amonoo, H.L., Longley, R.M., Okoro, F., Huffman, J.C., Celano, C.M., & Hoeppner, B. (2022). Can positive psychological interventions improve health behaviors? A systematic review of the literature. Preventive Medicine, 163, 107214.

Ghosh, A., & Deb, A. (2017). Positive psychology interventions for chronic physical illnesses: A systematic review. Psychological Studies, 62(3), 213–232.

Giurca, B., Lau, M., & Fallows, E. (2025). Lifestyle medicine: Bridging behavioural science and clinical care. Clinics in Integrated Care, 33, 100288.

Holt-Lunstad, J., & Uchino, B.N. (2015). Social support and health. In K. Glanz, B.K. Rimer, & K. Viswanath (Eds.), Health behavior (pp. 183–204). Wiley.

Huber, M., Knottnerus, J.A., Green, L., Van Der Horst, H., Jadad, A.R., Kromhout, D., Leonard, B., Lorig, K., Loureiro, M.I., van der Meer, J.W.M., Scnabel, P., Smith, R., van Weel, C., & Smid, H. (2011). How should we define health? BMJ, 343.

Huffman, J.C., Feig, E.H., Zambrano, J., & Celano, C.M. (2023). Positive psychology interventions in medical populations: Critical issues in intervention development, testing, and implementation. Affective Science, 4(1), 59–71.

Huffman, J.C., Legler, S.R., & Boehm, J.K. (2017). Positive psychological well-being and health in patients with heart disease: A brief review. Future Cardiology, 13(5), 443–450.

Kabat-Zinn, J., Wheeler, E., & Light, T. (1998). Influence of a mindfulness meditation based stress reduction intervention on rates on skin clearing in patients. Psychosomatic Medicine, 60, 625–632.

Keng, S.L., Smoski, M.J., & Robins, C.J. (2011). Effects of mindfulness on psychological health: A review of empirical studies. Clinical Psychology Review, 31, 1041–1056.

Labarthe, D.R., Kubzansky, L.D., Boehm, J.K., Lloyd-Jones, D.M., Berry, J.D., & Seligman, M.E.P. (2016). Positive cardiovascular health: A timely convergence. Journal of the American College of Cardiology, 68(8), 860–867.

Lianov, L.S. (2024). The role of positive psychology in lifestyle medicine. American Journal of Lifestyle Medicine, 18(5), 666–670.

Lianov, L.S., Barron, G.C., Fredrickson, B.L., Hashmi, S., Klemes, A., Krishnaswami, J., Lee, J., Le Pertel, N., Matthews, J.A., Millstein, R.A., Phillips, E.M., Sannidhi, D., Purpur de Vries, P., Wallace, A., & Winter, S.J. (2020). Positive psychology in health care: Defining key stakeholders and their roles. Translational Behavioral Medicine, 10(3), 637–647.

Lianov, L.S., Fredrickson, B.L., Barron, C., Krishnaswami, J., & Wallace, A. (2019). Positive psychology in lifestyle medicine and health care: Strategies for implementation. American Journal of Lifestyle Medicine, 13(5), 480–486.

Lippman, D., Stump, M., Veazey, E., Guimarães, S.T., Rosenfeld, R., Kelly, J.H., . . . & Katz, D.L. (2024). Foundations of lifestyle medicine and its evolution. Mayo Clinic Proceedings: Innovations, Quality & Outcomes, 8(1), 97–111.

Marchand, W.R. (2012). MBSR, Mindfulness-based cognitive therapy, and Zen meditation for depression, anxiety, pain, and psychological distress. Journal of Psychiatric Practice, 18, 233–252.

Muller, R., Gertz, K.J., Molton, I.R., Terrill, A.L., Bombardier, C.H., Ehde, D.M., & Jensen, M.P. (2016). Effects of a tailored positive psychology intervention on well-being and pain in individuals with chronic pain and a physical disability: A feasibility trial. The Clinical Journal of Pain, 32(1), 32–44.

O'Boyle, C.A., Lianov, L.S., Burke, J., Frates, B., & Boniwell, I. (2023). Positive health: An emerging new construct. In J. Burke, I. Boniwell, B. Frates, L.S. Lianov, & C.A. O'Boyle (Eds.), Routledge international handbook of positive health sciences (pp. 2–23). Routledge.

Ong, N.Y., Teo, F.J.J., Ee, J.Z.Y., Yau, C.E., Thumboo, J., Tan, H.K., & Ng, Q.X. (2024). Effectiveness of mindfulness-based interventions on the well-being of healthcare workers: A systematic review and meta-analysis. General Psychiatry, 37(3), e101115.

Ryff, C.D., Singer, B.H., & Dienberg Love, G. (2004). Positive health: Connecting well–being with biology. Philosophical Transactions of the Royal Society of London. Series B: Biological Sciences, 359(1449), 1383–1394.

Scheier, M.F., & Carver, C.S. (2018). Dispositional optimism and physical health: A long look back, a quick look forward. American Psychologist, 73(9), 1082–1094.

Schiavon, C.C., Marchetti, E., Gurgel, L.G., Busnello, F.M., & Reppold, C.T. (2017). Optimism and hope in chronic disease: A systematic review. Frontiers in Psychology, 7, 237584.

Shapiro, S.L., Walsh, R., & Britton, W.B. (2003). An analysis of recent meditation research and suggestions for future directions. Journal for Meditation and Meditation Research, 3, 69–90.

Steptoe, A., Deaton, A., & Stone, A.A. (2015). Subjective wellbeing, health, and ageing. The Lancet, 385(9968), 640–648.
Townsley, A.P., Li-Wang, J., Katta, R., Townsley, A., & Li-Wang, J. (2023). Healthcare workers' well-being: A systematic review of positive psychology interventions. Cureus, 15(1) e34102.
WHO. (1948). Official records of the World Health Organization No. 2. Summary report on proceedings. World Health Organization.
Witek-Janusek, L., Albuquerque, K., Rambo Chroniak, K., Chroniak, C., Durazo-Arvizu, R., & Mathews, H. (2008). Effect of mindfulness-based stress reduction on immune function, quality of life and coping in women newly diagnosed with early stage breast cancer. Brain, Behavior, and Immunity, 22, 969–981.

Chapter 10

Positive Economic Psychology

These are momentous times for Positive Economic Psychology! Launched in 2025 as a bold new interdisciplinary field integrating Positive Psychology and Economic Psychology (Hart & Hart, 2025), it is currently experiencing a period of rapid development, exploration and cross-field collaboration, and is attracting significant interest from academics, practitioners and the general public.

> **Positive Economic Psychology:** An interdisciplinary field integrating Positive Psychology and Economic Psychology to understand and promote financial and economic wellbeing.
>
> **Economic Psychology:** An interdisciplinary domain that integrates Psychology and Economics, which examines how psychological processes shape economic thinking and behaviour and how economic circumstances affect people's lives.

This chapter charts the intellectual landscape of this emerging discipline. It begins by briefly introducing Economic Psychology and then traces the factors that gave rise to Positive Economic Psychology, clarifying its core mission, scope and guiding principles. Finally, the chapter looks ahead, considering the field's likely trajectory.

Economic Psychology

> **Behavioural Economics:** A field rooted in Economics that incorporates psychological insights to explain decision-making.

Economic Psychology is a branch of Applied Psychology and an interdisciplinary field that brings together Psychology and Economics to understand how psychological processes shape economic decisions and behaviour and, in turn, how economic circumstances influence people's lives. Ranyard and De Mello Ferreira (2018) defined it as "the science of economic mental life and behaviour" (p. 4).

DOI: 10.4324/9781032663111-14

Behavioural Economics emerged to strengthen decision-making research by integrating psychological insights into economic models (Ranyard & De Mello Ferreira, 2018). As its scope broadened to financial behaviour, markets and policy, it increasingly overlapped with Economic Psychology, generating debates around the association between the two disciplines (Cartwright, 2011). Kirchler and Hoelzl (2018) explained that Behavioural Economics and Economic Psychology share substantial intellectual territory and similar aims, but emerged from different lineages: Economic Psychology is grounded in Psychology, whereas Behavioural Economics is rooted in Economics. Hence, they differ in their philosophical assumptions, methodological preferences and conceptual framing. Nevertheless, the boundaries between them have become increasingly blurred, as Cartwright (2011, p. 11) noted: "it seems fair to say that a lot of what has historically been called Behavioural Economics would probably be more appropriately called Economic Psychology." In light of this convergence, this chapter uses the term Economic Psychology as an umbrella term encompassing contributions from both traditions.

Defining Positive Economic Psychology

Positive Economic Psychology an interdisciplinary scientific and applied field that integrates Positive Psychology and Economic Psychology. Its central aim is to advance the understanding and promotion of financial and economic wellbeing by identifying the conditions and processes that enable economic prosperity and optimal economic functioning across individuals, groups and institutions. As such, financial and economic wellbeing sit at the core of its research and practice (Hart & Hart, 2025).

In this context, financial wellbeing is defined as a construct applicable at the individual and household level, whereas economic wellbeing pertains to broader entities such as organisations, communities and nations.

The Rise of Positive Economic Psychology

Positive Economic Psychology arose as a distinct field in response to Economic Psychology's long-standing emphasis on economic difficulties, dysfunctions and deficits. A survey of the landmark texts that have shaped the discipline, such as *Heuristics and Biases* (Gilovich et al., 2002), *Predictably Irrational* (Ariely, 2008), *Why Smart People Make Big Money Mistakes and How to Correct Them* (Belsky & Gilovich, 2010), *Misbehaving* (Thaler,

2015), *Noise* (Kahneman et al., 2021), and *Nudge* (Thaler & Sunstein, 2008), alongside leading textbooks and numerous publications highlights a persistent assumption within Economic Psychology that people are poorly equipped for sound financial decision-making and prudent economic behaviour, and that these errors in economic judgement and behaviours are largely inherent, arising from cognitive and psychosocial constraints.

Echoing the goals of Positive Psychology, Positive Economic Psychology seeks to expand Economic Psychology beyond its dominant focus on financial and economic deficits and dysfunction. Hart and Hart (2025) argued that the sustained emphasis on the negative side of economic behaviour has created a marked scholarly gap: Scarce research has examined prudent and productive economic behaviour, evidence-based approaches to building wealth, or psychologically informed ways of addressing the cognitive and psychosocial constraints identified by the field. This gap has been filled by the self-help industry, where recommendations and interventions are often weakly supported by research.

This critique frames Positive Economic Psychology as a corrective movement which seeks a more balanced account of economic behaviour by attending to strengths as well as shortcomings.

The Mission of Positive Economic Psychology

The mission of Positive Economic Psychology is to reorient research and practice in Economic Psychology towards evidence-based ways of cultivating positive economic functioning, financial wellbeing and prosperity. To support this shift, Hart and Hart (2025) proposed several key aims:

- To advance new research themes that foreground effective, skilled and strengths-based economic decision-making and behaviour.
- To design and rigorously test micro-level strategies and interventions that enhance financial wellbeing.
- To inform meso- and macro-level policies that promote prudent economic behaviour and strengthen financial and economic wellbeing across individuals, households and organisations.
- To reduce economic hardship and inequality by examining and addressing disparities in opportunities and outcomes across diverse groups.
- To develop a shared language to improve clarity, communication and cumulative knowledge-building in the field.
- To integrate positive and negative perspectives within applied contexts such as Economic Counselling and Financial Planning.

These aims position Positive Economic Psychology as both a scientific agenda and an applied programme for building resilient economic lives within fairer contexts.

The Principles of Positive Economic Psychology

Hart and Hart (2025) set out a series of principles that define Positive Economic Psychology's scope, philosophical foundations, aims and key areas of focus:

> **Homo economicus:** The traditional economic idea of people acting in a rational, self-interested way in the economic domain.

- **Positive assumptions about human nature in economic contexts:** Traditional and neoclassical Economics have been shaped by the concept of ***homo economicus*** – the idea that people are rational, self-interested maximisers. Although Economic Psychology challenged this concept by highlighting the complexity of economic behaviour (Kahneman, 2011), its agenda has often implied a more pessimistic view, emphasising ingrained shortcomings, ignorance and incompetence that lead to poor outcomes. By contrast, Positive Economic Psychology adopts a strengths-based stance, viewing people as oriented towards economic growth and prosperity and capable of ethical and effective economic choices. It also holds that individuals can overcome, with intentional effort, the common cognitive and psychosocial limitations observed by Economic Psychology scholars.
- **Positive aim:** Positive Economic Psychology seeks to identify and explain what underpins positive, adaptive, effective and satisfying economic decisions and behaviours.
- **Positive agenda:** The field centres on themes such as financial wellbeing, abundance, economic resilience, grit, self-regulation, economic intelligence and financial wisdom.
- **Positive processes:** The discipline emphasises mechanisms, often built into interventions, that develop skills for achieving economic goals and fostering growth, such as financial knowledge and literacy, self-discipline, self-awareness or mindfulness.
- **Focus on applications:** Positive Economic Psychology is explicitly intervention-oriented, using research to develop tools and programmes that strengthen financial wellbeing, prosperity and economic resilience.
- **Non-clinical target population:** The field primarily serves non-clinical populations.
- **Constructive lexicon:** Economic Psychology has often relied on deficit-laden terms (bias, ignorance, error, irrationality, and financial disorders; Kahneman, 2011; Thaler, 2015), whereas Positive Economic Psychology promotes a more balanced vocabulary that makes

room for the expression, exploration and discussion of the positive facets of human economic thinking and behaviour.

- **Non-directive value stance:** The field adopts a non-paternalistic, non-prescriptive approach that prioritises self-determination and supports people's agency in pursuing their economic goals. This contrasts with the **libertarian paternalism** of **"nudge"** approaches (Thaler & Sunstein, 2008), which aims to steer people's choices towards preferred outcomes.

Libertarian paternalism: An approach that seeks to steer people towards preferred choices.

Nudge: A way of influencing decisions by altering the choice environment so that people are steered towards certain options.

These principles position Positive Economic Psychology as a generative, strengths-based complement to existing approaches, one that retains the diagnostic insights of Economic Psychology while expanding the scientific and practical agenda towards capability-building, empowerment and sustained economic wellbeing. They also provide a coherent foundation for a wider programme of research and application that the field seeks to catalyse.

Current Developments

Several lines of research already integrate concepts from Economic Psychology and Positive Psychology and sit squarely within the remit of Positive Economic Psychology:

- **Happiness Economics:** A leading example is the extensive literature on the Economics of Happiness (Frey, 2018; Easterlin, 2014), which explores how economic factors (particularly money in its various forms) relate to happiness. In contemporary studies, happiness is often operationalised as subjective wellbeing drawing on Positive Psychology concepts (Tay et al., 2018). Although the inclusion of happiness initially surprised economists (Agrawal et al., 2023), it is now routinely used

Happiness Economics: A research area examining how economic factors such as income, wealth and spending relate to happiness.

in valuing public goods, underscoring Positive Psychology's influence on public policy (Diener, 2000) and the productive interdisciplinary collaborations between Positive Psychology and Economic Psychology scholars (Kahneman et al., 1999).

Syntheses of this literature (Fisher & Frechette, 2023) suggest that the money–happiness link is typically weak to moderate and differs by national economic context. The effects of money are most pronounced under conditions of privation, with evidence of a satiation point at higher levels of resources beyond which additional money yields little additional happiness. Moreover, spending patterns often matter more than income, and relative income or wealth tends to predict happiness more strongly than absolute resources. Finally, hedonic adaptation means that happiness gains from positive financial changes (such as a pay rise) are often short-lived as people adjust to their new circumstances.

> **Heuristics and biases:** Mental shortcuts that can lead to systematic errors in judgement and decision-making.
>
> **Planning fallacy:** The tendency to underestimate the time, effort or resources needed to complete tasks or plans.

- **Optimism:** Seminal work on **heuristics and biases** showed that people (including managers, entrepreneurs and investors) often make overly optimistic forecasts in economic decisions and organisational planning (Kahneman & Tversky, 1996). Lovallo and Kahneman (2003) described "delusional optimism" as a bias that fuels the **planning fallacy**, leading individuals to underestimate the resources required to execute a task while overestimating likely returns. In high-stakes contexts, such errors can contribute to dire organisational and market consequences (Kahneman & Tversky, 1996). However, in his later work, Kahneman (2011) drew on Positive Psychology research evidence on the benefits of optimism and argued that "when action is needed, optimism, even if the mildly delusional variety, may be a good thing" (Kahneman, 2011, p. 256). This evidence base indicates that optimism is associated with better physical health, stronger coping and social support, and higher psychological wellbeing and performance across domains including education, work and finance (Carver & Scheier, 2014; Forgeard & Seligman, 2012; Scheier & Carver, 2018). The tension between Lovallo and Kahneman's (2003) account and the wider evidence underscores the need for further research to distinguish adaptive optimism from maladaptive over-optimism.

- **Financial wellbeing:** A further, relatively nascent concept within the remit of Positive Economic Psychology is financial wellbeing. The CFPB (2017, p. 6) defined it as "a state of being wherein a person can fully meet current and ongoing financial obligations, can feel secure in their financial future, and is able to make choices that allow them to enjoy life." Yet, there is no agreed definition as Garcia-Mata and Zeron-Felix (2022) identified 18 competing definitions, and Riitsalu et al. (2023) noted the lack of consensus. Only one definition (Salignac et al., 2020) explicitly draws on Positive Psychology by defining financial wellbeing as "how happy people are with their current financial situation, and their ability to function economically" (p. 1583). This conceptual fragmentation is mirrored in diverse measurement approaches spanning objective and subjective indicators and related constructs, with no measure adopting Positive Psychology's wellbeing measurement approach.

  Prudent financial behaviour: Careful, thoughtful and adaptive financial behaviour that supports long-term wellbeing and stability.

  Despite these challenges, research has expanded rapidly, largely examining predictors of financial wellbeing rather than outcomes. This body of research suggests that multiple factors can predict financial wellbeing, with **prudent financial behaviour** emerging as a central predictor, shaped by personality traits, skills and financial literacy, economic conditions and wider socio-economic and policy contexts (Mahendru et al., 2022).

- **Boosting strategies:** Closely aligned with Positive Psychology's humanistic orientation, Hertwig and Grüne-Yanoff's (2021) boosting approach aims to strengthen people's capacities to make their own decisions. Unlike nudges, which steer choices by altering the decision environment, boosts prioritise empowerment and agency through education, alongside guidance that builds competence and self-sufficiency in economic life. Although the evidence base remains limited, findings are encouraging: Boosts have been shown to improve health decision-making (Hertwig & Grüne-Yanoff, 2017), strengthen digital judgements (Gerber et al., 2018), and enhance statistical understanding (Gigerenzer et al., 2007), though they are yet to be tested in the financial domain.

  Boosting: An approach that aims to strengthen people's own decision-making competences through education, guidance and skill-building.

- **Financial literacy:** Consistent with the boosting perspective, research on financial literacy has expanded sharply in recent decades (Kaiser &

> **Financial literacy:** Knowledge and understanding that help people make informed financial decisions.

Lusardi, 2024). However, outcomes are mixed, with some interventions producing only modest effects on financial behaviour (Fernandes et al., 2014; Kaiser et al., 2022). Recent work informed by Positive Psychology suggest stronger effects when programmes adopt a self-determined approach, build self-awareness, incorporate psychoeducation and motivational techniques, and account for readiness to change (Kaiser & Lusardi, 2024; Peeters et al., 2016).

- **Applications of Positive Psychology Interventions:** Klontz et al. (2023) recommend embedding several evidence-based Positive Psychology Interventions in Financial Planning client-facing contexts, but do not report evidence of successful implementation. To date, only one published multi-component positive financial intervention has been tested (Surana, 2025). It combines expressive writing about money, a financial gratitude exercise, meditation on money attitudes, charitable giving and future-oriented reflection, and aims to improve life satisfaction, self-efficacy, saving behaviour, financial anxiety and maladaptive money beliefs. The study reported significant improvements in most outcomes. This narrow evidence base underscores a clear gap that the new discipline is well placed to address.

These examples indicate that Positive Psychology and Economic Psychology are already meaningfully integrated. A key task for Positive Economic Psychology, therefore, is to consolidate these established strands, advance them and amalgamate them into a coherent body of knowledge.

Future Possibilities and Challenges

As a new discipline, Positive Economic Psychology faces the early task of defining its identity, building credibility and developing a robust evidence base, while also generating momentum, attracting scholars and demonstrating clear practical value. Its interdisciplinary character is a key strength, yet it also brings predictable challenges, reflecting differences in intellectual traditions, methodological preferences and underlying assumptions across the contributing fields.

Building on the strengths and limitations of both parent disciplines, the new discipline is well placed to combine what each does best across three areas:

- **A more balanced view of human capability:** Economic Psychology often emphasises bias, poor judgement and financial mistakes, while

Positive Psychology highlights strengths, growth and potential. Positive Economic Psychology brings these together, recognising both human limitations and the capacity to develop adaptive financial behaviours.
- **A broader lens:** Positive Psychology has been criticised for focusing too heavily on individual traits and overlooking structural constraints. By drawing on Economic Psychology's micro-, meso- and macro-level perspective, Positive Economic Psychology links personal agency with social, economic and policy realities.
- **Novel interventions:** Positive Psychology offers practical interventions, whereas Economic Psychology has been stronger at explaining behaviour than changing it. Positive Economic Psychology combines these strengths to design interventions that improve financial and economic wellbeing at the level of individuals, communities and systems.

Taken together, these features suggest that Positive Economic Psychology has significant promise: It can offer a distinctive framework for understanding and improving economic life in ways that are both scientifically grounded and practically relevant. Its longer-term contribution will depend on whether it can translate this integrative promise into coherent theory, credible evidence and interventions that are responsive to both human strengths and real-world constraints.

Conclusion

This chapter examined Positive Economic Psychology, an emerging discipline at the intersection of Positive Psychology and Economic Psychology. Its distinctive contribution is a clear commitment to advancing financial and economic wellbeing through interdisciplinary research and application. The field seeks to address gaps in its parent disciplines by developing underexplored themes, refining psychological constructs and designing innovative interventions.

Positive Economic Psychology is distinguished by its foundational view of human nature: Individuals are seen as capable of sound and ethical economic decisions, motivated by growth, prosperity and prosocial contribution. In contrast to deficit-oriented accounts and the libertarian paternalism often associated with Economic Psychology, it adopts constructive terminology, reframes financial challenges as manageable and foregrounds strengths and potential. It also takes a non-directive stance, prioritising agency over prescription while promoting adaptive financial behaviour, responsible organisational practice and empowering policy across individuals and communities.

Looking ahead, the field appears poised for growth, but will need to navigate challenges such as methodological integration, interdisciplinary collaboration and sustained relevance to real-world economic conditions.

Overall, Positive Economic Psychology offers a bold framework for understanding economic behaviour in relation to wellbeing, yet its development will require careful navigation to become a robust, impactful and genuinely transdisciplinary field.

References

Agrawal, S., Sharma, N., Bruni, M.E., & Iazzolino, G. (2023). Happiness economics: Discovering future research trends through a systematic literature review. Journal of Cleaner Production, 137860.
Ariely, D. (2008). Predictably irrational. HarperCollins.
Belsky, G., & Gilovich, T. (2010). Why smart people make big money mistakes and how to correct them. Simon and Schuster.
Cartwright, E. (2011). Behavioral economics. Routledge.
Carver, C.S., & Scheier, M.F. (2014). Dispositional optimism. Trends in Cognitive Sciences, 18(6), 293–299.
CFPB. (2017). CFPB financial well-being scale. Consumer Financial Protection Bureau.
Diener, E. (2000). Subjective well-being: The science of happiness and a proposal for a national index. American Psychologist, 55(1), 34–43.
Easterlin, R.A. (2014). Happiness and economic growth – the evidence. In W. Glatzer, L. Crayamfield, V. Moller, & M. Rojas (Eds.), Global handbook of quality of life (pp. 283–299). Springer.
Fernandes, D., Lynch Jr, J.G., & Netemeyer, R.G. (2014). Financial literacy, financial education, and downstream financial behaviors. Management Science, 60(8), 1861–1883.
Fisher, J., & Frechette, M. (2023). One more time, does money buy happiness? Applied Research in Quality of Life, 18(6), 3089–3110.
Forgeard, M.J.C., & Seligman, M.E.P. (2012). Seeing the glass half full: A review of the causes and consequences of optimism. Pratiques Psychologiques, 18(2), 107–120.
Frey, B.S. (2018). Economics of happiness. Springer.
Garcia-Mata, O., & Zeron-Felix, M. (2022). A review of the theoretical foundations of financial well-being. International Review of Economics, 69(2), 145–176.
Gerber, N., Gerber, P., & Volkamer, M. (2018). Explaining the privacy paradox: A systematic review of literature investigating privacy attitude and behavior. Computers & Security, 77, 226–261.
Gigerenzer, G., Gaissmaier, W., Kurz-Milcke, E., Schwartz, L.M., & Woloshin, S. (2007). Helping doctors and patients make sense of health statistics. Psychological Science in the Public Interest, 8(2), 53–96.
Gilovich, T., Griffin, D., & Kahneman, D. (Eds.). (2002). Heuristics and biases. Cambridge University Press.
Hart, R., & Hart, D. (2025). New frontier: Positive economic psychology. Open Psychology, 7(1), 20250004.
Hertwig, R., & Grüne-Yanoff, T. (2017). Nudging and boosting: Steering or empowering good decisions. Perspectives on Psychological Science, 12(6), 973–986.

Hertwig, R., & Grüne-Yanoff, T. (2021). Boosting and nudging: Two paths toward better financial decisions. In R. Viale, U, Filotto, B. Alemanni, & S. Mousavi (Eds.), Financial education and risk literacy (pp. 150–180). Edward Elgar Publishing.
Kahneman, D. (2011). Thinking fast and slow. Straus and Giroux.
Kahneman, D., Diener, E., & Schwarz, N. (Eds.). (1999). Well-being. Russell Sage Foundation.
Kahneman, D., Sibony, O., & Sunstein, C.R. (2021). Noise. Hachette.
Kahneman, D., & Tversky, A. (1996). On the reality of cognitive illusions. Psychological Review, 103(3), 582–591.
Kaiser, T., & Lusardi, A. (2024). Financial literacy and financial education: An overview. National Bureau of Economic Research, Working Paper 32355. NBER.
Kaiser, T., Lusardi, A., Menkhoff, L., & Urban, C. (2022). Financial education affects financial knowledge and downstream behaviors. Journal of Financial Economics, 145(2), 255–272.
Kirchler, E., & Hoelzl, E. (2018). Economic psychology: An introduction. Cambridge University Press.
Klontz, B., Chaffin, C.R., & Klontz, T. (2023). Psychology of financial planning: The practitioner's guide to money and behavior. John Wiley & Sons.
Lovallo, D., & Kahneman, D. (2003). Delusions of success: How optimism undermines executives' decisions. Harvard Business Review, 56–63.
Mahendru, M., Sharma, G.D., Pereira, V., Gupta, M., & Mundi, H.S. (2022). Is it all about money honey? Analyzing and mapping financial well-being research and identifying future research agenda. Journal of Business Research, 150, 417–436.
Peeters, N., Rijk, K., Soetens, B., Storms, B., & Hermans, K. (2016). Identifying successful elements for financial education: A literature review. CEBUD Working paper 1601. CEBUD.
Ranyard, R., & De Mello Ferreira, V.R. (2018). Introduction to economic psychology: The science of economic mental life and behavior. In R. Ranyard (Ed.), Economic psychology (pp. 3–18). Wiley.
Riitsalu, L., Atkinson, A., & Pello, R. (2023). The bottlenecks in making sense of financial well-being. International Journal of Social Economics, 50(10), 1402–1422.
Salignac, F., Hamilton, M., Noone, J., Marjolin, A., & Muir, K. (2020). Conceptualizing financial wellbeing: An ecological life-course approach. Journal of Happiness Studies, 21, 1581–1602.
Scheier, M.F., & Carver, C S. (2018). Dispositional optimism and physical health: A long look back, a quick look forward. American Psychologist, 73(9), 1082–1094.
Surana, P. (2025). Manage you money manage your mind. Robinsons.
Tay, L., Zyphur, M., & Batz, C.L. (2018). Income and subjective well-being: Review, synthesis, and future research. In E. Diener, S. Oishi, & L. Tay (Eds.), Handbook of well-being. DEF Publishers.
Thaler, R.H. (2015). Misbehaving. WW Norton & Company.
Thaler, R.H., & Sunstein, C. R. (2008). Nudge. Yale University Press.

Section 5

Key Methods

This Section in Summary

Chapter 11: Research Methods in Positive Psychology

- Positive Psychology broadly inherits the scholarly aims and methodological traditions of Psychology as its parent discipline, while adapting them to its own distinctive research questions;
- Quantitative methods remain dominant in the field, supported by widely used measures of central constructs and a strong reliance on statistical analysis;
- Experimental designs are commonly used to assess the effectiveness of interventions;
- Large-scale survey research provides insight at the population level;
- Qualitative approaches, although less prominent, add contextual depth through detailed analysis of spoken and written accounts;
- Mixed-methods designs are used when complex questions call for the integration of numerical and narrative forms of evidence;
- In addition to primary empirical studies, theoretical work and reviews synthesise evidence, refine conceptual frameworks and shape future research agendas;
- Research in Positive Psychology, especially quantitative, experimental, and cross-sectional work, has been the subject of sustained critique.

DOI: 10.4324/9781032663111-15

Chapter 11

Research Methods in Positive Psychology

Positive Psychology has matured into a wide-ranging scientific and applied enterprise, concerned with understanding and promoting wellbeing across individuals and systems, with a distinct emphasis on positive qualities, processes and outcomes. As the field has expanded, so too has the diversity of its research methods repertoire – from foundational measurement of core constructs to experimental and longitudinal studies testing interventions, to population-level analyses that inform policy and practice.

This chapter provides an overview of the research methods commonly applied by scholars in the field, situating them within the broader traditions of Psychology while highlighting the distinctive demands that arise when studying complex, context-sensitive aspects of human flourishing. The chapter maps the main research designs, measurement strategies and analytical approaches used in the field, highlighting recurring methodological critiques.

Research Methods: An Overview

Scientific research is a process of posing and answering questions about the world, with the central aim of generating new knowledge. Creswell (2014) characterised research as a systematic, stepwise endeavour that involves collecting information, analysing it, producing new knowledge and disseminating findings.

Scientific inquiry in the social sciences is characterised by three core features (Stanovich, 2013):

- **Systematic empiricism:** Scientific work is grounded in observation. Social scientists learn about the world by systematically searching, recording and analysing observations of events and phenomena.
- **Empirical questions:** These are questions about how the world operates that can be addressed through systematic observation.

DOI: 10.4324/9781032663111-16

- **Public knowledge:** By formulating empirical questions, conducting systematic observations and drawing conclusions, scientists generate new knowledge, with an accompanying responsibility to disseminate findings for the wider public good.

Within Psychology, scientific research has four interrelated goals (Danziger, 1994):

- To describe behaviours;
- To be able to make predictions about future behaviours;
- To be able to provide explanations of behaviours;
- To apply the knowledge learned through research to change people's lives for the better.

> **Empirical research:** Research based on systematic observation, measurement or experience rather than on opinion, theory alone or speculation.

Positive Psychology largely draws on the aims and methodological traditions of its parent discipline, Psychology, tailoring them to its distinctive research aims (Ong & Van Dulmen, 2007). Quantitative methods dominate the field, supported by widely used measures of key constructs and statistical analyses, while experimental designs are most often employed to evaluate interventions. Policy-oriented scholarship further extends the field's influence beyond academia, while large-scale surveys strengthen its evidence base by offering population-level insights. Qualitative approaches, though less prominent, contribute contextual richness through in-depth analysis of spoken or written texts, and mixed-methods designs are adopted where complex questions warrant the integration of numerical and narrative evidence. Beyond primary empirical research, theoretical contributions and reviews synthesise findings, refine conceptual frameworks and help to shape future research agendas. The sections that follow briefly outline these approaches.

Quantitative Research Methods

Quantitative methods are central to Positive Psychology, reflecting the field's commitment to measurement, hypothesis testing and cumulative evidence-building. These are systematic approaches that investigate research questions by collecting numerical data and analysing it using statistical techniques to describe patterns, test hypotheses and estimate relationships, effects or differences between groups. They typically involve structured designs (such as experiments, surveys or observational studies), standardised instruments (questionnaires with rating scales, tests or behavioural counts) and data collection and analysis procedures aimed at producing findings that are reliable, replicable and, depending on the sampling and design, generalisable to a wider population (Goodwin & Goodwin, 2016).

Operationalisation: The process of defining a concept in a specific, measurable way for research purposes.

Psychometric assessment: The process of testing whether a measure is reliable, valid and appropriate for assessing a construct.

Self-report measure: A measure in which participants provide information about their own thoughts, feelings or behaviour, usually through questionnaires.

Much of the quantitative enterprise begins with psychometric **operationalisation** of core constructs. One of the field's most significant achievements has been the development of a wide range of validated questionnaires designed to assess constructs such as psychological wellbeing (Butler & Kern, 2016), meaning (MacDonald et al., 2012) and character strengths (Niemiec, 2017) – measures that mostly did not exist before the emergence of Positive Psychology. This involved extensive scale development and validation work. Most of the measures used by scholars are self-report tools that collect subjective data, with fewer using informant ratings or objective data such as physiological measures, financial data or behavioural reports.

A key critique directed at these self-report scales is that they are vulnerable to social desirability, recall biases, mood-congruent responding and reference-group effects. Another critique is that closely related constructs are often confused and conflated, which can inform scale development and undermine comparisons across studies, complicating synthesis and cumulative science (Gaffaney & Donaldson, 2025).

An alternative data collection method applied by scholars in the field to avoid the limitations of questionnaires is Experience Sampling Methods (ESM) (Pavot, 2018), which capture moment-to-moment experiences in daily life through mobile technology and allow fine-grained modelling of affective, cognitive or behavioural patterns. These are well suited to constructs that are inherently dynamic (such as emotional experiences, flow, relational exchanges and meaning-making).

A wide range of **quantitative research** designs are used. Cross-sectional survey studies remain common for mapping correlations and testing theoretically derived predictive models using regression-based approaches, including **mediation** and **moderation analyses**. Examples of this line of work include examining the associations between personality traits and psychological wellbeing (see Chapter 3) (Ryff, 2018), considering whether meaning in life predicts physical health (Cross et al., 2018) and investigating the intricate association between income and happiness (see Chapter 4) (Tay et al., 2018). Researchers often use Structural Equation Modelling (SEM), a multivariate statistical framework for analysing the relationships between variables, that enables researchers to infer cause-and-effect relationships (Lin & Yeh, 2014).

Quantitative research: Research that uses numerical data and statistical analysis to test hypotheses, describe patterns or estimate relationships.

Correlation: A statistical relationship showing that two variables tend to change together, without necessarily meaning that one causes the other.

Mediation analysis: A statistical approach used to test whether the effect of one variable on another operates through a third variable.

Moderation analysis: A statistical approach used to test whether the strength or direction of a relationship depends on another variable.

Cross-sectional analyses: A study that collects data at one point in time, often used to examine correlations between variables.

Alongside this, the field includes comparative work that asks whether the same patterns hold across different groups, examining differences in average levels of variables such as psychological wellbeing, optimism and resilience, and whether the predictors of these variables operate similarly or differently across groups (Veenhoven, 2012).

Increasingly, researchers also employ longitudinal designs to examine temporal dynamics and change processes, with research on the benefits of happiness providing a prime example (Lyubomirsky et al., 2005a).

Experimental research, including **quasi-experimental designs** and randomised controlled trials, is especially prominent in evaluating interventions, with most experiments conducted in laboratory settings and comparatively fewer carried out in real-world environments (such as workplaces, schools or communities) (see Chapter 5). Classic experimental paradigms test whether specific activities such as writing a gratitude diary (Emmons & Shelton, 2002), savouring positive life experiences (Bryant & Veroff, 2017) or performing acts of kindness (Curry et al., 2018) produce improvements in a selected outcome. Intervention research also extends to multi-session programmes, including school-based resilience programmes (Gillham et al., 2013), mindfulness training (Kabat-Zinn, 2003) and clinically adjacent approaches such as Wellbeing Therapy (Fava, 2016). Methodologically, well-conducted intervention studies use randomised controlled trials that incorporate randomisation, active control groups and adequate follow-up periods.

At a larger scale, population surveys contribute complementary evidence by enabling cross-national and policy-relevant analyses, as reflected in work that uses happiness or wellbeing indicators to inform public decision-making. Much of this evidence comes from large, repeated national or international surveys, such as the Gallup (2024) World Poll, the World Happiness Report (Helliwell et al., 2025), and the UK Census (ONS, 2019) which collects nationally representative data (see Chapter 3 and 4).

This substantial body of quantitative research has attracted sustained methodological critique. A considerable proportion of the literature remains cross-sectional, which makes it difficult to disentangle causes from consequences. As a result, claims about effects can exceed what the evidence is currently able to support (Van Zyl et al., 2024). Although Positive Psychology Interventions represent one of the field's flagship areas, the quality of trials varies considerably, raising concerns about their robustness, durability and practical significance, while the exploration of mechanisms and processes of change remains weak (Van Zyl et al., 2019). In addition, measures developed in Western contexts often encounter problems of translation and differing cultural norms surrounding the phenomena under investigation, which can weaken comparability across settings (Van Zyl et al., 2024). Relatedly, much of the evidence still derives from **WEIRD samples** (Western, Educated, Industrialised,

Longitudinal design: A research design that follows participants over time in order to examine change, development or temporal patterns.

Cross-sectional analyses: A study that collects data at one point in time, often used to examine correlations between variables.

Experimental design: A research design in which a researcher manipulates one or more variables to examine their effects on outcomes.

Quasi-experimental design: A design that tests intervention effects without full random assignment to conditions.

Randomised controlled trial: An experimental design in which participants are randomly allocated to conditions, often used to test interventions.

WEIRD populations: Samples drawn mainly from Western, Educated, Industrialised, Rich and Democratic populations, which may limit the broader applicability of findings.

Rich and Democratic; Henrich et al., 2010), frequently involving university students or otherwise relatively advantaged populations, which may bias conclusions about what works and for whom (Van Zyl et al., 2024). Finally, like other areas of Psychology, Positive Psychology research has also been subject to critiques concerning **publication bias** and **replicability** (see below).

Publication bias: The tendency for studies with statistically significant or theory-supporting results to be more likely to be published than null or contradictory findings.

Replicability: The extent to which research findings can be reproduced in new studies.

These critiques clarify what is required for quantitative research to sustain a credible and socially relevant evidence base. Continued progress depends on stronger design choices, greater transparency, clearer construct definitions and measurement standards, broader sampling and a more explicit integration of structural and cultural contexts into theory, methods and interpretation.

The Replicability Crisis

The **replicability crisis** in Psychology refers to the finding that many published psychological studies cannot be reproduced with similar results when the same methods are used again, raising concerns about the reliability of the field's evidence base (Nosek et al., 2022). Positive Psychology has not been insulated from Psychology's broader replicability challenges, underscoring the need for transparency and stronger statistical practices.

Replicability crisis: The recognition that many published psychological findings cannot be reproduced reliably when studies are repeated.

Qualitative Research Methods

Qualitative research in Positive Psychology provides an essential complement to the field's predominantly quantitative tradition. Whereas quantitative methods typically prioritise measurement, prediction and causal inference, qualitative research methods are approaches used to explore how people make sense of their experiences, focusing on meaning, context and process rather than numerical measurement. They typically involve collecting rich, detailed data, most often words, texts, images or observations, through techniques such as interviews, **focus groups**, participant observation, diaries, open-ended questionnaires and analysis of documents or media posts. Researchers then interpret patterns in the data using analytic approaches such as **Thematic Analysis**, **Grounded Theory**, **Narrative Analysis**, Discourse Analysis or **Interpretative Phenomenological Analysis**, aiming to develop nuanced descriptions or theory (Creswell, 2014).

In general, qualitative work prioritises depth over breadth and detail over broad depiction. Data collection and analysis are flexible and iterative (data collection and analysis often inform each other) and pay close attention to reflexivity (how the researcher's role and assumptions shape the study).

A range of qualitative designs are used in Positive Psychology. Semi-structured interviews are common as a data collection method, allowing researchers to explore lived experience. Interview-based work has been especially valuable for investigating complex phenomena such as flow (Csikszentmihalyi, 2014) and posttraumatic growth (Hefferon, 2012), where the subjective texture of experience and the language people use provide important theoretical

Qualitative research: Research that explores meaning, experience and context using text-based data, such as interviews, texts or observations.

Focus group: A qualitative research method in which a small group of participants discuss a topic so that researchers can explore their views, experiences and shared meanings.

Thematic Analysis: A qualitative method used to identify and interpret recurring patterns or themes in data.

Grounded Theory: A qualitative approach that develops theory inductively from patterns found in the data.

Narrative Analysis: A qualitative approach that examines how people construct meaning through stories and personal accounts.

Interpretative Phenomenological Analysis (IPA): A qualitative approach focused on how individuals make sense of lived experiences.

Reflexivity: Awareness of how the researcher's own assumptions, role and perspective may shape the research process and interpretation.

> **Document analyses:** Systematic analysis of written documents to derive a mapping of key themes.

insights. Focus groups have been used to examine shared experiences or meanings, for example, how groups understand resilience (Matheson et al., 2016) or social support (Wong et al., 2014). **Document analyses** have been used to investigate what the term "positive" means in early Positive Psychology publications (Pawelski, 2016), how wellbeing is framed in policy (Higgins & Goodall, 2021), and the critique voiced against Positive Psychology (Van Zyl et al., 2023). Other types of text analyses have been used to explore optimistic and pessimistic thinking styles in social media posts (Manley, 2016), and how parents perceive their children's happiness and strengths (Park & Peterson, 2006).

Critics have argued that quantitative Positive Psychology research can overemphasise intra-individual factors while giving insufficient attention to structural conditions such as inequality, discrimination, labour markets and access to resources. This can lead to incomplete explanations and, in applied contexts, interventions that are misaligned with real-world constraints (Lomas & VanderWeele, 2023). Qualitative studies can help address this issue by capturing people's lived experiences and illuminating how these contextual factors shape their lives.

> **Triangulation:** The use of multiple methods, sources or perspectives to strengthen the credibility of research findings.

Methodological rigour in qualitative research relies on transparent sampling rationales, systematic analytic procedures, reflexivity about researcher assumptions and credibility checks such as **triangulation**, audit trails and participant validation where appropriate.

Used thoughtfully, qualitative research strengthens the Positive Psychology research enterprise by deepening the understanding of people's lived experiences and by highlighting depth and nuance not captured in quantitative research. It can also be used to enhance conceptual clarity and highlight components of concepts or models. Mechanism analysis is another benefit of qualitative inquiry, and it can also improve cultural and contextual sensitivity, enriching the evidential base that informs theory, intervention and policy.

Mixed-Methods

Mixed-methods research occupies an important place in Positive Psychology since many of its central phenomena, such as wellbeing, meaning, strengths, resilience and optimism, are measurable as well as deeply subjective and experiential. Mixed-methods integrate quantitative and qualitative approaches within a single programme of inquiry, enabling researchers to combine breadth (prevalence, effect sizes and predictive models) with depth (lived experiences, mechanisms, meaning making and contextual influences) (Creswell, 2014). In Positive Psychology, this integration is particularly valuable for strengthening inference, improving construct validity and producing findings that are both theoretically informative and practically actionable.

Mixed-methods research: Research that combines quantitative and qualitative approaches within one study or programme of inquiry.

A common starting point in the use of mixed-methods is the decision about how the methods will be combined and how they inform and complement each other. In scale development, quantitative scale development can be enriched by conducting preliminary qualitative work that clarifies how participants understand a construct, which indicators feel meaningful and how cultural or contextual factors shape interpretation. For example, in developing a measure for flow, interviews were first conducted to facilitate the creation of questionnaire items (Csikszentmihalyi, 2014). This is followed by quantitative testing using factor analysis, validity and reliability assessment and measurement invariance. This sequence helps reduce the risk that standardised measures inadvertently reflect narrow or culturally specific assumptions.

Mixed-methods are also widely used in intervention research. Quantitative components typically assess outcomes and effect sizes using experimental designs. Qualitative components can explore acceptability, engagement, perceived mechanisms of change and contextual enablers or barriers, and therefore play a key role in the initial testing of new interventions. They can also be used summatively to understand engagement and unintended consequences, issues that may not be apparent in outcome measures (Walsh et al., 2018; Hoffmann et al., 2023).

Classic mixed-methods studies illustrate the value of combining narrative indicators with quantitative outcomes. For example, in the renowned nun study, Danner et al. (2001) analysed the nuns' diaries to assess the emotional tone of entries, and this qualitative analysis was then quantified and assessed for its association with later-life outcomes collected through surveys, including health indicators and longevity. Similarly, Harker and Keltner (2001) analysed women's types of smiles in their yearbook photos, and this analysis was then linked to data collected through surveys that examined their wellbeing, social life, marital status and satisfaction. More recent work (Cebral-Loureda et al., 2023) used text mining analysis of Twitter posts to examine human flourishing. These multimodal approaches demonstrate how qualitative indicators can complement quantitative models.

Mixed-methods research also responds directly to methodological critiques of the field. By moving beyond exclusive reliance on self-report scales and cross-sectional associations, mixed-methods can provide richer evidence about processes, cultural meanings and structural influences (Van Zyl et al., 2023). However, high-quality mixed-methods work requires explicit integration, coherence between research questions and design choices and sufficient expertise across methods. Rigour also depends on transparent analytic procedures, careful sampling and an integration strategy that makes clear how the combined evidence supports conclusions.

When designed with genuine integration, mixed-methods studies can sharpen conceptual clarity, strengthen intervention development and produce evidence that is both empirically robust and practically meaningful.

Publication Bias

Publication bias in Psychology refers to the tendency for studies with statistically significant, novel or theory-supporting results to be more likely to be written up, submitted, accepted and published than studies reporting null, negative or contradictory findings. This creates a distorted scientific literature in which the published evidence can make effects appear stronger, more consistent, and more reliable than they actually are (Francis, 2012).

Theoretical Research and Reviews

> **Theoretical research:** Research that develops concepts, models and explanatory frameworks rather than collecting primary data.

Theoretical research is a core pillar of Positive Psychology, providing the conceptual scaffolding that organises empirical findings, clarifies key constructs and guides the development of interventions and policy applications. While the field is often associated with measurement and intervention studies, its progress depends equally on theory-building. For example, specifying what psychological wellbeing (Ryff, 2018), resilience (Long & Bonanno, 2018), character strengths (Peterson & Seligman, 2004) or mindsets (Dweck, 2017) mean, and unpacking the key components of such concepts, identifying mechanisms that explain how interventions lead to cognitive or behavioural changes (Layous & Lyubomirsky, 2014), and articulating testable theories that can be examined across contexts and populations. Examples include theories that explain how flow emerges (Csikszentmihalyi, 2014), what determines happiness (Lyubomirsky et al., 2005b), and Fredrickson's (2001) Broaden-and-Build Theory of positive emotions.

Theoretical research also includes conceptual or critical work and model-building that synthesise evidence to propose new frameworks or refine existing ones. Examples include Lomas et al.'s (2024) work on the conceptualisation on wellbeing and Hart and Hart's (2026) work on decluttering the work/er wellbeing literature.

It also includes programme-building scholarship that identifies research priorities, settles between competing models and proposes standards for evidence and application. Examples include Linley et al.'s (2006) paper on the future of Positive Psychology, Van Zyl (2025) responses to the critiques on Positive Psychology and Lomas et al.'s (2020) analysis of the third wave in Positive Psychology. In this sense, theoretical work functions as the connective tissue of the discipline, enabling cumulative knowledge. These frameworks, in turn, stimulate a large body of research, illustrating how theory can generate shared constructs and hypotheses that anchor a diverse research agenda.

Reviews are also central to the field, with varied types often applied by scholars in the field. **Narrative reviews** are commonly used in Positive Psychology. They describe and appraise previous work but do not describe the specific methods by which the reviewed studies were identified, selected and evaluated. They are often used to provide overviews, discussions and critiques of previous work, clarify concepts, identify current gaps in knowledge or serve as a rationale for new research. Examples include Duncan et al.'s (2021) on hope in the context of lifestyle medicine and Sinclair et al.'s (2020) review of the dangers of positivity in the context of domestic abuse. One of their limitations is that biases occurring in the selection and assessment of the literature remain unspecified.

> **Narrative reviews:** A review that summarises and discusses a body of research without using a fully systematic search and selection procedure.
>
> **Systematic review:** A review of a body of research that uses systematic methods to search for, select and critically analyse relevant studies.

Systematic reviews are a type of literature review that systematically collects and critically analyses multiple research papers in order to offer readers an overview of a topic, a summary of findings or to enable researchers to reach a conclusion regarding the usefulness or effectiveness of a concept, a questionnaire or an intervention. Allen et al.'s (2021) review of interventions that combine mindfulness and positive activities and Yan et al.'s (2020) review of strengths interventions in people with chronic illnesses exemplify this type of review. A systematic review is often confined to quantitative studies, although at times it may include qualitative research (meta-synthesis).

Meta-analyses are quantitative evidence-synthesis methods that statistically combine results from multiple empirical studies addressing a related psychological question to estimate an overall effect. They are commonly used to summarise the effects of interventions. For example, Curry et al. (2018) examined the effects of kindness interventions, Davis et al. (2016) investigated the effects of gratitude interventions, whereas Bolier et al.'s (2013) synthesised evidence on a variety of Positive Psychology Interventions. Meta-analysis typically involves a systematic search and selection of studies, extraction of effect sizes and the use of weighting to compute a pooled estimate, alongside confidence intervals and tests of heterogeneity to examine whether effects vary across studies.

Meta-analyses: A quantitative review method that statistically combines results from multiple studies to estimate an overall effect.

Scoping reviews synthesise research evidence and are often used to categorise or group existing literature in a given field and characterise it in terms of its nature, features and volume. Scoping reviews offer an assessment of the potential size and scope of the available body of literature on a particular topic or in a particular field. They can be used to clarify working definitions and conceptual boundaries of a topic or field, or to identify gaps in the existing literature (Tricco et al., 2016). Examples include Rusk and Waters' (2013) analysis of the size, reach, impact and breadth of Positive Psychology research and the mapping of its key topics (see Chapter 2) and Wang et al.'s (2023) bibliometric analysis of Positive Psychology research in the past decade.

Scoping review: A review used to map the size, scope and characteristics of research on a topic.

Review of reviews: A systematic synthesis of findings from multiple existing reviews or meta-analyses on the same topic to provide an overarching summary of the evidence.

A review of reviews is a type of evidence synthesis that systematically collects, appraises, and summarises findings from multiple existing reviews. For instance, Carr et al. (2024) conducted a mega-analysis of meta-analyses to assess the impact of Positive Psychology Interventions, whereas Kaleta et al. (2025) conducted a review of reviews on the effects of nature-based interventions. Its purpose is to provide a high-level map of what is known, where results converge or conflict across reviews and an assessment of the methodological quality of the included reviews (Grant & Booth, 2009).

Conclusion

This chapter has outlined the principal research methods that underpin Positive Psychology, spanning quantitative designs, qualitative inquiry, mixed-methods, theoretical scholarship and policy research grounded in large-scale surveys. Taken together, these approaches reflect a field that has moved beyond early conceptual enthusiasm to build an increasingly diverse methodological repertoire capable of addressing questions about positive experiences, traits, cognitions, emotions and behaviours across varied contexts and levels of analysis.

At the same time, the chapter has highlighted methodological challenges that continue to shape the field's credibility and future direction. These critiques are best understood not as reasons to retreat from Positive Psychology's agenda, but as prompts to refine it through stronger designs.

Looking ahead, the methodological development of Positive Psychology will be central to its scientific and societal impact. The field is well positioned to strengthen cumulative knowledge by embedding novel methods. By doing so, the field can continue to mature as a rigorous, integrative and practically relevant science of human flourishing.

References

Allen, J.G., Romate, J., & Rajkumar, E. (2021). Mindfulness-based positive psychology interventions: A systematic review. BMC Psychology, 9(1), 116.

Bolier, L., Haverman, M., Westerhof, G., Riper, H., Smit, F., & Bohlmeijer, E. (2013). Positive psychology interventions: A meta-analysis of randomized controlled studies. BMC Public Health, (13), 119.

Bryant, F.B., & Veroff, J. (2017). Savoring. Psychology Press.

Butler, J., & Kern, M.L. (2016). The PERMA-profiler: A brief multidimensional measure of flourishing. International Journal of Wellbeing, 6(3), 1–48.

Carr, A., Finneran, L., Boyd, C., Shirey, C., Canning, C., Stafford, O., Lyons, J. Cullen, K., Predergast, C., Corbett, C., Drumm, C., & Burke, T. (2024). The evidence-base for positive psychology interventions: A mega-analysis of meta-analyses. The Journal of Positive Psychology, 19(2), 191–205.

Cebral-Loureda, M., Hernández-Baqueiro, A., & Tamés-Muñoz, E. (2023). A text mining analysis of human flourishing on Twitter. Scientific Reports, 13(1), 3403.

Creswell, J.W. (2014). Research design (4th ed.). Sage.

Cross, M.P., Hofschneider, L., Grimm, M., & Pressman, S.D. (2018). Subjective well-being and physical health. In E. Diener, S. Oishi, & L. Tay (Eds.), Handbook of well-being. DEF Publishers.
Csikszentmihalyi, M. (2014). Flow and the foundations of positive psychology: The collected works of Mihaly Csikszentmihalyi. Springer.
Curry, O.S., Rowland, L.A., Van Lissa, C.J., Zlotowitz, S., McAlaney, J., & Whitehouse, H. (2018). Happy to help? A systematic review and meta-analysis of the effects of performing acts of kindness on the well-being of the actor. Journal of Experimental Social Psychology, 76, 320–329.
Danner, D.D., Snowdon, D.A., & Friesen, W.V. (2001). Positive emotions in early life and longevity: Findings from the nun study. Journal of Personality and Social Psychology, (80), 804–813.
Danziger, K. (1994). Constructing the subject: Historical origins of psychological research. Cambridge University Press.
Davis, D.E., Choe, E., Meyers, J., Wade, N., Varjas, K., Gifford, A., Quinn, A., Hook, J.N., Van Tongeren, D.R., Griffin, B.J., & Worthington, E.L., Jr. (2016). Thankful for the little things: A meta-analysis of gratitude interventions. Journal of Counselling Psychology, 63(1), 20–31.
Duncan, A.R., Jaini, P.A., & Hellman, C.M. (2021). Positive psychology and hope as lifestyle medicine modalities in the therapeutic encounter: A narrative review. American Journal of Lifestyle Medicine, 15(1), 6–13.
Dweck, C. (2017). Mindset – Updated edition. Hachette UK.
Emmons, R.A., & Shelton, C.M. (2002). Gratitude and the science of positive psychology. In C.R. Snyder, & S.J. Lopez (Eds.), Handbook of positive psychology (pp. 459–471). Oxford University Press.
Fava, G.A. (2016). Well-being therapy. Karger.
Francis, G. (2012). Publication bias and the failure of replication in experimental psychology. Psychonomic Bulletin & Review, 19(6), 975–991.
Fredrickson, B.L. (2001). The role of positive emotions in positive psychology: The broaden-and build theory of positive motions. The American Psychologist, 56(3), 218–226.
Gaffaney, J., & Donaldson, S.I. (2025). Addressing the criticisms and critiques of positive psychology: Recommendations for improving the science and practice of the field. Frontiers in Psychology, 16, 1548612.
Gallup. (2024). Global life evaluation index. Gallup.
Gillham, J.E., Abenavoli, R.M., Brunwasser, S.M., Linkins, M., Reivich, K.J., & Seligman, M.E.P. (2013). Resilience education. In S.A. David, I. Boniwell, & A.C. Ayers (Eds.), The Oxford handbook of happiness (pp. 609–630). Oxford University Press.
Goodwin, K.A., & Goodwin, C.J. (2016). Research in psychology. Wiley.
Grant, M.J., & Booth, A. (2009). A typology of reviews: An analysis of 14 review types and associated methodologies. Health Information & Libraries Journal, 26(2), 91–108.
Harker, L., & Keltner, D. (2001). Expressions of positive emotion in women's college yearbook pictures and their relationship to personality and life outcomes across adulthood. Journal of Personality and Social Psychology, (80), 112–124.
Hart, R., & Hart, D. (2026). Cutting through the clutter: Cleaning the lens on work-related wellbeing concepts. Behavioral Sciences, 16, 3, 373.

Hefferon, K. (2012). Bringing back the body into positive psychology: The theory of corporeal posttraumatic growth in breast cancer survivorship. Psychology, 3(12A), 1238–1242.
Helliwell, J.F., Layard, R., Sachs, J.D., De Neve, J.E., Aknin, L.B., & Wang, S. (2025). World happiness report 2025. Gallup.
Henrich, J., Heine, S.J., & Norenzayan, A. (2010). The weirdest people in the world? Behavioral and Brain Sciences, 33(2–3), 61–135.
Higgins, J., & Goodall, S. (2021). Transforming the wellbeing focus in education: A document analysis of policy in Aotearoa New Zealand. International Journal of Qualitative Studies on Health and Well-being, 16(1), 1879370.
Hoffmann, A., Pilger, S., Olbrecht, T., & Claassen, K. (2023). Qualitative evaluation of a brief positive psychological online intervention for nursing staff. Archives of Psychiatric Nursing, 44, 38–45.
Kabat-Zinn, J. (2003). Mindfulness-based interventions in context: Past, present, and future. Clinical Psychology, 10(2), 144–156.
Kaleta, B., Campbell, S., O'Keeffe, J., & Burke, J. (2025). Nature-based interventions: A systematic review of reviews. Frontiers in Psychology, 16, 1625294.
Layous, K., & Lyubomirsky, S. (2014). The how, why, what, when, and who of happiness. In J. Gruber, & J.T. Moskowitz (Eds.), Positive emotion (pp. 473–495). Oxford University Press.
Lin, C.C., & Yeh, Y.C. (2014). How gratitude influences well-being: A structural equation modeling approach. Social Indicators Research, 118(1), 205–217.
Linley, P.A., Joseph, S., Harrington, S., & Wood, A.M. (2006). Positive psychology: Past, present, and (possible) future. The Journal of Positive Psychology, 1(1), 3–16.
Lomas, T., Pawelski, J.O., & VanderWeele, T.J. (2024). A flexible map of flourishing: The dynamics and drivers of flourishing, well-being, health, and happiness. International Journal of Wellbeing, 13(4), 3665, 1–38.
Lomas, T., & VanderWeele, T.J. (2023). The complex creation of happiness: Multidimensional conditionality in the drivers of happy people and societies. The Journal of Positive Psychology, 18(1), 15–33.
Lomas, T., Waters, L., Williams, P., Oades, L.G., & Kern, M.L. (2020). Third wave positive psychology: Broadening towards complexity. The Journal of Positive Psychology, 16(5), 660–674.
Long, K., & Bonanno, G.A. (2018). An integrative temporal framework for psychological resilience. In J.G. Noll, & I. Shalev (Eds.), The biology of early life stress (pp. 121–146). Springer.
Lyubomirsky, S., King, L., & Diener, E. (2005a). The benefits of frequent positive affect: Does happiness lead to success? Psychological Bulletin, (131), 803–855.
Lyubomirsky, S., Sheldon, K.M., & Schkade, D. (2005b). Pursuing happiness: The architecture of sustainable change. Review of General Psychology, 9(2), 111–131.
MacDonald, M.J., Wong, P.T., & Gingras, D.T. (2012). Meaning in life measures and development of a brief version of the Personal Meaning Profile. In P.T. Wong (Ed.), The human quest for meaning (pp. 357–382). Routledge.

Manley, D. (2016). Personality and positive psychology in social media and post-secondary education. Journal of Professional Communication, 4(2), 77–92.
Matheson, C., Robertson, H.D., Elliott, A.M., Iversen, L., & Murchie, P. (2016). Resilience of primary healthcare professionals working in challenging environments: A focus group study. British Journal of General Practice, 66(648), e507–e515.
Niemiec, R.M. (2017). Character strengths interventions. Hogrefe.
Nosek, B.A., Hardwicke, T.E., Moshontz, H., Allard, A., Corker, K.S., Dreber, A., Fideler, F., Hilgard, J., Kline Struhl, M., Nuijten, M.B., Rohrer, J.M. Romeo, F. Scheel, A.M. Scherer, L.D. Schonbrodt, F.D., & Vazire, S. (2022). Replicability, robustness, and reproducibility in psychological science. Annual Review of Psychology, 73, 719–748.
Ong, A.D., & Van Dulmen, M.H. (2007). Introduction. In A.D. Ong, & M.H. Van Dulmen (Eds.), Oxford handbook of methods in positive psychology (pp. xxii–xix). Oxford University Press.
ONS. (2019). Measuring national well-being in the UK. Office of National Statistics.
Park, N., & Peterson, C. (2006). Character strengths and happiness among young children: Content analysis of parental descriptions. Journal of Happiness Studies, 7(3), 323–341.
Pavot, W. (2018). The cornerstone of research on subjective well-being: Valid assessment methodology. In E. Diener, S. Oishi, & L. Tay (Eds.), Handbook of well-being. DEF Publishers.
Pawelski, J.O. (2016). Defining the 'positive' in positive psychology: Part II. A normative analysis. The Journal of Positive Psychology, 11(4), 357–365.
Peterson, C., & Seligman, M.E.P. (2004). Character strengths and virtues. APA.
Rusk, R.D., & Waters, L.E. (2013). Tracing the size, reach, impact, and breadth of positive psychology. The Journal of Positive Psychology, 8(3), 207–221.
Ryff, C.D. (2018). Eudaimonic well-being: Highlights from 25 years of inquiry. In K. Shigemasu, S., Kuwano, T., Sato, & T. Matsuzawa (Eds.), Diversity in harmony – Insights from psychology (pp. 375–395). Wiley.
Sinclair, E., Hart, R., & Lomas, T. (2020). Can positivity be counterproductive when suffering domestic abuse?: A narrative review. International Journal of Wellbeing, 10(1), 26–53.
Stanovich, K.E. (2013). How to think straight about psychology. Pearson.
Tay, L., Zyphur, M., & Batz, C.L. (2018). Income and subjective well-being: Review, synthesis, and future research. In E. Diener, S. Oishi, & L. Tay (Eds.), Handbook of well-being. DEF Publishers.
Tricco, A.C., Lillie, E., Zarin, W., O'Brien, K., Colquhoun, H., Kastner, M., & Straus, S.E. (2016). A scoping review on the conduct and reporting of scoping reviews. BMC Medical Research Methodology, 16(1), 1–10.
Van Zyl, L.E. (2025). Exploring the potential solutions to the criticisms of positive psychology: But can the bold, idealistic visions of positive psychologists survive real-world scrutiny? Frontiers in Psychology, 16, 1511128.

Van Zyl, L.E., Efendic, E., Rothmann Sr, S., & Shankland, R. (2019). Best-practice guidelines for positive psychological intervention research design. In Positive psychological intervention design and protocols for multi-cultural contexts (pp. 1–32). Springer.

Van Zyl, L.E., Gaffaney, J., van der Vaart, L., Dik, B.J., & Donaldson, S.I. (2024). The critiques and criticisms of positive psychology: A systematic review. The Journal of Positive Psychology, 19(2), 206–235.

Veenhoven, R. (2012). Cross-national differences in happiness: Cultural measurement bias or effect of culture? International Journal of Wellbeing, 2(4), 333–353.

Walsh, S., Szymczynska, P., Taylor, S.J., & Priebe, S. (2018). The acceptability of an online intervention using positive psychology for depression: A qualitative study. Internet Onterventions, 13, 60–66.

Wang, F., Guo, J., & Yang, G. (2023). Study on positive psychology from 1999 to 2021: A bibliometric analysis. Frontiers in Psychology, 14, 1101157.

Wong, A.G., Ki, P., Maharaj, A., Brown, E., Davis, C., & Apolinsky, F. (2014). Social support sources, types, and generativity: A focus group study of cancer survivors and their caregivers. Social Work in Health Care, 53(3), 214–232.

Yan, T., Chan, C.W., Chow, K.M., Zheng, W., & Sun, M. (2020). A systematic review of the effects of character strengths-based intervention on the psychological well-being of patients suffering from chronic illnesses. Journal of Advanced Nursing, 76(7), 1567–1580.

Section 6

Key Impacts

This Section in Summary

Chapter 12: Taking Stock and Major Impacts

- Positive Psychology has largely achieved its founding aim of rebalancing Psychology by establishing the scientific study of the bright side of human psychology as a legitimate and growing mainstream field.
- The discipline now has substantial research, teaching, institutional, and publishing infrastructures, including journals, associations, degree programmes and a large international body of scholarship.
- It has developed a broad evidence base of interventions and applied practices that have extended into education, organisations, healthcare and therapeutic practices.
- Positive Psychology has had major interdisciplinary and societal impacts by shaping how wellbeing is understood, measured and applied across policy and professional practice.
- Its concepts and language have become widely diffused in public discourse, self-help and the wellness industry.
- Despite its achievements, the field continues to face important critiques concerning conceptual clarity, methodological limitations, short-term intervention effects and the risks of simplification and commodification.

DOI: 10.4324/9781032663111-17

Chapter 12

Taking Stock and Major Impacts

This chapter takes stock of Positive Psychology's evolution by examining how far it has progressed in establishing itself as a distinct discipline and applied practice, the degree to which it has achieved the goals that stimulated its emergence, and its major impacts.

Since its formal beginnings, the field has sought to expand the focus of psychological science beyond disorder and dysfunction, directing sustained attention towards the bright side of human psychology and the conditions that enable individuals and communities to flourish. Looking back, we can regard with awe its many achievements and impacts.

The chapter begins by evaluating the extent to which Positive Psychology has fulfilled its central aims and reviews key developments that have influenced its trajectory. The chapter then reviews its key impacts, highlighting the many ways in which the field has shaped research and applied practice in Psychology and beyond, as well as public understanding, impacting individuals, organisations, communities and policy.

Evaluating Positive Psychology's Progress Towards Its Goals

A central aim of Positive Psychology was to correct the imbalance within Applied Psychology by bringing a new set of topics and questions into Psychology's scientific agenda, particularly those concerned with healthy functioning. A review of its scientific development suggests that Positive Psychology has firmly established itself as a distinct field, with its core institutional and operational structures now in place. There is a substantial and continuously expanding body of research produced by hundreds of scholars across 46 countries (Donaldson et al., 2015). Wang et al. (2023) estimated that approximately 5,000 English-language journal articles were published during the first 23 years following the field's formal emergence, with publication trends continuing to rise.

DOI: 10.4324/9781032663111-18

In addition, a considerable number of academic books, handbooks, textbooks and book chapters have been published, either on Positive Psychology as a whole or on its core themes.

At present, there are eight international journals, three interdisciplinary journals and six regional journals dedicated to Positive Psychology, although much of the field's research continues to appear in broader Psychology journals.

Academic journal – peer reviewed: A scholarly publication in which research articles are evaluated by independent experts in the same field before being accepted for publication.

Furthermore, 25 national and international Positive Psychology associations support the field by promoting research and practice, organising regular conferences and other knowledge dissemination opportunities, and bringing researchers and practitioners together (Hart, 2020).

Academic association: A professional organisation that brings together scholars and researchers in a particular academic field to support research, collaboration, networking, and knowledge sharing.

Knowledge exchange: The process of sharing academic knowledge, research findings, and expertise with academic and non-academic partners and communities to create practical, social, economic, or policy impact.

This extensive research activity and exchange of knowledge have significantly broadened and deepened understanding of the topics at the heart of the field, the factors that make life worth living and the conditions that promote or hinder valued outcomes. The discipline has also progressed beyond foundational and exploratory work, with the development and testing of new conceptual models, research methods, empirically supported interventions and measurement tools (see Chapters 5–11).

The remarkable growth in scholarly output strongly suggests that the original imbalance within Psychology has been substantially reduced. Research on the positive dimensions of human life has become increasingly mainstream and normalised within Psychology and related disciplines.

Furthermore, as Kim et al. (2018) observed, during the second wave of Positive Psychology (see Chapter 1), the field's focus expanded beyond the study of positive experiences and traits alone to include their relationship with psychological dysfunction and wider social issues. This development has helped address one of the major criticisms directed at the first wave of Positive Psychology, namely, that it concentrated too narrowly on positive aspects of human life while overlooking the more difficult and negative realities of human life and society.

Despite this impressive progress, and perhaps partly because of it, Positive Psychology's research enterprise has been subject to sustained critique (see Chapter 5). These critiques have attended to its theoretical foundations, core concepts, research methods, empirical findings and particularly the ways in which these have been communicated, and have instigated further growth and improvement.

An essential aspect of its research enterprise is academic presence and teaching. Currently, 18 universities offer postgraduate degrees in Positive Psychology in English, including master's and doctoral programmes, while a further 13 offer equivalent degrees in other languages. In addition, numerous universities provide certificate courses or individual modules on Positive Psychology topics at undergraduate and postgraduate levels.

Beyond formal degree provision, several leading universities now offer Massive Open Online Courses (MOOCs) on Positive Psychology topics, often as certificate-bearing courses, and these have attracted thousands of participants.

> **MOOCs – Massive Open Online Courses:** Online courses that are open to large numbers of learners, often free or low-cost, and accessible remotely through digital platforms. These are offered mainly by universities.

A further important development is the growing availability of non-credit courses delivered by universities as well as private institutions. These programmes have considerably widened access to Positive Psychology beyond formal degree pathways and accredited professional training. They frequently combine psychoeducation with interventions, offering participants opportunities not only to learn about key theories and concepts but also to apply evidence-informed practices in their daily lives. In many cases, such courses are designed for broad public audiences as well as for practitioners seeking personal or professional development outside conventional academic structures. A large proportion of these courses are delivered digitally, making them flexible, scalable and accessible.

Notably, the questions and themes explored by Positive Psychology now occupy a prominent place not only within the scientific agenda but also within global and national policy and public health agendas. In line with early calls from leaders in the field (Diener, 2000), many countries, particularly in the West, have incorporated measures of core concepts in Positive Psychology into national and international surveys, including indicators such as life satisfaction, happiness, wellbeing, meaning in life, relationships and mental illness (see, for example, ONS, 2019; OECD, 2017). This has provided policymakers with valuable data for assessing the effects of policies and for making comparisons across time and between geographical contexts.

The self-help industry has also been significantly influenced. Numerous self-help books have been authored by Positive Psychology scholars who draw on scientific evidence to support the concepts and interventions they present (e.g., Seligman, 2006; Lyubomirsky, 2011; Fredrickson, 2010). This has enabled the field to disseminate its research findings more widely and to extend its reach beyond academia.

Positive Psychology also continuously attracts substantial media attention as a philosophy, a scientific enterprise and a broader movement. Scholarly work is regularly featured in the media, further amplifying its public visibility. In addition, the field has established a strong presence across the internet and social media platforms amounting to millions of websites and posts. This presence illustrates the wide diffusion, public salience and global reach of the field and its related concepts and concerns.

This extensive public visibility suggests that Positive Psychology has had considerable discursive influence. One of the field's key aims was to develop a shared language that could support communication, integration and coherence across its diverse areas of inquiry. In this respect, the field appears to have contributed meaningfully to the establishment of a common vocabulary through which its ideas can be articulated, communicated and advanced.

Discursive influence: The ability to shape how a topic is discussed, understood, and framed by influencing the language, concepts, and narratives used by others.

Another key aim of Positive Psychology was to design and empirically evaluate interventions intended to enhance wellbeing and other positive outcomes. Considerable progress has been made in this area (see Chapter 5), and scholars have devoted substantial effort to the development, refinement and testing of interventions. Importantly, this work has contributed to establishing Positive Psychology not only as a science concerned with understanding optimal functioning but also as an applied discipline seeking to translate knowledge into practical benefit. Nevertheless, a key critique of these interventions is that most have small to moderate effects and short-term impacts (see Chapter 5).

Translational science: Research that aims to turn scientific discoveries and academic knowledge into practical applications, interventions, policies, or improvements in real-world settings.

The development of this intervention literature has also broadened the reach of the field considerably. Positive Psychology Interventions are now disseminated through many educational, training, coaching, healthcare and therapeutic pathways (see Chapters 6–10). They are also widely communicated through self-help and popular psychology books and through digital formats, making interventions more accessible, scalable and adaptable to everyday life. Although the depth and quality of engagement vary across settings, the widespread uptake of these interventions indicates that the field has made substantial progress towards its aim of developing practical, evidence-based approaches for fostering positive outcomes at both individual and collective levels.

One of the most ambitious aims of Positive Psychology was to integrate the study of positive functioning within therapeutic and other applied settings. This has arguably been among the most challenging goals for the field, since it required engagement beyond its own boundaries and collaboration with established applied professions, including Counselling, Clinical Psychology, Coaching and Psychiatry. Progress in this area has nevertheless been substantial (see Chapter 6). The literature indicates growing efforts to incorporate Positive Psychology concepts, models and interventions into therapeutic and practice-based work. In this way, Positive Psychology has increasingly contributed to a more balanced applied perspective that attends not only to distress, dysfunction and symptom reduction but also to strengths, meaning, resilience, hope and the cultivation of wellbeing. This integrative movement has developed unevenly across domains, and in some areas, the incorporation of Positive Psychology has matured into more clearly established interdisciplinary applied fields, while in others it remains at an earlier stage of conceptual or practical integration (see Chapter 6).

In parallel, the field has developed beyond its original psychological foundations through the emergence of an increasing number of interdisciplinary subfields and applied domains (see Chapters 7–10). Positive Education and Positive Work and Organisations are now firmly established, while in newer areas such as Positive Health and Positive Economic Psychology, this expansion is still ongoing. Beyond these areas, a number of additional interdisciplinary subfields are currently emerging (see Chapter 2).

Overall, the review suggests that Positive Psychology has made substantial progress towards its original goals. It has succeeded in establishing itself as a recognised scientific and applied field, expanding the scope of psychological inquiry, generating and disseminating a large and growing body of research, creating research and training infrastructures, developing evidence-based interventions and contributing a shared conceptual language that now extends well beyond academia. It has also made important advances in influencing policy, public discourse and applied practice, including efforts to integrate positive and negative perspectives within therapeutic work.

Key Impacts

Since its launch, Positive Psychology has generated effects that extend well beyond the creation of a new subfield within Psychology. Its impact is visible not only in theory, research and practice but also in interdisciplinary mergers, institutional practices, professional markets, policy agendas and public discourse. Key areas of impact are summarised below.

> **Academic impact:** The influence and reach of academic work, assessed through measures such as publications, citations, research quality, collaboration, knowledge exchange, policy or practice influence, public engagement, and wider social, cultural, or economic benefits.

- **Impact on Psychology:** Positive Psychology played an important role in rebalancing Applied Psychology's long-standing focus on disorder, deficit and dysfunction by legitimising the scientific study of the positive dimensions of human experience. In this respect, it broadened the core agenda of Psychology. The field also stimulated significant theoretical innovation in relation to the concept of wellbeing, including distinctions between hedonic and eudaimonic wellbeing and the emergence of integrative frameworks such as PERMA (see Chapter 3). These conceptual developments were accompanied by the creation of a wide range of psychometric instruments designed to measure wellbeing and other positive constructs (see Chapter 11). This marked a significant departure from earlier approaches in which wellbeing was commonly inferred from the absence of pathology.
- **Impact on other disciplines and interdisciplinary mergers:** The field has merged productively with adjacent areas including Education, Management Studies, Health and Economic Psychology:
  - Within Education, Positive Education broadened educational practice from its focus on academic achievement to the cultivation of wellbeing, strengths, resilience, positive relationships and holistic development. In practice, this shift impinges on school cultures and priorities, informs curriculum design and content and contributes to the training of teachers. It therefore affects the everyday experiences of schools, with direct implications for teachers, parents and children alike (see Chapter 7).
  - In organisational scholarship, its influence was especially visible in the emergence of Positive Work and Organisational approaches, which broadened the focus of management from performance,

efficiency and profits to employee wellbeing, and highlighted employers' responsibilities to cultivate work environments that are meaningful, growth-oriented and fulfilling. On the practical side, this contributed to a shift in how organisations understand employee wellbeing, moving away from narrower health and safety framings or remedial psychological responses towards more holistic conceptions of wellbeing and a broader range of employee support services (see Chapter 8).

- Its interdisciplinary influence on health has been evident in the rise of Positive Health, which reframed health from a focus on disease treatment and management to also incorporating prevention and the promotion of healthy lifestyles. On the applied side, this integration instigated a gradual shift in healthcare towards a more holistic and preventive framing of wellbeing (see Chapter 9).
- The development of Positive Economic Psychology marks a further interdisciplinary extension by challenging the predominantly deficiency-focused orientation of Economic Psychology and redirecting attention to the competencies and potentials embedded in human economic behaviour (see Chapter 10).
- Beyond these established intersections, Positive Psychology has also influenced a wide range of disciplines, from economics and public policy to sociology, international relations and the arts. Its concepts, frameworks and measures have increasingly been adopted across these areas. This wider uptake has helped establish wellbeing as a genuinely cross-disciplinary object of inquiry and has encouraged the adaptation of Positive Psychology concepts to diverse theoretical, methodological and applied contexts.

- **Impact on practice and on other applied fields:** The discipline has accelerated the translation of wellbeing science into practical interventions. It has influenced applied domains including Coaching, Counselling, Psychotherapy and Psychiatry. In these domains, its impact has been about enriching them with resource-oriented, preventive and growth-focused perspectives (see Chapter 6). These developments suggest that Positive Psychology has begun to influence how applied work itself is understood and practised. Its contribution therefore lies not only in demonstrating efficacy but also in helping to reshape applied work in Psychology around a more complete model of human functioning.
- **Impact on national and global surveys:** One of Positive Psychology's most visible societal impacts has been the normalisation of wellbeing and happiness measurement in official statistics. Major institutions now treat life satisfaction, affect and related wellbeing indicators as

legitimate survey content, and over time this expanded to the measurement of other Positive Psychology concepts. Crucially, such indicators increasingly came to be seen as important complements to traditional economic measures such as GDP for understanding societal progress and quality of life (Diener et al., 2015).

- **Impact on policy:** Positive Psychology contributed to a broader policy shift in which wellbeing came to be treated as a legitimate policy outcome rather than a by-product of economic growth. The OECD (2025), for example, noted that subjective wellbeing data are used by a growing number of governments to monitor trends and inform decision-making, indicating that wellbeing has become policy-relevant internationally.
- **Impact on higher education:** The discipline has had a substantial impact on higher education through the creation of degree programmes and modules focused on Positive Psychology topics. Universities also increasingly use ideas drawn from the field as a framework for assessing student experience, especially in response to concerns about student distress. In this sense, higher education has been both a site of scholarship production and a major dissemination channel for its ideas (Williams et al., 2018).
- **Impact on the training, coaching, and consultancy markets:** Positive Psychology has been highly influential in the growth of a training and consultancy ecosystem built around its key concepts. In Coaching, Positive Psychology became one of the most visible evidence-based frameworks, especially Positive Psychology Coaching. Consultancy and executive development markets also use its concepts extensively, although this commercial uptake has often run ahead of the evidence base and has attracted criticism for oversimplification and commodification (Biswas-Diener & Dean, 2007).
- **Impact on the self-help industry:** Positive Psychology strongly shaped the self-help industry by giving scientific legitimacy to positive themes and by providing an expanding research base that self-help authors, programmes and products could draw upon for evidence and credibility. However, its migration into self-help also created tensions between scientific nuance and marketable simplification, contributing to concerns about the "happiness industry" (Parks, 2015).
- **Impact on the wellness industry:** Positive Psychology has influenced the products of the wider wellness industry. Its concepts have been incorporated into phone and web applications, workshops, retreats, journals and products, often blurring the line between science-based intervention and lifestyle branding. This diffusion increased visibility and accessibility, but also risks commercial dilution and the presentation of wellbeing as an individual consumer project rather than a social and political matter (Allem, 2024).

- **Impact on individuals:** Its ideas have reached large publics through books, online courses, workbooks, talks, coaching tools and digital content, greatly expanding lay access to this body of knowledge. This has made its key concepts and interventions part of everyday practice for many people, even outside formal therapy or education settings, and these are increasingly taken up within communities, schools, workplaces and organisations. Such public reach is therefore one of its major impacts, although the quality and fidelity of what people encounter vary.
- **Impact on language:** The discipline has changed the vocabulary through which many people discuss mental health and wellbeing. Terms such as flourishing, strengths, gratitude, resilience, meaning and engagement have become mainstream beyond academic and professional discourse. This linguistic shift matters because it has reoriented discussion from illness towards capabilities and resources. At the same time, the popularisation of this language has sometimes detached terms from their original conceptual precision, especially in commercial and self-help contexts.

Overall, the impact of Positive Psychology has extended far beyond its original goals: It has reshaped psychological theory, influenced measurement and policy, spread into education, health, organisations and coaching, and entered popular culture, public language and wellbeing-oriented markets, albeit not without critique regarding commercialisation, individualism and uneven scientific fidelity (see Chapter 1).

Conclusion

Positive Psychology can be deemed a remarkably influential intellectual and applied project. Since its launch, it has moved well beyond its original aspiration of correcting Psychology's imbalance towards pathology by establishing a substantial research base, institutional infrastructure, educational presence and intervention literature. It has also contributed to a broader reorientation in how wellbeing, mental health and human functioning are conceptualised across Psychology and neighbouring fields. At the same time, its development has not been linear or uncontested. The field's expansion has exposed conceptual, methodological and ethical tensions, particularly around the strength of its evidence base, the durability of intervention effects and the risks of simplification, commodification and excessive individualism. These critiques highlight the growing pains of the field.

Taking stock, the major impact of Positive Psychology lies not only in the knowledge it has produced but also in the way it has altered agendas, institutions and public discourse. It has helped legitimate wellbeing as a scientific, educational, organisational and policy concern, fostered interdisciplinary innovation and provided a shared language through which its concepts can be discussed. Its ideas now circulate through universities, schools, workplaces, healthcare, policy frameworks, professional training, self-help markets and the media. Few recent developments in Psychology have achieved such broad diffusion. Yet this reach also brings responsibility. The future contribution of Positive Psychology will depend on its capacity to retain scientific rigour, deepen contextual sensitivity and continue integrating positive and negative dimensions of human experience into a more complete and mature science of flourishing.

References

Allem, J.P. (2024). The need for research on the wellness industry's impact on health decisions. American Journal of Preventive Medicine, 67(4), 627–630.

Biswas-Diener, R., & Dean, B. (2007). Positive psychology coaching. Wiley.

Diener, E. (2000). Subjective well-being: The science of happiness and a proposal for a national index. American Psychologist, 55(1), 34–43.

Diener, E., Oishi, S., & Lucas, R.E. (2015). National accounts of subjective well-being. American Psychologist, 70(3), 234.

Donaldson, S.I., Dollwet, M., & Rao, M.A. (2015). Happiness, excellence, and optimal human functioning revisited: Examining the peer-reviewed literature linked to positive psychology. The Journal of Positive Psychology, 10(3), 185–195.

Fredrickson, B. (2010). Positivity. Oneworld Publications.

Hart, R. (2020). Positive psychology: The basics. Routledge.

Kim, H., Doiron, K., Warren, M., & Donaldson, S.I. (2018). The international landscape of positive psychology research: A systematic review. International Journal of Wellbeing, 8(1), 50–70.

Lyubomirsky, S. (2011). The how of happiness. Penguin.

OECD. (2017). How's life? Measuring well-being. OECD Publishing.

OECD. (2025). OECD guidelines on measuring subjective well-being. OECD Publishing.

ONS. (2019). Measuring national well-being in the UK. Office of National Statistics.

Parks, A.C. (2015). Putting positive psychology into practice via self-help. In S. Joseph (Ed.), Positive psychology in practice (pp. 237–248). Wiley.

Seligman, M.E.P. (2006). Learned optimism. Vintage.

Wang, F., Guo, J., & Yang, G. (2023). Study on positive psychology from 1999 to 2021: A bibliometric analysis. Frontiers in Psychology, 14, 1101157.

Williams, N., Horrell, L., Edmiston, D., & Brady, M. (2018). The impact of positive psychology on higher education. The William & Mary Educational Review, 5, 83–94.

Section 7

Key Emerging Areas

This Section in Summary

Chapter 13: Future Developments

- Positive Psychology followed a path of partial integration within Psychology alongside continued specialisation and retaining a distinct identity.
- The next phase of the field is likely to be shaped less by novelty and more by consolidation, refinement, replication and critical re-evaluation of existing constructs, measures, models, interventions and methods.
- Future research is expected to move towards more culturally grounded, context-sensitive and systems-oriented approaches, with stronger theory building and clearer conceptual foundations.
- Applied and interdisciplinary domains are likely to expand further, but their progress will depend on better integration between the allied disciplines, stronger evidence, clearer mechanisms and more routine embedding of interventions in real-world settings.
- The future credibility and influence of Positive Psychology will also depend on its professionalisation pathways, including clearer standards for training and client-facing practice.

DOI: 10.4324/9781032663111-19

Chapter 13

Future Developments

In an early reflection on the development of Positive Psychology, Linley et al. (2006) observed that "it is clear from many perspectives that Positive Psychology has arrived. Yet in our view, this is just the beginning, and what has been achieved so far, while both laudable and remarkable, may be just an historical footnote to what is to follow" (p. 8). These words remain strikingly relevant today, albeit with even greater force given the field's subsequent expansion in visibility, influence and application. At the same time, it stands at a pivotal stage in its development, one that is likely to shape its longer-term trajectory and legacy.

This chapter explores several possible future directions for Positive Psychology. It begins by considering the field's relationship with its parent discipline of Psychology, and then delineates its future scientific trajectory and emerging domains of practice. Finally, the chapter considers the field's growing development as a formalised area of practice.

Positive Psychology: Integration, Specialisation or Dissolution?

Positive Psychology is at a critical juncture. Since its formal emergence in 1998 as a reformist and, in many ways, rebellious movement within Psychology, it has rapidly evolved into an influential intellectual and social force that has captured the attention of both the scientific community and the wider public. As the preceding chapters in this volume have shown, the field has expanded dramatically

> **Reformist:** A movement that seeks gradual change within an existing social, political, or institutional system rather than replacing it entirely.
>
> **Rebellious:** A movement that challenges or resists existing authority, rules, or institutions, often seeking more fundamental or disruptive change.

DOI: 10.4324/9781032663111-20

since its inception, as reflected in the growth of publications, readership, research output, academic courses, student engagement, media attention and public interest (see Chapter 12). Conversely, it has also been suggested that Positive Psychology may ultimately disappear and, somewhat paradoxically, such a dissolution would be seen by some as evidence of its success.

At the heart of Positive Psychology's development lies an enduring tension between two opposing impulses: The desire to establish and preserve its own identity, and the competing pull towards integration within the broader discipline of Psychology, particularly across applied areas. The field is therefore entering a decisive period, one that may determine its longer-term form and future relevance. Will Positive Psychology endure in its current form, evolve, become integrated into other Applied Psychology disciplines or gradually fade away?

Linley et al. (2006) outlined three possible trajectories for the future of Positive Psychology. The first was complete integration into other areas of Psychology, leading ultimately to the disappearance of Positive Psychology as a separate field. From this perspective, such an outcome would not represent failure, but fulfilment: The core principles of Positive Psychology would have become so thoroughly embedded in psychological research, teaching and practice that a distinct identity would no longer be necessary. As Diener (2003) expressed it, "my hope is that Positive Psychology will eventually disappear because it becomes part of the very fabric of Psychology. Thus, it will fade as a campaign precisely because it has been so successful" (p. 120).

The second possibility is partial integration alongside continued specialisation. Viewed from the perspective of full integration, this outcome might be seen as an incomplete achievement of the field's original mission to redress Psychology's imbalance. Linley et al. (2006) suggested that, under this model, Positive Psychology would continue to pursue that corrective role while maintaining its distinctiveness. However, others have regarded this pathway more favourably. Lomas et al. (2014) argued not only for the incorporation of Positive Psychology concepts and interventions across Psychology, but also for the development of professional chartered status and accreditation for Positive Psychology practitioners, separate from, though comparable to, other Applied Psychology specialisms.

The third trajectory is one of little or no integration, coupled with continued specialisation. Linley et al. (2006) warned that this would suggest that Positive Psychology had failed to achieve the wider disciplinary influence it originally sought and might therefore persist only as a specialist but increasingly marginalised area, "locked out of the major psychological agendas" (p. 10). A central risk in such a scenario is that Positive Psychology would become vulnerable to the very criticism that prompted its creation: Namely, that by focusing too narrowly on the positive dimensions of human experience, it risks becoming conceptually narrow, partial and imbalanced.

When these possible trajectories are considered in light of the field's progress and achievements to date (as detailed in this volume), it appears that Positive Psychology has largely followed the second path: Partial integration combined with continued specialisation. Moreover, it has already made substantial advances on both fronts (see Chapter 12).

The Next Phase of Positive Psychology Research and Applied Work

Against the backdrop of the field's achievements, criticisms and current challenges, attention can now turn to the next phase of development in Positive Psychology research and applied work.

Over the past decade, Positive Psychology appears to have reached a degree of saturation in some areas, with innovation proceeding more slowly than during its first wave. This is reflected in the relatively small number of new concepts, measures and interventions that have emerged in recent years. This pattern may indicate that the next decade will be characterised less by novelty, and more by the consolidation, refinement and critical re-evaluation of existing constructs, scales, models and interventions, with greater attention to revision and replication, especially in the context of Psychology's replication crisis (see Chapters 1 and 11).

The future development of Positive Psychology research is likely to involve a move away from relatively decontextualised and individualised models of wellbeing towards more culturally grounded,

Decontextualised models of wellbeing: Approaches that explain wellbeing largely without considering the wider social, cultural, economic, political, or environmental contexts in which people live.

Individualised models of wellbeing: Approaches that locate wellbeing primarily within the individual, emphasising personal attitudes, behaviours, choices, and psychological characteristics rather than structural or collective factors.

System-orientated approaches: Approaches that understand wellbeing as shaped by interconnected individual, social, organisational, economic, political, and environmental factors within a wider system.

context-sensitive and systems-oriented approaches. This direction reflects the field's third wave, which, according to Lomas et al. (2020), extends the earlier dialectical turn through broader interdisciplinary engagement, deeper inquiry and an increasing willingness to address more complex questions.

Positive Psychology has been criticised for lacking a coherent metatheoretical foundation capable of anchoring its underlying philosophical assumptions. As a result, the field has sometimes struggled to articulate a sufficiently integrated framework through which its diverse theories, methods and aims can be situated. Addressing this limitation is likely to become an important priority in the coming decade, with greater attention given to the development of overarching frameworks that can bring more philosophical and theoretical coherence to the field.

> **Meta-theory:** A framework for examining, comparing, and organising theories by addressing their underlying assumptions.

A related issue concerns the lack of clarity surrounding several of Positive Psychology's core concepts, as well as the continuing debates over their definitions, constituent components and measurement. Future progress is therefore likely to depend on more precise conceptual refinement and on the systematic mapping of relationships among concepts and models into a more coherent body of knowledge. Recent work on the conceptualisation of wellbeing offers an early indication of this direction and suggests that such integrative efforts are already underway (see Chapter 3).

> **Conceptual refinement:** The process of clarifying, specifying, and improving a concept so that its meaning, boundaries, and relationships with other concepts are more precise.
>
> **Systematic concept mapping:** A structured method for identifying, organising, and visually representing concepts and the relationships between them within a field or topic.

Research methods in Positive Psychology, especially its quantitative approaches, have come under sustained scrutiny. Critics have argued that the field has too often relied on weak measurement practices and an overuse of cross-sectional designs based on relatively small and unrepresentative samples, while underutilising more methodologically robust approaches. Such tendencies have raised questions about the validity, credibility and generalisability of the evidence base (see Chapter 5). However, these concerns are not exclusive to Positive

Psychology, but are shared more broadly across Psychology and the Social Sciences. In the coming years, the field is likely to move towards a more routine use of technological and data-intensive methods, including mobile data collection, large-scale surveys, and big data and data-mining techniques, enabling the integration of both objective and subjective forms of data.

Big data: Extremely large and complex datasets that can be analysed to identify patterns, trends, relationships, and behaviours that may not be visible in smaller datasets.

Data mining: The process of analysing large datasets using statistical and computational techniques to discover meaningful patterns, relationships, and previously unknown insights.

In line with this trajectory, intervention research is likely to develop more efficient and ecologically valid ways of testing interventions, enabling evaluation in naturalistic settings while reducing the costs and time demands typically associated with traditional research designs. From a theoretical perspective, future intervention research is likely to focus on understanding the mechanisms through which interventions exert their effects, the factors that moderate their effectiveness and the development of overarching typologies based on key intervention features. This would provide a stronger basis for practitioners to judge which interventions are most suitable for particular individuals, groups and contexts.

A long-standing criticism of the field is that it has largely privileged Western perspectives in its research and applications, with a substantial proportion of its research conducted in WEIRD contexts (Western, Educated, Industrialised, Rich and Democratic; Henrich et al., 2010). This has led to concerns about whether the field's dominant models and measures are adequately transferable to other cultural settings. Future research is therefore likely to pay closer attention to the social, cultural and contextual conditions.

With respect to Positive Psychology's interdisciplinary subdomains (see Chapters 7–10), all of these fields would benefit from a stronger research base. More specifically, there is a need for more rigorous work examining the degree of integration between each of the disciplines involved, alongside more robust evidence on how these approaches are implemented and what their short- and long-term outcomes are. Positive Economic Psychology, as the newest subdiscipline, is likely to see an expansion in both conceptual and empirical work. In contrast, Positive Work and Organisational scholarship may require sustained and coordinated efforts to overcome its current stagnation and enable the production of more original research to increase its impact. With regard to applications, it is hoped that interventions in Positive Education, Positive Health, and Positive Work and Organisations will become more systematically integrated into everyday practice, rather than remaining peripheral or supplementary additions. It is also likely that new interdisciplinary subdomains will continue to emerge, giving rise to research in areas such as Positive Body, Positive Ageing, Positive Neuroscience, Positive Environments and Architecture, and Positive Tourism.

In applied interdisciplinary domains such as Positive Psychology Coaching, Positive Psychotherapy and Positive Psychiatry (see Chapter 6), many approaches remain in need of further development and consolidation. Future progress will likely depend on stronger theoretical integration, more detailed investigation of underlying mechanisms and a more robust evidence base regarding efficacy. There is also a need for clearer professional guidance concerning who should be permitted to deliver these approaches and what training and accreditation standards ought to apply.

With respect to academic teaching, expansion over the past decade has been limited, raising concerns that current provision, predominantly at MSc level and with relatively few opportunities for doctoral training, may not adequately prepare the future cohort of scholars and lecturers in Positive Psychology.

At the same time, there has been a substantial increase in non-accredited training, alongside growing concerns about its quality and empirical grounding. These developments have contributed to efforts to professionalise the field through greater emphasis on course accreditation and provider **certification** (see below).

Professionalising Positive Psychology

At present, Positive Psychology is an unregulated and unaccredited field of practice, with no universally accepted standards governing how its concepts and interventions should be applied in client-facing settings. Consequently, Positive Psychology training and interventions can be offered by anyone through a variety of means, including books, websites and mobile applications. As the field matures, however, calls for

Professionalisation: The process of developing a field into a more formal profession through accreditation, standards, ethical oversight and recognised training routes.

professionalisation through accreditation and regulation have become increasingly prominent.

In 2021, the Leadership Team of the Work and Organisation Division within the International Positive Psychology Association (IPPA) responded to these calls by launching the **Professionalising Positive Psychology** policy consultation process. Following these consultations, in 2022 a survey was developed to gather members' views on how the field should be professionalised, including preferred routes and the perceived benefits and risks.

The survey considered four pathways:

- **Accreditation of courses** involving the evaluation of educational programmes against established criteria;
- **Credentialing practitioners** based on completion of specified courses;
- **Certifying practitioners** comprising formal assessment of practitioners' skills and competencies;
- **Licensing**, requiring practitioners to acquire legal authorisation to practise.

Accreditation: The formal evaluation and approval of educational programmes against agreed standards.

Credentialing: The awarding of recognised status to practitioners based on completion of specified training or qualifications.

Licensing: Legal authorisation to practise professionally in a regulated field.

Certification: A formal process of assessing whether practitioners have demonstrated specified skills or competencies.

The findings showed that accreditation was the preferred route, followed by credentialing. Although support for the initiative was generally strong, some opposition was also expressed (Hart & Donaldson, 2025).

Following the survey, in 2023 IPPA established an Accreditation Taskforce to develop a multi-level accreditation framework for Positive Psychology programmes. The initiative responded to growing demand, uneven programme quality and the absence of regulatory oversight, all of which pose risks to the field's credibility and may allow unverified or ethically questionable practices to spread. Accreditation was seen as necessary to protect learners and to ensure research-based education.

The Task Force's work included a review of comparable programmes and market analysis, culminating in the proposal of an accreditation framework centred on four core competencies: Positive Psychology content, scientific literacy, ethical decision-making and psychological assessment. It also outlined standards relating to faculty qualifications, teaching quality, student support, and diversity, equity, and inclusion, together with mechanisms for ongoing evaluation through student assessment and regular programme review.

The overall aim was to create an international benchmark for excellence in Positive Psychology education, with launch anticipated in the near future.

Taken together, these developments suggest that the future of Positive Psychology as a scientific and applied enterprise will depend not merely on generating more research and applied work, but on the consolidation, refinement and critical reappraisal of its existing constructs, scales, models and interventions, with stronger emphasis on revision, replication and conceptual precision, and more robust research methods. Its next phase is also likely to be characterised by more robust theory building, greater critical self-reflection, deeper interdisciplinary engagement and increased sensitivity to context, culture and contradiction. Alongside this, the professionalisation of the field is likely to become increasingly important, through the development of clearer standards for training and client-facing practice.

Conclusion

Positive Psychology has travelled a remarkable distance in a relatively short time. From its beginnings as a call to rebalance Psychology's concerns, it has developed into an influential body of scholarship and practice that has reshaped how the positive aspects of human life are studied and applied. The task before it now is not simply to grow further, but to grow wiser: To consolidate its achievements, confront its limitations and build a more conceptually coherent, methodologically robust, culturally sensitive and professionally accountable future.

Ultimately, Positive Psychology speaks to one of the oldest and most important human concerns: What constitutes a life well-lived. This concern transcends disciplinary boundaries and ensures that the field's future will continue to matter far beyond academia. In a time when the world faces profound psychological, social and environmental challenges, the need for thoughtful, evidence-based and ethically grounded work on flourishing has never been greater. The future of Positive Psychology will therefore be shaped not only by the questions it asks, but by the courage, reflexivity and imagination with which it pursues them. Much has been achieved, but the deeper promise of the field still lies ahead.

References

Diener, E. (2003). What is positive about positive psychology: The curmudgeon and Pollyanna. Psychological Inquiry, (14), 115–120.

Hart, R., & Donaldson, S. (2025). White paper: Professionalising positive psychology: Survey report. The International Positive Psychology Association, the Work and Organisation Division.

Henrich, J., Heine, S.J., & Norenzayan, A. (2010). The weirdest people in the world? Behavioral and Brain Sciences, 33(2–3), 61–135.

Linley, P.A., Joseph, S., Harrington, S., & Wood, A.M. (2006). Positive psychology: Past, present, and (possible) future. The Journal of Positive Psychology, 1(1), 3–16.

Lomas, T., Hefferon, K., & Ivtzan, I. (2014). Applied positive psychology: Integrated positive practice. Sage.

Lomas, T., Waters, L., Williams, P., Oades, L.G., & Kern, M.L. (2020). Third wave positive psychology: Broadening towards complexity. The Journal of Positive Psychology, 16(5), 660–674.

Index

Note: Page numbers in *italic* indicate a figure and page numbers in **bold** indicate a table on the corresponding page.